Before Homosexuality in the Arab-Islamic World, 1500–1800

Before Homosexuality in the Arab-Islamic World, 1500–1800

KHALED EL-ROUAYHEB

The University of Chicago Press CHICAGO AND LONDON

Khaled El-Rouayheb is a British Academy Postdoctoral Research Fellow at the Faculty of Divinity, University of Cambridge.

The University of Chicago Press, Chicago 60637
The University of Chicago Press, Ltd., London

Printed in the United States of America

14 13 12 11 10 09 08 07 06 05   1 2 3 4 5

ISBN: 0-226-72988-5 (cloth)

Parts of chapter 2 appeared as "The Love of Boys in Arabic Poetry of the Early Ottoman Period, 1500–1800," *Middle Eastern Literatures* 8, no. 1 (January 2005): 3–22, © Taylor & Francis Ltd.

Library of Congress Cataloging-in-Publication Data

El-Rouayheb, Khaled.
Before homosexuality in the Arab-Islamic world, 1500–1800 : Khaled El-Rouayheb.
p. cm.
Revision of the author's thesis (doctoral)—University of Cambridge.
Includes bibliographical references and index.
ISBN 0-226-72988-5 (cloth : alk. paper)
1. Homosexuality—Arab countries—History. 2. Sodomy—Arab countries—History. 3. Homosexuality in literature. I. Title.
HQ76.3.A65E576 2005
306.76′6′09174927—dc22

2005008022

♾ The paper used in this publication meets the minimum requirements of the American National Standard for Information Sciences—Permanence of Paper for Printed Library Materials, ANSI Z39.48-1992.

To discover from the history of thought that there are in fact no such timeless concepts, but only the various different concepts which have gone with various different societies, is to discover a general truth not merely about the past but about ourselves.

QUENTIN SKINNER,
"Meaning and Understanding in the History of Ideas"

Contents

Acknowledgments

The present work is a revised version of a PhD dissertation submitted at the University of Cambridge. I would like to thank Corpus Christi College, the Cambridge European Trust, and the Board of Graduate Studies of the University of Cambridge for jointly funding my PhD research. Without their generous support, the present study would not have been possible.

My supervisor, Basim Musallam, was a constant source of support and advice during the years spent writing my dissertation. Abd al-Rahim Abu-Husayn of the American University of Beirut first supported me in my belief that a study such as this would be feasible, and introduced me to the sources of the period. Michael Cook, Geert Jan van Gelder, James Montgomery, Samir Seikaly, and Tarif Khalidi kindly read earlier versions of this work, and their comments and suggestions saved me from many a mistake and oversight. Two anonymous reviewers for the University of Chicago Press also wrote detailed and helpful reviews of the penultimate version. My thoughts on the topic have benefited from discussions with David M. Halperin, Saleh J. Agha, Joseph Massad, Martha Mundy, Annabel Keeler, Jacob Skovgaard-Petersen, Emran Mian, Frédéric Lagrange, and Mohammad Rihan. Douglas Mitchell of the University of Chicago Press gave crucial support to the idea of publishing this work. Russell Harper carefully edited the manuscript I submitted, correcting or pointing out a number of stylistic infelicities and obscurities. Christine Schwab conscientiously supervised the book through the proofreading stage. My work is much the better for the kind contributions of everyone mentioned. I have, however, undoubtedly failed to do justice to all comments and suggestions, and the remaining shortcomings are my own.

My research would not have been possible were it not for the resources of the following libraries, kindly made available to me by their curators, librarians, and staff: Cambridge University Library; the Library of the Faculty of Oriental Studies in Cambridge; the British Library; the Jafet Library of the American University of Beirut; the Library of the London School of Oriental and African Studies; the Berlin Staatsbibliothek (Preussischen Kulturbesitz); the Princeton University Library; and the Chester Beatty Library in Dublin. During my research trips, I enjoyed the hospitality of family and close friends: Mona El-Rouayheb, Marwan El-Rowayheb, Malek Shareef, and Nisreen Salti. Maher Jarrar, Samer Traboulsi, Suleiman Mourad, and Amal Ghazal kindly helped me to obtain out-of-the-way books and copies of manuscripts.

Special thanks to Manja Klemenčič, for her support and patience; and to my parents, for . . . everything.

Introduction

The present study is an attempt to reconstruct the way in which male homosexual behavior and feelings were conceived and evaluated in the Arab-Islamic Middle East between 1500 and 1800, the centuries immediately preceding the beginnings of modernization and westernization in the nineteenth century. My central contention is that Arab-Islamic culture on the eve of modernity lacked the concept of "homosexuality," and that writings from the period do not evince the same attitude toward all aspects of what we might be inclined to call homosexuality today. An appreciation of this point is crucial to understanding attitudes toward homosexuality in the premodern Arab-Islamic world.

Tolerance of Homosexuality?

The Arabic literature of the early Ottoman period (1516–1798) is replete with casual and sometimes sympathetic references to homosexual love. Biographical dictionaries, poetic anthologies, and belletristic works on profane love relate, usually without any hint of disapproval, the pederastic love affairs of prominent poets, religious scholars, and political notables. Much if not most of the extant love poetry of the period is pederastic in tone, portraying an adult male poet's passionate love for a teenage boy. A popular topic amongst poets and belletrists was whether beardless or downy-cheeked youths were more appropriate objects of passionate love. The general picture suggested by such passages is reinforced by European travel accounts of the period. Many travelers were of course silent on the issue, but several noted, usually with astonishment or disgust, that local men openly flaunted their amorous feelings for boys.[1] For example, the Englishman Joseph Pitts, a sailor who was a captured and sold into slavery at Algiers in 1678, to escape fifteen years later, noted:

> This horrible sin of Sodomy is so far from being punish'd amongst them, that it is part of their ordinary Discourse to boast of their detestable Actions of that

kind. 'Tis common for Men there [Algiers] to fall in Love with Boys, as 'tis here in England to be in Love with Women.[2]

The French traveler C. S. Sonnini, who visited Egypt between 1777 and 1780, made a similar observation:

> The passion contrary to nature . . . the inconceivable appetite which dishonored the Greeks and Persians of antiquity, constitute the delight, or, to use a juster term, the infamy of the Egyptians. It is not for the women that their amorous ditties are composed: it is not on them that tender caresses are lavished; far different objects inflame them.[3]

To be sure, such testimony from often bigoted travelers should be treated with caution.[4] However, their claims receive support from the fact that Muslim travelers who "rediscovered Europe" in the first half of the nineteenth century found it noteworthy that the men there did *not* court or eulogize male youths. For example, the Moroccan scholar Muḥammad al-Ṣaffār, who visited Paris in 1845–46, wrote:

> Flirtation, romance, and courtship for them take place only with women, for they are not inclined to boys or young men. Rather, that is extremely disgraceful to them.[5]

The Egyptian scholar Rifāʿah al-Ṭahṭāwī, who was in Paris between 1826 and 1831, noted:

> Amongst the laudable traits of their character, similar really to those of the Bedouin [*ʿarab*], is their not being inclined toward loving male youths and eulogizing them in poetry, for this is something unmentionable for them and contrary to their nature and morals. One of the positive aspects of their language and poetry is that it does not permit the saying of love poetry of someone of the same sex. Thus, in the French language a man cannot say: I loved a youth (*ghulām*), for that would be an unacceptable and awkward wording. Therefore if one of them translates one of our books he avoids this by saying in the translation: I loved a young female (*ghulāmah*) or a person (*dhātan*).[6]

The surprise expressed by Saffār and Ṭahṭāwī suggests that they came from societies in which "flirtation, romance, and courtship" with boys was quite familiar, as was composing "amorous ditties" for male youths.

It is perhaps tempting to view such passages as evidence of a widespread tolerance of homosexuality or—to be more precise—pederasty in the pre-nineteenth-century Islamic world. Such an interpretation has been advanced by modern historians. In his pioneering comparative study *Sexual Variance in Society and History* (1976), Vern L. Bullough propounded the view that Islam, in contrast to Christianity, is a "sex-positive" religion, and that homosexuality was widely tolerated in medieval Muslim societies.[7] John Boswell, in his *Christianity, Social Tolerance, and Homosexuality* (1980), similarly contrasted an increasingly homophobic cultural climate in medieval Europe with what he saw as widespread tolerance for homosexuality in Muslim Spain.[8] Specialists in Arab-Islamic history have made similar, if more nuanced, claims. For instance, Marshall Hodgson, in his influential *The Venture of Islam,* wrote that in medieval Islamic civilization,

> despite strong Sharʿi [i.e., Islamic legal] disapproval, the sexual relations of a mature man with a subordinate youth were so readily accepted in upper-class circles that there was often little or no effort to conceal their existence . . . The fashion entered poetry, especially the Persian.[9]

Bernard Lewis made the same point in his recent *Music from a Distant Drum:*

> Homosexuality is condemned and forbidden by the holy law of Islam, but there are times and places in Islamic history when the ban on homosexual love seems no stronger than the ban on adultery in, say, Renaissance Italy or seventeenth-century France. Some [classical Arabic, Persian, and Turkish] poems are openly homosexual; some poets, in their collected poems, even have separate sections for love poems addressed to males and females.[10]

Both Hodgson and Lewis suggest that what was cultivated openly in society is precisely that which Islamic law prohibited. As I hope to make clear in the course of this study, this assumption is questionable. What Islamic law prohibits is sexual intercourse between men, especially anal intercourse. It is hardly credible to suggest that such illicit intercourse was carried out in public. What unfolded in public was presumably such things as courting and expressions of passionate love. It may seem natural for modern historians to gloss over the distinction between committing sodomy and expressing passionate love for a youth, and to describe both activities as manifestations of "homosexuality." But this only goes to show that the term is anachronistic and unhelpful in this particular context. Islamic religious scholars of the period were committed to the precept that sodomy (*liwāṭ*) was one of the most abominable sins a man could commit. However, many of them clearly did not believe that falling in love with a boy or expressing this love in verse was therefore also illicit. Indeed, many prominent religious scholars indulged openly in such activity. The example that follows is a case in point.

The Egyptian scholar ʿAbdallah al-Shabrāwī (d. 1758) was for over thirty years Rector (*Shaykh*) of the Azhar college in Cairo, perhaps the most prestigious Islamic college in the Arabic-speaking world. He was also an accomplished poet, and his collected poetry (*Dīwān*) was, according to a scholar writing two generations later, "well known among people."[11] The *Dīwān* consists overwhelmingly of love poetry, much of which clearly depicts a young male beloved. An example is the following poem, in which the gender of the beloved is indicated both by the allusion to beard-down in the third verse, and more clearly by the last verse, which reveals the beloved's name to be Ibrāhīm:

> My lord, by Him who has granted you comeliness, splendor and beauty.
> And who in your bewitching eyes has permitted lovers some licit magic.
> And who has bestowed on your cheeks that thing which lovers have disputed at such length.
> Grant nearness to a lover for whom infatuation is a strict duty and forgetfulness is impossible.
> O gazelle! No! You are even more exalted, whose neck puts the gazelle to shame.
> O namesake of al-Khalīl [the epithet of the Prophet Ibrāhīm], you are cold and yet set my heart ablaze.[12]

Another poem commemorates the growth of beard-down (*ʿidhār*) on the cheeks of an Ibrāhīm in the year 1110 of the Muslim era (i.e., 1698–99 CE). The poem ends with the following words, containing the date of composition in letter-code: "The hill flowers delight on the cheeks of Ibrāhīm."[13] Yet another poem is introduced by the poet himself with the following words: "I also said a love poem of a youth (*qultu mutaghazzilan fī shābb*) who studied with me the sciences of language, addressing him dallyingly."[14]

It is difficult to believe that Shabrāwī was openly committing a cardinal sin in composing such poetry. Of course, a religious scholar may sometimes fail to live up to the principles he preaches. Yet in such cases one would expect some discretion, not a public flaunting of the transgression. It is much more likely that Shabrāwī simply did not believe that what he was doing fell into the same category as the sodomy that was so strictly prohibited by Islamic law. Indeed, the love poetry of the *Dīwān* repeatedly insists on the chaste nature of the poet's affection: "he [i.e., the poet] has no wish for that which is prohibited"; "I have chastity by natural disposition, not affectation"; "my conscience desists from sin."[15] Shabrāwī seems not to have had an attitude toward "homosexuality" at all, but apparently drew a central distinction between, on the one hand, falling ardently in love with a boy and expressing this love in verse and, on the other hand, committing sodomy with a boy. Until quite recently, it was common in Europe to tolerate or even value ardent love between an unmarried man and an unmarried woman but to condemn premarital sex. This combination of attitudes is only contradictory if one wrongheadedly insists on interpreting the coexisting judgments as expressions of both tolerance and intolerance of "heterosexuality."

Constructionism and Essentialism

The assumption that it is unproblematic to speak of either tolerance or intolerance of homosexuality in the premodern Middle East would seem to derive from the assumption that homosexuality is a self-evident fact about the human world to which a particular culture reacts with a certain degree of tolerance or repression. From this perspective, writing the history of homosexuality is seen as analogous to writing, say, the history of women. One assumes that the concept "homosexual," like the concept "woman," is shared across historical periods, and that what varies and may be investigated historically is merely the changing cultural (popular, scientific, legal, etc.) attitude toward such people. In contrast to this "essentialist" view, a number of anthropologists, sociologists, and historians, inspired in the main by the late French philosopher Michel Foucault, have recently emphasized the "constructed," or historically conditioned, nature of our modern sexual categories. They claim that the concept of homosexuality (and heterosexuality) was developed in Europe in the late nineteenth century, and that though its meaning may overlap with earlier concepts such as "sodomite" or "invert," it is not, strictly speaking, synonymous with these. For example, Foucault stressed that the term "sodomite" applied to the perpetrator of an act; someone who was tempted to commit sodomy but refrained out of moral or religious considerations was thus not a sodomite. By contrast, the category "homosexual" would include someone who has the inclination, even if it is not translated into action.[16] On this account, homosexuality is no more a synonym for sodomy than heterosexuality is equivalent to fornication.

Foucault's "constructionist" claim has inspired much recent work in the history of homosexuality, but it has also provoked sometimes heated "essentialist" rejoinders. It is generally acknowledged that the term "homosexualität" was coined in the late 1860s by the Austro-Hungarian writer Karl Maria Kertbeny, and that the first English equivalent first appeared in print some twenty years later. "Essentialists" insist that though the term "homosexuality" was new, the concept was not. Rejecting Foucault's claim of conceptual discontinuity, they believe that the new term corresponds in meaning to earlier terms such as the medieval Latin *sodomia* or the classical Arabic *liwāṭ*.[17]

The adjudication of the dispute between constructionists and essentialists should of course be based on a careful investigation of the historical evidence. To avoid prejudging the issue, close attention will have to be paid to the premodern—in this case Arabic—terms and phrases used in various contexts to designate acts and actors that we would be inclined to call "homosexual." Only then will it be possible to determine whether such terms and phrases are equivalent in meaning to the English term "homosexual." Unfortunately, modern scholars are often not so careful. For instance, one recent author translates the Arabic medical term *ubnah* as "homosexuality," even though he himself acknowledges that the term only applied to the male who desired to be anally penetrated.[18] A man who regularly anally penetrated other men was not thought to have *ubnah* but would presumably be deemed a "homosexual" today. The two terms are simply not synonymous. Recent general histories of homosexuality find a "disparity" between the proclaimed ideals and actual behavior of some Islamic scholars who, on the one hand, condemned "homosexuality" but, on the other, wrote "strongly homoerotic poetry."[19] What Islamic scholars condemned was not "homosexuality" but *liwāṭ*, that is, anal intercourse between men. Writing a love poem of a male youth would simply not fall under the juridical concept of *liwāṭ*.

What such examples show is that care should be taken before translating as "homosexual" any Arabic term attested in the texts. The possibility at issue is precisely whether pre-nineteenth-century Arab-Islamic culture lacked the concept of homosexuality altogether, and operated instead with a set of concepts (like *ubnah* or *liwāṭ*) each of which pick out some of the acts and actors we might call "homosexual" but which were simply not seen as instances of one overarching phenomenon. In the course of this study I hope to show that this was indeed the case. I argue that distinctions not captured by the concept of "homosexuality" were all-important from the perspective of the culture of the period. One such distinction is that between the "active" and the "passive" partner in a homosexual encounter—these were typically not conceptualized or evaluated in the same way. Another distinction is that between passionate infatuation (*ʿishq*) and sexual lust—emphasizing this distinction was important for those who would argue for the religious permissibility of the passionate love of boys. A third distinction centers on exactly what sexual acts were involved—Islamic law prescribed severe corporal or capital punishment for anal intercourse between men, but regarded, say, kissing, fondling, or non-anal intercourse as less serious transgressions.

The State of the Field

Much of what has been written on homosexuality in Arab-Islamic civilization shirks the conceptual point discussed in the previous section.[20] Proceeding on the basis of an unquestioned "essentialist" assumption, many historians have assumed that their task is to point out the extent to which "pederasty" or "homosexuality" was practiced or tolerated, and perhaps to offer explanations of this phenomenon. The tendency is very much in evidence already in Sir Richard Burton's remarks on "Pederasty" in the "Terminal Essay" to his translation of *The Arabian Nights* in 1886. Writing before the term "homosexuality" was introduced into the English language, Burton still assumed that he was faced with one phenomenon, "pederasty," which he claimed was widespread in the Islamic world and regarded as at worst a peccadillo. He believed that this was due to the "blending of masculine and feminine temperaments" in the region.[21] More recent commentators often proceed in the same fashion. The article "Liwāṭ" in the *Encyclopaedia of Islam,* published exactly one hundred years after Burton's essay, notes that homosexuality was prohibited by Islamic law but nevertheless widely practiced and tolerated in Islamic history after the eighth century. This is traced back to the "corruption of morals" by luxury and the "rapid process of acculturation" following in the wake of the Islamic conquest of the Middle East.[22] Similarly, one historian has sought to explain what he believed to be widespread pederasty or homosexuality in Arab-Islamic civilization by invoking supposedly "oversatiated" heterosexual appetites among the upper classes of society.[23] At least one other historian has advanced the exact opposite explanation: widespread homosexuality was supposedly caused by gender segregation and the resulting frustration of heterosexual appetites.[24] One may suspect that such "explanations" reveal very little besides the moral prejudices of those who offer them, and their sense of what stands in need of explanation and what does not. More crucially, however, such studies do not seem to suspect that the culture under discussion may not have shared our concept of homosexuality, and may thus have seen as unrelated certain phenomena that we are inclined to conflate.

A broadly "constructionist" approach to the issue of homosexuality in Arab-Islamic history has recently been suggested by writers such as Arno Schmitt, Everett Rowson, and Thomas Bauer.[25] They emphasize that the modern concept of homosexuality was absent from premodern Arab-Islamic culture, which, like classical Greek and Roman culture, tended to categorize and evaluate people according to whether they were active or passive in a sexual relation, and not according to the gender of their partners. This study offers some support for their claim, but argues that the distinction between active and passive was merely one of several distinctions that are not captured by the modern concept of homosexuality but are nevertheless crucial to understanding the attitudes underlying the texts that have come down to us. An exclusive emphasis on the distinction between active and passive will not allow us to understand the attitude of the majority of writers of the period who, like ʿAbdallah al-Shabrāwī, did not have a single attitude even toward "active" homosexuality, but held the distinction between, for example, passionate infatuation and lust, or between passionate kissing and anal intercourse, to be important.

The secondary literature on attitudes toward homosexuality in Arab-Islamic civilization consists overwhelmingly of brief discussions that try to encompass the entire geographic and historical span of this civilization. Even the few studies that focus on a text or a selection of thematically related texts usually try to supply a context in the form of general remarks about homosexuality in Arab-Islamic civilization. Such general discussions or remarks are based on a highly selective use of sources spanning many centuries and different geographic regions. All too often, sweeping claims are based on no more than a handful of sources, and sometimes even a single text.[26] For instance, in a recent article which displays an admirable awareness of the need to avoid anachronism when discussing attitudes toward homosexuality in Arab-Islamic culture, J. T. Monroe nevertheless states that "Islamic jurisprudence" regards homosexual attraction to be "entirely normal and natural," in sharp contrast to "Christianity," which holds that such attraction is a "pathological character defect."[27] The claim is supported by a single statement by a twelfth-century Islamic scholar to the effect that a man who claims that he can gaze at a handsome beardless youth without feeling lust is lying. Some qualified version of Monroe's claim may perhaps be defensible, but it is surely desirable to consider both the context of such a statement and a much larger number of texts before putting forward such a general claim.

The existing secondary literature also suffers from another kind of selectivity. It tends to focus on evidence from one or two particular genres, for instance poetry or juridical texts or medical works. There has as yet been no sustained effort to investigate the evidence from a whole range of genres and bring out their interrelations. This may be due to the fact that modern scholars tend to specialize in one particular field, such as Middle Eastern history or Arabic poetry or Islamic law or Sufism, and are understandably reluctant to venture beyond it. However, such an "interdisciplinary" approach is necessary. The textual evidence relevant to the study of attitudes toward homosexuality in Arab-Islamic history straddles such genres as biographical dictionaries, Islamic law, commentaries on the Qur'an, belles-lettres, Sufism, and medicine.

The source material that is relevant if one wishes to survey attitudes in Islamic, or even just Arab-Islamic, civilization from the seventh to the twentieth century is dauntingly large. A study that is less selective with regard to the amount and the genres of textual evidence it takes into account will also be a study that has a somewhat reduced geographic and temporal scope. In the present study I focus on the Arabic-speaking parts of the Ottoman Empire from the early sixteenth to the early nineteenth century. The nineteenth century saw the beginning of the encroachment of Western values and ideas upon the region. As I will briefly discuss in my conclusion, the encounter with European Victorian morality was to have profound effects on local attitudes toward what came to be called "sexual inversion" or "sexual perversion" (*shudhūdh jinsī*). The present work should hopefully set the stage for a study of this profound change.

I should perhaps add that the imposed geographic and temporal limits do not imply any commitment on my part to the uniqueness of attitudes in that area and period. However, I also do not want to claim that each and every point I make will be valid for earlier periods of Arab-Islamic history. For instance, the love poetry of the period I study predominantly portrayed a chaste and unreciprocated love for a person whose gender is usually either indeterminate or male. This may or may not be true of earlier periods of Arabic history. Also, Islamic scholars of the period I study typically deemed composing love poetry of beardless youths religiously permissible. Again, this may or may not have been true of earlier periods. In general, it seems to me that the best approach to recovering the history of attitudes toward homosexuality in Arab-Islamic civilization is to conduct a series of more narrowly defined studies. Only then will the exact balance of continuity and change between various periods and regions become clear.

Overview of the Present Study

The present study is conceived as a work of cultural and intellectual history. The focus will not be on homosexual behavior in the past, but on how such behavior was perceived and represented. I should perhaps emphasize this point. In particular, I do not wish to suggest that the sexual behavior of individuals must conform in a straightforward way to the dominant sexual categories or concepts used in their society. For example, I shall be arguing that biographical and bawdy works from the period tend to distinguish conceptually between the active pederast and the effeminate pathic. This need not imply that individuals always acted in ways that fit neatly with this distinction. By the same token, it might be possible to establish that in the dominant discourse of the modern West, people tend to be classified according to the gender of their preferred sexual partners, and not according to their preferred role (insertive or receptive) in sexual intercourse. Even if this is the case, it does not follow that certain individuals do not act in ways that confound the dominant categorization—for example, pursuing both women and teenage boys, but never accepting to play the "receptive" role. On the other hand, it does not seem plausible to think of the distinction between representations and behavior as a rigid dichotomy, and to maintain that the former is completely unresponsive to the latter and the latter completely uninfluenced by the former. I therefore think that much of what I have to say about dominant perceptions will also reveal something about broad behavioral patterns.

The culture I shall be studying is the one shared by urban, literate Muslim men in the Arabic-speaking parts of the Ottoman Empire between 1500 and 1800. The textual evidence that I consider was almost invariably written in urban centers such as Cairo, Damascus, Aleppo, Mosul, Baghdad, Mecca, and Medina. By textual evidence I mean primarily Arabic literary sources such as chronicles, biographical dictionaries, belletristic works in verse and prose, and Islamic mystical and legal works. This will inevitably imply a bias toward the attitudes and values of the learned male elite, by whom and for whom such works were written. One obviously cannot assume that such values and attitudes can without further ado be thought to apply to other social groups. On the other hand, there would seem to be positive reasons for not supposing that the main cultural strands I shall discuss were narrowly confined to the elite. The cultural significance given to the distinction between active and passive partners was hardly an elite phenomenon. It is still apparent today amongst all social classes in the Middle East. The courting of boys by adult men also does not seem to have been an elite phenomenon. The literary sources suggest that men of non-elite status—bakers, tailors, street-sellers, and "rabble" attending the Saints Fairs of Egypt—could behave likewise. There is also no reason to believe that acceptance of the authority of Islamic law—even if one occasionally failed to live up to all the demands of this authority—was confined to the sociopolitical elite. The attitudes I discuss may have been more significantly correlated with gender than with social class. Unfortunately the literary sources of the period give almost no information on female attitudes to love and sex.

If the focus on the learned male elite seems somewhat narrow, speaking of the Arab-Islamic part of the Ottoman Empire between 1500 and 1800 could appear too broad. It might reasonably be asked whether it is legitimate to assume that there was no significant evolution and/or regional differences in attitudes within the geographic and temporal boundaries of this study. I believe not, and my approach will be essentially systematic rather than diachronic. I should emphasize that I have not started by assuming uniformity within the geographic and temporal scope of my study. The supposition that the culture of the literate classes in the period and area under consideration displayed an overall stability in time and uniformity from city to city is one that I believe is largely substantiated by the textual evidence. This does not preclude the existence of individual differences in outlook, but it is not possible to correlate such differences with period or region; they exist equally between two individuals of the same generation or city. In fact, the geographic and temporal continuity almost certainly extends beyond the limits of this study. I would expect that many of the points I make (though probably not all) are valid for Turkey and Persia between 1500 and 1800, as well as for the Arab-Islamic world in the Abbasid and Mamluk periods (750–1516).

The questions raised concerning the scope of the present study are certainly legitimate, especially given the above-mentioned tendency to make undifferentiated statements about attitudes in "Islam" or "Islamic civilization." However, a justified suspicion of this approach can easily lead to an overemphasis on the differences between periods, regions, or social groups. Current discussions of attitudes toward homosexuality in Arab-Islamic history often present "religious scholars" and "Sufis" and "poets" and "the upper classes" as distinct groups with distinct and competing mentalities and values. However, this is a caricature of social reality.[28] At least in the period under consideration, a substantial number of individuals were all of these things at once. A person might be an Islamic religious jurist, and as such committed to the principles of Islamic law. However, being an Islamic religious jurist would almost certainly be one of several social roles he assumed. The same individual would also think of himself as a "man," as opposed to a woman or a child or an "effeminate" man. This social role carried with it certain demands on behavior that were independent of, and sometimes in tension with, the demands of Islamic law. Similarly, the same individual might also think of himself as a "refined" and "urbane" individual, in contrast to "rustic" and "coarse" common people, peasants, and nomads. This again involved certain expectations as to behavior, taste, and demeanor, expectations that had little or nothing to do with religion. In other words, a literate, urban male Muslim would be under the influence of distinct cultural strands. These cultural strands were independent of each other, and embodied values and assumptions that were potentially or actually in tension with each other. A study that ignores this fact will fail to do justice to this complex reality.

Rather than trying to recover attitudes that were supposedly characteristic of particular social groups, I will focus on distinct but coexisting strands in the culture of the urban elite.[29] In particular, I will focus on three cultural strands that were relevant to perceptions and evaluations of what we might be inclined to call homosexual behavior or sentiments. In the first chapter of the study, I will present one cultural strand according to which the "active" or "insertive" role in sexual intercourse was uniquely appropriate to a man, and the "passive" or "receptive" role was uniquely appropriate to a woman. A man who willingly assumed the latter role was violating conventional gender roles, and was often stereotyped as effeminate and thought to suffer from an abnormal or pathological condition. However, a man who sought to have "active" or "insertive" intercourse with a beardless male youth was not violating gender roles, nor was he stereotyped in the same way. In the second chapter, I will present another cultural strand, one which valued passionate love and a general aesthetic sensibility toward human beauty in the form of women or beardless youths. Such a sensibility was thought to be the hallmark of urbane and refined people, and to lie at the root of evocative love poetry. In some Islamic mystical circles, such an aestheticist regard for beautiful women or handsome youths was given a metaphysical dimension, and held to be a means of personally experiencing the overwhelming beauty of God. In the third chapter, I discuss the cultural strand that receives expression in Islamic law, and the related disciplines of commentaries on the Qur'an and on the canonical sayings (*ḥadīth*) of the Prophet Muḥammad. This strand perceived sexual relations between men as a transgression of Holy Law, though according to most schools of law only anal intercourse was deemed a cardinal sin. Anything that could be perceived to be the first step along the slippery slope to such transgressions, such as gazing at beardless youths or being alone with them, became deeply problematic. However, jurists were also committed to the principle that one ought not prohibit what God has made licit, or think ill of one's fellow Muslims, and the efforts of especially zealous jurists to prohibit outright such "preliminaries" of sodomy met with resistance from other jurists. Most jurists did not deem that a man's passionate love of a youth was in itself a sin, and permitted the composition of pederastic love poetry.

CHAPTER ONE

Pederasts and Pathics

Sex as Polarization

Toward the end of the year 1701, a Druze chieftain (Emir) from the Wādī al-Taym area in Syria came to Damascus to be officially invested as head military official (*Yāyābāshī*) of his home region by the governor of the city. According to a contemporary chronicler, the Emir was a notorious womanizer, who "in Damascus was determined to conduct himself with his characteristic lewdness." Once, while at the house of a local woman, he was surprised by around twenty Turcoman soldiers, who gang-raped him and robbed him of his clothes, leaving him barefoot and clad only in his inner garments. "He who encroaches upon the womenfolk (*ḥarīm*) of the Muslims deserves more than this," they reportedly said before letting him go. "News of the incident," the chronicler added, "reached the women and children [of the city], and songs about him [i.e., the Emir] were composed and performed by singers . . . He then departed to the land of the Druzes, his home, and it was said that the woman remained untainted [i.e., she was not dishonored before the arrival of the soldiers], and thus God forsook the damned Emir at the hands of the Turcomans."[1] The quoted remarks make it clear in what terms the chronicler, and the Muslim population of Damascus in general, viewed the reported action of the soldiers. An outsider, and a non-Muslim at that, by his attempt to seduce or rape a local woman, had threatened the honor of the community at large. The threat was not only averted, but the potential dishonorer was himself dishonored by being buggered, and the Turcoman troops came in this particular case to be seen as instruments of poetic justice. Underlying the interpretation, of course, is a tacit identification of sexual penetration, both the one averted and the one committed by the soldiers, with dishonor. This assumption is one that will be all too familiar to anyone acquainted with the more bawdy or ribald aspects of present-day Arab (and Mediterranean) culture, as manifested for example in jokes and insults: to penetrate phallically is to dominate, subjugate, and ultimately to humiliate. According to the oneiromantic handbook of the Damascene scholar ʿAbd al-Ghanī al-Nābulusī

(d. 1731), to dream that one is sexually penetrating a rival or enemy forebodes that one will get the better of him in real life, whereas being penetrated by him is ominous, signifying the reverse.[2] A strikingly uncompromising expression of this way of conceiving phallic penetration is contained in the following defamatory poem in which Ibrāhīm al-Ghazālī (d. 1678), deputy judge at one of the courts of Damascus, lampooned a contemporary:

> By God ask, on my behalf, the gross character: "Of what do you disapprove in so-and-so?" and you will be amazed.
>
> You will not find the reason to be other than that I did not fuck him since he has long disgusted me.
>
> And had I inflicted upon him my penis and given it to him, he would not have reckoned I had any faults.
>
> But I now cauterize his ulcerous arse with the fire of my penis, and ascend the ranks [of virtue] in his eyes.
>
> I impose on my self what is contrary to its preference; before me many did what I am now doing . . .
>
> O penis! Arise! Put on your armor, and enter his interior like a raider, and give us his guts as spoils.
>
> Make him wide as you hump and shake within him, and if you cannot, delegate in your place a piece of wood.[3]

As described in this context, the act of penetration can hardly be called "sexual," as it is dissociated, not only from love and intimacy, but also from desire and pleasure. It is explicitly stated that the penetrator has to overcome his feeling of disgust and impose on his self "what is contrary to its preference," whereas the fact that the penetrated is said to derive pleasure from the act simply adds to the insult. "You who closes his thighs around the manhood from pleasure! You pasture-ground of penises!" a seventeenth-century Egyptian scholar wrote to an adversary.[4] As has been noted by the psychiatrist T. Vanggaard, it seems to be a misconception to assume that men are only able to sustain an erection and have intercourse if they are attracted sexually (in any ordinary sense of the word) to the person in question. In some cases, the erection may be sustained by feelings of aggressive hostility.[5] The possibility of what Vanggaard calls "phallic aggression" seems to have been conceived in the premodern Arab East. The Iraqi scholar Maḥmūd al-Alūsī (d. 1854), for example, stated that some people in his time used sodomy as a way of getting revenge in vendettas (*akhdhan li-al-tha'r*).[6] In addition, some of the traditions which were invoked by Muslim religious scholars to explain the rise of sodomy among "the people of Lot" (*Qawm Lūṭ*) stated that they started to sodomize strangers as a way of driving them off their land, "without having any sexual desire to do that (*min ghayr shahwah bihim ilā dhālik*)."[7]

Instead of references to desire and pleasure, the quoted verses of Ibrāhīm al-Ghazālī contain a remarkable profusion of metaphors derived from the language of violence and war: infliction, fire, armor, raid, spoils. Conversely, literary descriptions of battles in classical Arabic often conjure up, perhaps unconsciously, the imagery of sexual intercourse: the defeated soldiers "turn tail" (*wallaw al-adbār*); the swords of the victorious ravage the turned tails (*fataka* or *ʿamila fī adbārihim*) of their enemies; the sword of the powerful military commander was said to "make courageous men into women" (*yuʾannithu al-buhm al-dhukūr*) or to "make male enemies menstruate" (*jaʿala al-dhukūr min al-aʿādī ḥuyyaḍan*).[8] The word *futūḥ* can be used equally of military conquest and of sexual penetration or deflowering. If the act of penetration can be seen as a uniting of two persons or as "making love," it can also be perceived as a deeply "polarizing" experience, which distinguishes the dominant from the dominated, the dishonorer from the dishonored, and the victorious from the defeated.[9] Some recent writers seem to want to juxtapose the two views, and attribute the former to the modern West and the latter to the Mediterranean–Middle Eastern area.[10] Yet the idea of sex as *jimāʿ* (i.e., bringing together, combining) was not foreign to the premodern Middle East, nor is the idea of "screwing" in the sense of defeating or insulting in any way absent in the contemporary West. Having said this, it is still undeniable that the aggressive, masculine-centered view featured much more prominently in the public (male-dominated) discourse of the early Ottoman Arab East than the affectionate-androgynous view. In the ongoing rivalries for posts, money, status, and influence in the exclusively male public sphere, allusions to phallic penetration were always near at hand. When the poet Māmāyah al-Rūmī (d. 1579) was appointed as interpreter at one of the courts of Damascus at the expense of the previous holder of the position, a Turk by the name of Amrallah, he composed the following lines in celebration:

> Thanks to God, I achieved my desired aim, and the opponent was discharged.
> And I received what I had hoped for, and God's will (*amr Allah*) was done (*mafʿūlan*).[11]

Since *mafʿūl bihi* is the term usually used to denote the passive sexual partner, the allusion is very clear in Arabic: Amrallah has been "screwed" by his successful rival for the post.

The modern concept of "homosexuality" elides a distinction that, in the Middle East, was (and still is) fraught with symbolic significance: that between the penetrator and the penetrated. Not surprisingly, in ordinary language there was no corresponding concept that would apply to both those who preferred the active-insertive role and those who preferred the passive-receptive role in a homosexual act. The term *lūṭī* was typically used of the former, while *mukhannath* or *ma'būn* or (more colloquially) *ʿilq* was reserved for the latter. It is worth dwelling on this point, since there is a persistent tendency among some modern scholars to overlook this distinction and render the indigenous term *lūṭī* as "homosexual."[12] In Islamic law, the *lūṭī* is a man who commits *liwāṭ* (i.e., anal intercourse with another man), regardless of whether he commits it as an active or passive partner.[13] However, in ordinary, nontechnical language (as manifested in, for example, bawdy-satirical anecdotes) the term *lūṭī* almost always meant "pederast." One short anecdote illustrates the fact that a stereotypical *lūṭī* was thought to be interested in active-insertive anal intercourse with boys: ". . . of another person it was related that he was a *lā'iṭ* [variant of *lūṭī*], and so his wife told him: I have what boys have (*ʿindī mā ʿind al-ghilmān*). He replied: Yes, but it has an unpleasant neighbor [i.e., the vagina]."[14] A tradition related by the Shīʿī scholar Muḥammad al-Ḥurr al-ʿĀmilī (d. 1693) also confirms that *liwāṭ* was normally understood to be equivalent to sodomizing boys: a heretic (*zindīq*) asked ʿAlī ibn Abī Ṭālib (the Prophet Muḥammad's son-in-law) for the reason behind the religious prohibition of *liwāṭ*. ʿAlī supposedly answered: "If carnal penetration of a boy (*ityān al-ghulām*) were permitted, men would dispense with women, and this would lead to the disruption of procreation."[15] In the Egyptian version of the popular, orally transmitted epic *Sīrat Baybars,* the term *lūṭī* is used of adult males who make sexual advances to beardless youths, and the term is used interchangeably with the colloquial term *bitāʿ al-ṣighār,* which roughly translates as "he who is for youngsters."[16] According to an anonymous and tongue-in-cheek couplet cited in both a late seventeenth-century Egyptian and a late eighteenth-century Damascene text:

> The lover of beardless boys is known among people as a *lūṭī,* and the lover of young women is called a fornicator [*zānī*].
>
> So, out of chastity, I turned to those with beards, and thus I am neither a *lūṭī* nor a *zānī*.[17]

The Egyptian scholar and poet Aḥmad al-Khafājī (d. 1659) complained in verse of the age in which he was living, claiming that it was similar to "the people of Lot" in giving preference to young upstarts at the expense of the older and venerable.[18] In a love poem, the Iraqi scholar ʿAbd al-Bāqī al-ʿUmarī (d. 1697/8) said of the eulogized female that, "if the people of Lot had seen her beauty, they would never have turned to a boy."[19]

The image of "the people of Lot" in the Islamic tradition was, to be sure, not entirely uniform. In commenting on the just-quoted verse of ʿAbd al-Bāqī al-ʿUmarī, the Iraqi scholar Muḥammad Amīn al-ʿUmarī (d. 1788) reminded readers that the people of Lot not only sodomized boys but also adult male strangers.[20] This was the standard dual image of the "people of Lot" in the Qurʾanic commentaries of the time: on the one hand they were portrayed as pederasts and, on the other, as an aggressive people who anally raped trespassers.[21] In both cases, however, they were assumed to be the "active" or "insertive" party, and this assumption tended to reflect back on the juridical literature itself. The Palestinian religious scholar Muḥammad al-Saffārīnī (d. 1774), for example, defined *liwāṭ* or "the act of the people of Lot" (*ʿamal qawm Lūṭ*) as "carnal penetration of males in the anus (*ityān al-dhukūr fī al-dubur*)."[22] Though Saffārīnī was committed to the idea that the man who willingly assumes the passive-receptive role in anal intercourse has committed sodomy and may be prosecuted accordingly, it still seemed natural for him to define sodomy in a way which suggests that it is only the active-insertive party who commits it. Similarly, the Egyptian jurist Ibrāhīm al-Bājūrī (d. 1860) stated that *liwāṭ* was "the act committed by the people of Lot (*fiʿl qawm Lūṭ*), for they were the first to sodomize men (*fa-innahum awwal man atā al-rijāl fī adbārihim*)." He went on to claim that the habit disappeared after the destruction of Sodom, and was only resurrected after the Islamic conquest of the Middle East. Many soldiers were away from their women, and availed themselves of native, subservient males instead, and so they "did it to them and treated them as women" (*faʿalū bihim wa ajrawhum majrā al-nisāʾ*).[23] Bājūrī's remarks are not particularly valuable as a historical observation, but again reveal that even jurists were prone to make the tacit assumption that *liwāṭ* ("the act of the people of Lot") was active rather than passive sodomy, and that the paradigmatic *lūṭī* was therefore the active-insertive partner. The assumption was articulated clearly in nonjuridical discourse, such as the following defamatory poem by the Aleppine poet Ḥusayn al-Jazarī (d. ca. 1624):

> Does the offspring of al-Naḥḥās Fatḥallah seek satisfaction for his
> scratchy arse?
> Trust my maternal cousin in *liwāṭ* and trust his extended, erect prick.
> Take it and forgo my penis, for I see no one suitable for that effeminate man
> (*mukhannath*) except that *lūṭī*.[24]

The confusion resulting from the assumption that *lūṭī* translates as "homosexual" may be seen, for example, in a modern discussion of the collection of erotic anecdotes entitled *Nuzhat al-albāb fīmā lā yūjad fī kitāb* by the

Egyptian scholar Aḥmad al-Tīfāshī (d. 1253). Having apparently been misled by a French translation, Robert Irwin asserts, in his absorbing and rewarding book *The Arabian Nights: A Companion,* that the sixth chapter of Tīfāshī's work deals with homosexuals, and goes on to give the "characteristic features" attributed to them:

> The homosexual should have a pleasant lodging, well-furnished with books and wine, and made pleasanter yet by the presence of doves and singing birds. A homosexual can be recognized by the way he stares directly at one, this direct gaze often being followed by a wink. The typical homosexual has thin legs with hairy ankles and tends to wear robes which reach right down to the ground. When he walks, his hands and his legs sway.[25]

Chapters 6–8 of al-Tīfāshī's book are in fact devoted to *al-lāṭā* (plural of *lūṭī*) and *al-murd al-mu'ājirīn.* Even a cursory reading of the Arabic text (to which Irwin did not have access) reveals that the former term refers to adult men who desire to sodomize boys—that is, to "pederasts" rather than "homosexuals"—while the term *murd mu'ājirīn* refers to beardless boy prostitutes who render sexual services to *al-lāṭā.* The quoted account of "characteristic features" runs these two categories together: it is the pederast who should have pleasant lodgings, books and wine, but it is the boy prostitute who may be recognized by his gaze, his legs, and the way he walks.[26] What is even more damaging to the assumption that the term *lūṭī* is synonymous with "homosexual" is the fact that a later chapter of Tīfāshī's work (chapter 12) deals with *al-khināth*—that is, effeminate adult men who desire to be sodomized by (preferably very masculine) men. This category is clearly treated by the author as distinct from the previously mentioned *lāṭā* and *mu'ājirīn* (the latter are beardless boys and their motives are depicted as pecuniary). It should be clear by now that the modern term "homosexual" hopelessly muddles certain native distinctions, and that insisting on using it in translation or paraphrase leads to serious misunderstanding.[27] It is also clear that Tīfāshī's work cannot be invoked, as Irwin does, in support of the idea that some medieval Arabs thought of homosexuality as a "single condition" shared by those who prefer the active role and those who prefer the passive, nor of the idea that this single condition was considered by some to be "a form of illness." There does not seem to be any support at all for the idea that pederasts were thought to suffer from an illness. One may admittedly encounter a few passages in which *liwāṭ* was called a *dā',* and the latter term may in appropriate contexts mean "disease." However, the term *dā'* was frequently used in a loose sense to cover any habit or character trait that was held to be reprehensible. The very passages or works that use the term *dā'* of *liwāṭ* also use it, for example, of stinginess (*bukhl*) or ignorance of religious stipulations (*jahl*).[28] There were no medical discussions of *liwāṭ* or any other indication that a tendency to commit *liwāṭ* was held to be a disease in the strict sense, with a physiological basis, physical symptoms, and natural remedies.[29] The *lūṭī* was instead widely represented as a morally dissolute person, a libertine (*fāsiq*), and this latter word was sometimes used as its synonym. Being a pederast was often spoken of in the same breath as being a drinker of wine: "he is suspected of drinking wine and being inclined to beardless boys"; "[he] loves boys and drink"; "he became famous for drinking wine and loving boys"; "both of them are unscrupulous wine-drinkers and rakes, well known for their carousing, and famous among rich and poor for kissing fair boys and fair girls."[30] As in the case of drinking alcohol, the antidote to pederasty was repentance. A story in a collection of humorous anecdotes, perhaps dating from the seventeenth century, started thus: "It was related that one of the *lūṭīs* repented (*tāba*) from sodomy (*liwāṭ*)."[31] In the romance of Baybars, men who make sexual advances to the young hero and his groom ʿUthmān are regularly beaten up until they say: "I repent at your hands, and swear by your head and eyes that I will no longer meet youngsters and commit *liwāṭ*," or, "My master! I repent and recant for what I did, and regret and repent at your hands from this time on, and if I should revert to anything of the kind then kill me."[32] The following couplet by the poet Māmāyah al-Rūmī also illustrates the tendency to assimilate pederasty to sins such as (heterosexual) fornication and drinking alcohol:

> My career in pursuit of fancy is ruined, so have mercy on me, O Bestower and Benefactor!
> I've lost this world and the next, on fornication, booze, and beardless boys in my time.[33]

It was the *ma'būn* or *mukhannath* who was viewed as a pathological case. The Arabic medical tradition, following the Greek, tended to regard the male who desires to be anally penetrated as being afflicted with a disease—*ubnah*—at least from the time of Abū Bakr al-Rāzī (d. ca. 925), and this continued to be the verdict of the medical treatises of the early Ottoman period.[34] *Ubnah* was classified as a disease with prescribed remedies in the medical works of ʿAbd al-Wahhāb al-Shaʿrānī (d. 1565), Dāwūd al-Anṭākī (d. 1599), and Aḥmad al-Qalyūbī (d. 1658).[35] Of the three, only Anṭākī discussed the etiology of the disease. He considered it to be caused by the presence of a boric substance (*māddah būrāqiyyah*) in the veins of the rectum, which burns and tickles the anus until it becomes like an itching wound, inducing the person with the disease to seek to have his anus penetrated. Though usually inherited (*mawrūth*), the disease could also be caused by being subjected to penetration, since the anal itch could be the effect of especially pungent semen. The person with *ubnah* was most often effeminate, and typically suffered from flabbiness, cough, a dull, languid look, dried lips, a fleshy face, and a large posterior. As a remedy, Anṭākī mentioned liquid potions of lapis lazuli, agaric, aloe, mastic, or clove with yogurt, all of which supposedly counteract pungent humors. He also suggested the efficacy of rubbing the anus with ash obtained by burning hair from the right thigh of a hyena.[36]

Even outside a strictly medical context, the desire of the passive sodomite was perceived as anomalous and as requiring a special explanation, for example in terms of a worm-infected anus.[37] Of course, the fact that passive sodomy was widely regarded as disease-induced did not imply that it ceased to be judged as morally and religiously reprehensible. However, it was not simply a sin that in principle anyone could commit—like, say, drinking alcohol or stealing. *Ubnah* was something a *ma'būn* had or suffered from, whereas *liwāṭ* was simply something a *lūṭī* did. The difference is strikingly illustrated in jurists' discussion of insults that qualify as formal accusations of illicit sexual intercourse. Calling a man a *lūṭī* always qualified as such an accusation, but in the case of calling someone a *ma'būn* opinions were less uniform. The Egyptian jurist Manṣūr al-Buhūtī (d. 1641), for example, asserted that the latter insult did not qualify as an accusation of illicit sexual intercourse, since it referred to a condition of the insulted person and did not explicitly claim that he acted in accordance with it (*al-ubnah al-mushār ilayhā lā tu'tī annahu yaf'al bi-muqtaḍāhā*).[38]

The concept of *liwāṭ* was thus to a large extent "behavioristic," whereas *ubnah* was more likely to be seen as an inner condition that gave rise to, and hence explained, peculiar behavior. *Ubnah* was a pathological or abnormal state which, permanently or recurrently, overwhelmed the person afflicted: "I would see him drink alcohol until he was intoxicated . . . and his *ubnah* would be aroused and he would remain restless until he would be done in his anus"; "I heard of a person of honorable status who was afflicted with the disease of *ubnah,* so, fearing that this would be divulged . . . he had a piece of wood in the shape of a penis made, and when the disease would be roused he would seclude himself . . . and lock the doors from fear of being discovered and treat himself with the wood . . . [afterwards] he would implore of God . . . that this disease would cease."[39] At least during the phase in which his disease is active, the *ma'būn* was seen as being thoroughly saturated with his deviant sexual preference, and he was typically portrayed in the works of bawdy comedy (*mujūn*) as insatiable and indiscriminately promiscuous (except perhaps for his preference for virile and well-endowed men).[40] Such a stock association is reiterated in a defamatory poem composed by the Damascene poet ʿAbd al-Ḥayy al-Khāl (d. 1715) of a contemporary whom he accused of being a passive sodomite (*ʿilq*):

> You of wide and generous posterior—and how many marks have we left on it!
> You who, if a penis appears in the Hijaz and the land of Rāmah,
> Cries and wails, saying, "I am tired of my residence [in Damascus]."
> Or if he smells a penis in al-Yamāmah says: "By God, to al-Yamāmah!"
> He prefers to everlasting bliss with wine [in paradise],
> A penis as the neck of a camel and as long as the legs of an ostrich.
> If the pricks that he has used to quench his cravings were put end to end,
> And he mounted them, he would reach the sky, and truly exceed the stars in stature.[41]

A common insult (attested for sixteenth- and seventeenth-century Damascus, seventeenth-century Cairo, and seventeenth- and eighteenth-century Mosul) which denigrated the passive male sodomite, and associated him with a ravenous sexual appetite, is the term *wasīʿ*, or "wide[-arsed]."[42]

The mentioned differences in the stereotypes of the *lūṭī* and the *maʾbūn* seem to be related to the fact that only the latter was perceived as being at odds with the ideal of masculinity. Effeminacy was not a part of the image of the *lūṭī*. Soldiers, for instance, had a reputation for being active sodomites.[43] The *Sakbāns,* mercenary soldiers who roamed the Syrian countryside in the early seventeenth century, were according to a contemporary source notorious pederasts and took many boys captive when they looted the suburbs of Damascus in 1606, as did the Egyptian troops of Muḥammad Bey Abū al-Dhahab after their sacking of Jaffa in 1775.[44] The Ottoman historian and belletrist Muṣṭafā ʿAlī (d. 1600), who visited Egypt in 1599, held that a large proportion of the cavalrymen (*jundīs*) there were pederasts.[45] According to the above-mentioned poet Māmāyah al-Rūmī:

> The art of *liwāṭ* is the way of masculinity (*fuḥūliyyah*), and might (*ʿizz*), so leave to Majnūn Laylah, and with Kuthayyir ʿAzz[ah],
> And go up to every handsome beardless boy, strip him, and, even if he cries, present him with your prick and fuck him by force.[46]

Liwāṭ was simply one of the temptations to which a man was exposed. On the other hand, a preference for the passive-receptive role in sexual intercourse was seen as the very antithesis of masculinity. A common synonym for *maʾbūn* was *mukhannath,* an effeminate man. The two terms were, to be sure, not perfect synonyms. A person suffering from *ubnah* could hide this fact and thus not behave in a way likely to be considered effeminate by his peers. It was also recognized that it was possible to be outwardly effeminate without being a passive sodomite. However, it seems misguided to expect a strictly literal use of what were, after all, very derogatory epithets. That the two terms were usually used interchangeably is clear from the bawdy-erotic literature, and is also confirmed by jurists of the period who discussed insults that qualify as formal accusations of illicit sexual intercourse. The Egyptian scholar Aḥmad al-Dardīr (d. 1786), for example, asserted that someone who calls a man a *mukhannath* has made such an accusation, and is thus bound to substantiate his claim or face punishment for slander. This is so, wrote Dardīr, even if the person swears that he only intended the strict lexical meaning of the term, because according to the prevalent norm (*ʿurf*), the term *mukhannath* was used of the passive sodomite.[47] The Damascene jurist ʿAlāʾ al-Dīn Muḥammad al-Ḥaṣkafī (d. 1677) also explicated the term *mukhannath* as "he who is penetrated like a woman" (*man yuʾtā ka-al-marʾah*).[48]

The passive male sodomite was seen as being in possession of a female sex drive, but without any of the constraints imposed on women in a patriarchal, gender-segregated society, and his image in bawdy-humorous works is similar to the image of promiscuous women (*al-qiḥāb*).[49] The parallel is also revealed at the level of insults: a woman could be called "wide" (*wasīʿah*) and the passive sodomite a "slut" (*qaḥbah*); or at the level of folk-etiology: the sex drive of the nymphomaniac could also be explained by a worm-induced itch.[50] The existence of the *maʾbūn* or *mukhannath* challenged what was, in the premodern Middle East, one of the most sharp and consequential of boundaries: the distinction between genders. Lying outside the bounds of normality, *ubnah* was seen as a force that was powerful and uncontrollable (capable of overturning the familiar order of things) but also comparatively rare. When jurists of the Ḥanafi school sought to defend their ruling that sodomy was not a subvariety of fornication (*zinā*)—and was therefore not subject to the same punishment—one of the arguments to which they resorted was that the incitement to fornication typically came from both parties, whereas the incitement to sodomy came from one party only.[51]

The conceptual distinction between the active and passive sodomite, and the association of the latter—but not the former—with the transgression of gender roles, is hardly distinctive of the early Ottoman Arab East. The same could more or less be said of contemporary Arab, southern European, or Latin American culture, or, for that matter, the culture of classical Greece and Rome, Viking-age Scandinavia, or pre-Meiji Japan. One is clearly dealing with a conceptualization that is very widespread, both geographically and historically. Transgressions of culturally sanctioned gender roles tend to provoke particularly strong feelings of unease and condemnation, and this is especially so in the case of men who, in strongly patriarchal societies like those mentioned above, adopt behavior seen as proper only to women.[52] The contempt and ridicule aroused by the *maʾbūn* thus tended to be greater than the disapproval allotted to the *lūṭī*. It was generally understood that one would rather be known as an active than a passive sodomite, as is clear from the following anecdote:

> It was related that a certain man entered his home with a beardless boy . . . when the beardless boy came [back] out he claimed that he had been the active party, so this was related to him [the man], so he said: "Trustworthiness is debased and sodomy is [therefore] forbidden except in the presence of two witnesses."[53]

It should be pointed out that it would be rash to assert on the basis of this passage, or the story of the rape of the Druze chieftain, or the defamatory poem of Ibrāhīm al-Ghazālī, that the active, "male" role in homosexual intercourse was regarded as being entirely free of opprobrium. Such an assertion has nevertheless been made, and an analogy is often drawn to what has been called the "double-standard" of traditional Mediterranean societies: outside of marriage (and historically also slavery) sexual relations are dishonoring for the female (the penetrated) but not for the male (the penetrator). As is to be expected, moral valuations are somewhat more complex than such a neat contrast suggests. First, the very distinction between male/penetrator and female/penetrated is much less relevant in one—hardly unimportant—context, namely the religious-juridical. It is in such contexts than one may encounter the otherwise atypical use of the word *lūṭī* to designate the passive as well as the active sodomite.[54] Second, there is abundant evidence that to say or insinuate of a man that he was a fornicator or an active sodomite was perceived and intended as a derogatory remark. For example, in a defamatory poem, the Damascene scholar Badr al-Dīn al-Ghazzī (d. 1577) said of his rival Muḥammad al-Ījī (d. 1577):

> and how many times has he not crept up on a beardless boy at night, and
> caused an opening in the upper part of the porch [*riwāq*—an allusion to the boy's rear].[55]

That this was not only the attitude of puritanical scholars is clear from the way the biographer Ḥasan al-Būrīnī (d. 1615) relates the following incident in his entry on the Damascene scholar Ismāʿīl al-Nābulusī (d. 1585):

> He was falsely suspected of [an affair with] a boy . . . and the religious scholars (*ʿulamāʾ*) supported him in this ugly affair but he encountered during that

> time extreme coldness from both elite and commoners, and this was because the boy went up to the hall of the governor . . . with blood flowing down his legs, claiming that this was due to his being penetrated.[56]

The different popular reactions to the reported act of Ismāʿīl al-Nābulusī in the late sixteenth century, and to the reported act of the Turcoman soldiers in the early eighteenth, is a testimony, not to changed sensibilities in the intervening period, but to the fundamentally context-dependent nature of the perception and evaluation of homosexual intercourse. In the first case, it is the alleged penetrator, a distinguished notable and scholar, who is highlighted and bears the brunt of public disapproval, whereas the identity and moral character of the penetrated boy is left out of consideration as being of secondary interest. In the second case, the reverse is true: the Emir occupies center stage, while the soldiers remain more or less anonymous. The social status of the people involved was thus one factor determining the interpretation and judgment of a particular case. In the oneiromantic handbook of ʿAbd al-Ghanī al-Nābulusī, dreaming that one is being anally penetrated by a social equal or inferior (a rival, a younger brother, a slave) usually has an inauspicious portent, while being penetrated by a social superior (the Sultan or one's father) is a good omen.[57] It is as if the aggressive, polarizing significance of phallic penetration, and therefore the humiliation of being the passive partner, is toned down in a situation in which the penetrated is already clearly a social inferior, whereas it is emphasized when the status of the partners is roughly equal, or when the penetrated is socially superior to the penetrator. An illustration of this point is contained in the following anecdote in an anonymous collection of humorous stories that seems to date from the seventeenth century: Satan assumes the form of a beautiful boy to lead a repentant sodomite astray. After he has succeeded, he reassumes his original form—that of an ugly, one-eyed old man—and reveals his true identity, whereupon the initially disappointed sodomite says: "Look at my prick up your hole."[58] What was merely sodomy with some boy became an act of "screwing"—and thus a cause of pride—when the passive partner turned out to be none other than Satan himself.

Where the attitude toward the passive partner tended to be unequivocally negative, the evaluation of the active partner was more ambivalent. From the perspective of the ideal of masculinity, the penetrator emerges from the sexual encounter with his honor unimpaired, if not enhanced. From the perspective of the ideal of conformity with the religious-moral norms of society, the penetrator is dishonored. It would be misleading to try to establish a correspondence between these two points of view and specific social groups. The religious scholars could, as we have seen, make unabashed use of the language of aggressive masculinity, while religious considerations were hardly irrelevant to the moral evaluations of the man on the street. Which perspective was adopted had more to do with the particularities of each concrete case than with the social background of the evaluator. Moral judgments are not, as is often supposed, a matter of the automatic application of clear and consensual principles. Rather, they typically involve selective and sometimes contestable use of the stock of generally accepted and usually loosely integrated maxims by individuals and social groups according to a myriad of contextual factors that cannot be exhaustively enumerated.[59] Within one culture (and subculture), the same act may be appraised differently according to the interest of the observer, the way in which the act becomes public knowledge, whether it is carried out discreetly or flauntingly, whether the perpetrator is male or female, young or old, a friend or a rival, a prominent religious scholar or a common soldier, and so on. In the words of the anthropologist J. Pitt-Rivers:

> A system of values is never a homogeneous code of abstract principles obeyed by all the participants in a given culture and able to be extracted from an informant with the aid of a set of hypothetical questions, but a collection of concepts which are related to one another and applied differentially by the different status groups defined by age, sex, class, occupation, etc. in the different social . . . contexts in which they find their meaning.[60]

Transgenerational Homosexuality

The significance attributed to biological gender seems to vary both geographically and historically. Whereas some cultures are relatively androgynous, other cultures have strongly developed gender roles, sometimes to the point of "gender polarity"—that is, valuing, on the whole, opposing character traits in the two sexes, such as timidity in women and assertiveness in men. The early Ottoman Arab East evidently belonged to the latter category, with its separate and clearly demarcated male and female spheres, which legitimately overlapped only in certain well-defined contexts. Merely by virtue of his biological sex, a man was expected to participate in a world from which women were in principle excluded. This was the public world in which men competed and cooperated in the pursuit of money, status, and power. Succeeding in this world was to succeed as a male, to live up to the demands of masculinity, and was thus on the symbolic level linked to virility. Defeat, on the other hand, was symbolically equivalent to calling into question male gender identity, to emasculation.[61] Hence, the pervasiveness of sexual allusions to express nonsexual rivalries between men. The victor (e.g., the abovementioned poet Māmāyah) figuratively "screws" the defeated (e.g., Māmāyah's rival Amrallah), depriving him of his gender and transforming him into a woman. Male honor was symbolically associated with the biological expressions of masculinity, shame with their diminishment or loss. According to the oneiromantic handbook of ʿAbd al-Ghanī al-Nābulusī, an increase in the size of the penis or testicles in a dream forebodes an increase in the dreamer's reputation, honor, and money. A decrease indicates the reverse: impoverishment and humiliation.[62]

In the "homosocial" world of the early Ottoman Arab East, sexual symbolism was thus never far from the surface. Yet actual sexual intercourse between adult men was clearly perceived as an anomaly, linked either to violence (rape) or disease (*ubnah*). Homosexual relations in the early Ottoman Arab East were almost always conceived as involving an adult man (who stereotypically would be the "male" partner) and an adolescent boy (the "female"). The latter—referred to in the texts as *amrad* (beardless boy); *ghulām* or *ṣabī* (boy); or *fatā, shābb,* or *ḥadath* (male youth)—though biologically male, was not completely a "man" in the social and cultural sense; and his intermediate status was symbolized by the lack of the most visible of male sex characteristics: a beard. The cultural importance of beards and/or moustaches in the early Ottoman Arab East is attested by both the European travel literature and the indigenous literature. The beard or moustache was a symbol of male honor, something one swore by or insulted. Slaves were expected not to wear a beard, and in early Ottoman Egypt at least, the phrase "he let his beard grow" (*arkhā liḥyatahu*) was a standard way of designating a master's emancipation of his slave.[63] The appearance of a beard on the cheeks of a youth was frequently celebrated in verse, and was often used in the biographical literature as an age marker, the third stage, after *tamyīz* (i.e., the age of discernment—traditionally set at around seven) and *bulūgh* (puberty). The association of the beard or moustache with male virility is a circum-Mediterranean trait, and is clearly brought out in the dream analysis of ʿAbd al-Ghanī al-Nābulusī:

> The beard in a dream means for the man wealth and honor, so if he sees it grow in length to an agreeable, handsome, not immoderate extent, he will encounter honor, prestige, beauty, money, power, and comfort . . . He who sees it [the beard] sparse to an ugly extent, his prestige and standing among people will diminish.

By comparison:

> The penis of a man is his reputation and honor among people, and an increase in its size indicates an increase in these . . . and he who sees that his penis is transformed into a vagina, his fortitude and strength will become impotence, weakness, feebleness, and submissiveness.

The symbolic equivalence of beard and penis is underlined in the following:

> It is said that if a woman dreams that she has a penis or beard or wears the clothes of men, she will become impudent toward her husband.[64]

Corollary to the tacit association of coarse facial hair with masculinity was the relative feminization of the teenage boy whose beard was as yet absent or soft and incomplete. This feminization must have been enhanced by the fact that, in the urban centers at least, women's faces were normally veiled in public.

The feminization of male youths is apparent in pederastic courtship, which tended to follow the typical heterosexual pattern in societies in which premarital contact between unrelated men and women is not hindered by gender segregation and arranged marriages. The part of the pursuer was assumed by the man; that of the pursued by the boy. The latter would walk a tightrope between being considered haughty and arrogant (a frequent complaint in the love poetry of the period) and being "easy" or "cheap." It was apparently the latter sort of boys that the Damascene poet Abū al-Fatḥ al-Mālikī (d. 1567/8) frequented, to the detriment of his reputation.[65] Similarly, the Egyptian poet Ismāʿīl al-Khashshāb (d. 1815), who himself fell in love with a young scribe during the brief Napoleonic rule of Egypt, warned a friend who had become infatuated with a boy not to fall for a worn hackney (*mubtadhal*).[66] A boy's reputation for being "easy" would be an embarrassing liability in his older days, upon which opponents and detractors could pounce. In a defamatory poem, the Damascene Amīn al-Dīn Muḥammad al-Ṣāliḥi al-Hilālī (d. 1596) said of a rival:

> . . . and who was in his youth a female camel, led to the worst of men and ridden.[67]

Though it was clearly held disreputable for the boy to display too much enthusiasm for his role as a coveted object, there are indications that many boys made the most of the interest shown in them by adult men. While they submitted to the sexual desires of men only at a peril to their reputation, they could hold a lover (or several lovers) suspended in hope, conceding a rendezvous or a kiss now and then, and playing admirers off against each other. Some boys clearly lorded it over their lovers, refusing to speak to them unless they composed a love poem, or asking them to prove their love by slitting a wrist or jumping into a moat.[68] A man could be taunted by other men if the boy he pursued ended up bestowing his favors upon another. The Yemeni poet Shaʿbān al-Rūmī (d. 1736) was, for example, teased by an acquaintance when a handsome shopkeeper he loved moved store and started showing favor to another man called al-Iṣfahānī:

O Shaʿbān, we have noticed the dark-lashed, tender-handed [fellow]
leave your quarter so as not to see you, and treat his eyes with Iṣfahānī [kohl] (*al-Iṣfahānī*).[69]

The family of the boy was expected to shield him from the sexual interests of older men, and were liable to be dishonored if they failed to do so. This is underlined in the following anonymous couplet purporting to address a handsome boy:

Your beauty has deprived the gazelle of his attributes, and all beauty has gathered in you.
You have his neck, eyes, and shyness, but as to the [cuckold's] horns, they are your father's.[70]

The Meccan jurist Ibn Ḥajar al-Haytamī (d. 1566) asserted that fornication was not only a transgression of the law of God but could also be seen as a crime against other persons, since it reflected dishonorably on the relatives of the passive-receptive party—the woman or the sodomized (*al-malūṭ bihi*).[71] The Egyptian scholar Ibn al-Wakīl al-Mallawī (d. ca. 1719) related with unconcealed sympathy a number of pederastic love stories that unfolded in Egypt in his own time. A recurrent feature of these stories is the intervention of fathers to prevent the adult lovers from frequenting their sons.[72] A mother in sixteenth-century Aleppo ended her son's apprenticeship with a tailor when she learned that the master had developed a liking for him, and one of the students of the Aleppine scholar Raḍī al-Dīn ibn al-Ḥanbalī (d. 1563) was evicted from the doorsteps of his beloved's home by the boy's father.[73] Other parents seem to have been willing to look the other way, especially if the suitor came from a socioeconomic class far above their own. The attention of a rich notable would often translate itself into concrete material benefits for both the boy and his parents. The Damascene judge Aḥmad al-Shuwaykī (d. 1598) was, according to a colleague, in the habit of paying regular subsidies to the youths he courted, as well as conferring certain "worldly benefits" upon their parents.[74]

The outlined pattern of pederastic courtship could suggest that boys functioned as ersatz women, and thus at first sight lend support to the oft-heard idea that (supposedly) widespread "homosexuality" in the Arab world is caused by the segregation of women. Men did not, however, simply turn to boys because of the unavailability of women. There are indeed a few remarks in the biographical literature that linked a person's interest in boys with his unmarried status. For example, the aforementioned biographer Ḥasan al-Būrīnī said of the Damascene poet Aḥmad al-ʿInāyātī (d. 1606) that "he did not marry throughout his long life, and did not incline toward a female beloved (*khalīlah*) who would fortify him (*tuḥṣinahu*) against having a male beloved (*khalīl*)."[75] Būrīnī's use of the term *tuḥṣinahu* reflects the assumption that marriage could provide protection (*iḥṣān*—a widely used synonym for marriage) against the temptation to have paramours (male or female). However, it is far from clear that Būrīnī believed that ʿInāyātī was unable to marry, and thus turned to boys only as an alternative sexual outlet. It is more likely that ʿInāyātī's unmarried status was voluntary, and that Būrīni believed that he might have gotten involved in fewer love affairs with boys had he married. The case of Māmāyah al-Rūmī lends support to the idea that sexual interest in boys was not necessarily the effect of the segregation—and hence "unavailability"—of women, but could just as well be the result of a considered decision to remain unmarried. In a long poem in his *Dīwān,* he described how he had been hounded into divorcing his wife by his mother-in-law and her family. He concluded the poem by expressing his resolve to avoid women and to resort to beardless boys when lust got the better of him.[76] In any case, even if it was widely believed that most unmarried men would be interested in boys (either because they constituted an alternative sexual outlet for unmarried men, or because men who chose to remain unmarried were not sufficiently interested in women), this does not show that it was also believed that most of those who were interested in boys were unmarried. Many of those who courted boys were married, and this was not depicted by the sources as in any way remarkable or strange. At most, the husband's pederastic escapades were said to have led to domestic discord because of resentment and jealousy on the part of the wife.[77] What little evidence we have of marital norms in the premodern Middle East suggests that marriage was nearly universal and was, moreover, usually entered into at a relatively early age, often at the onset of puberty.[78] The Egyptian scholar and historian ʿAbd al-Raḥmān al-Jabartī (d. 1825/6), for example, was married at the age of fourteen, while his grandfather died at the age of sixteen, one month after his wife had given birth.[79] To be sure, not all scholars married that early, and some remained unmarried all their lives, but this was unusual enough to be considered noteworthy in the biographical notices dedicated to them. It is possible that early marriage was the prerogative of the wealthier segment of the population, but the abundant evidence we have concerning pederasty in the premodern Arab East relate primarily to this social class, so that the purported explanation of widespread "homosexuality" in terms of the unavailability of women still fails to gain any credence. It is also worth mentioning that there is evidence for the availability of female prostitutes in the major Arab cities during the centuries under consideration.[80] It is thus far from clear that there were no heterosexual outlets even for the minority of adult men who were unmarried. There may indeed be some connection between gender segregation and widespread pederasty in the premodern Middle East. However, crude notions of blocked heterosexual libido being diverted toward boys fail to do justice to the complexity of the connection. Gender segregation in public, and arranged marriages, did not prevent women from being sexually available to adult men, but they may have severely restricted the possibilities for heterosexual courtship. One could suppose that courting fulfils certain emotional (rather than sexual) needs on the part of the courter, such as the thrill of fancying someone who is not straightforwardly available for sexual intercourse (in contrast to wives and prostitutes), the challenge of trying to win the favor of that someone, and the satisfaction of succeeding. In the premodern Middle East such needs could most easily be met by courting boys, not women.[81] An explanation along these lines was offered by the French traveler Volney, who visited Egypt in the 1780s. Speaking of the Mamluk elite of that country, he wrote: "They are, above all, addicted to that abominable wickedness which was at all times the vice of the Greeks . . . It is difficult to account for this taste, when we consider that they all have women, unless we suppose they seek in one sex that poignancy of refusal which they do not permit the other."[82] The connection between pederasty and gender segregation will be taken up again in the following chapter.

It is not a straightforward affair to determine the age during which a male youth was considered to be sexually attractive to adult men. The relevant terms, such as *amrad* or *ghulām,* tend to be impressionistic and somewhat loosely employed in the sources. For example, the term *amrad* (beardless boy) could be used to refer to prepubescent, completely smooth-cheeked boys, as opposed to adolescent, downy-cheeked youths, but it could also refer to all youths who did not yet have a fully developed beard, and hence to youths who were as old as twenty or twenty-one. According to a saying attributed to the first Umayyad Caliph Muʿāwiyah (d. 680) and quoted in an eighteenth-century dictionary:

> I was beardless for twenty years, fully bearded for twenty years, I plucked gray hairs from it for twenty years, and dyed it for twenty years.[83]

If the upper age limit was physical maturity at around twenty, the lower age limit for the sexual interest of the pederasts seems to have been the recognized transition from childhood to youth, at the age of seven or eight. The weight of the available evidence tends to support the conclusion that the pederasts' lust tended to be directed at boys whose age fell within this interval, and that the boy's attractiveness was usually supposed to peak around halfway through, at fourteen or fifteen. The Egyptian Yūsuf al-Shirbīnī, writing in the late seventeenth century, opined that a boy's attractiveness peaks at fifteen, declines after the age of eighteen, and disappears fully at twenty, by which time he will be fully hirsute: "So infatuation and passionate love is properly directed only at those of lithesome figure and sweet smile from those who are in their tens (*awlād al-ʿashr*)."[84] Similarly, an anonymous poem cited by the Damascene chronicler Ibn Kannān al-Ṣāliḥī (d. 1740) on the natural ages of man associated the "son of ten" (*ibn al-ʿashr*—presumably in the sense of "in his tens" rather than "exactly ten years old") with incomparable beauty, the "son of twenty" with the heedless pursuit of pleasure, the "son of thirty" with the apogee of strength, etc.[85] In love poetry and rhymed prose, the age of the beloved was often said to be fourteen, probably a standard rhetorical device engendered by the conventional comparison of the face of the beloved with the moon, which reaches its apogee around the fourteenth of each month of the Muslim lunar calendar.[86] However, there is independent evidence from European travel accounts that catamites were "likely of twelve, or fourteene years old, some of them not above nine, or ten."[87] Much depended, however, on the eye of the beholder as well as the individual rate of maturation. As will be seen in the next chapter, the comparison of the respective charms of beardless and downy-cheeked youths was a conventional topic in the belles-lettres of the period. Many poets expressed the opinion that a boy ceased to be attractive already at the appearance of beard-down (*ʿidhār*) on his cheeks, which would imply a somewhat lower upper age limit. The Damascene scholar and biographer Muḥammad Khalīl al-Murādī (d. 1791) seems to have had enough beard-down by the age of fourteen to merit a poem celebrating the occasion. A grandson of ʿAbd al-Ghanī al-Nābulusī was seventeen, and a son of the Iraqi scholar Maḥmūd al-Alūsī eighteen, when they elicited similar poems.[88] The prominent Syrian mystic Muḥammad ibn ʿIrāq (d. 1526) veiled his son ʿAlī between the age of eight and sixteen, "to keep people from being enchanted by him," suggesting that by the latter age his features were deemed by the father to be developed enough to make him unattractive to other men.[89] On the other hand, the chronicler Ibn Ayyūb al-Anṣārī recorded the death of a seventeen-year-old Damascene youth who left behind a host of lamenting male admirers.[90] The Iraqi poet Qāṣim al-Rāmī (d. 1772/3) traced in verse the development of a boy from the age of ten, when he "became settled in the sanctuary of beauty," to the age of sixteen, when he (disreputably) started to pluck the hairs from his cheeks.[91] Plucking beard-down from the face seems to have signaled, in a too direct and indiscreet manner, that the boy actually enjoyed being coveted by men, and was in no hurry to become a bearded adult. To that extent, it was associated with the behavior of boy prostitutes or effeminate males. The above-mentioned Yūsuf al-Shirbīnī thus stated that the term *natīf* (literally "plucked") was used of the beardless boy who, "if his beard starts to grow, and he enjoys being effeminate (*al-khināth*) or—God forbid—he has *ubnah,* will constantly shave his beard and beautify himself for the libertine (*fāsiq*) . . . for souls incline toward the beardless boy as long as his cheeks are clear."[92]

Interestingly, an adolescent youth was himself expected to be sexually attracted to women and it seems to have been a common ploy of those desirous of a youth to adopt a woman as bait.[93] It is also possible that adolescent youths themselves regularly courted younger, prepubescent boys. "Serial" relationships (*al-ʿishq al-musalsal*), in which the beloved of one man is himself the lover of a woman or boy, are not unknown to the Arabic lore on profane love.[94] According to a couplet by the Damascene Ibrāhīm al-Suʾālātī (d. 1684):

> The beloved has fallen in love with a gazelle like himself, and is afflicted by amorous rapture.
> He was a beloved and is now a lover, and thus love has passed its judgment [both] for and against him.[95]

The "male" sexual potential of an adolescent youth was not confined to intercourse with women or younger boys. Behind closed doors, one could not tell for certain whether the man or the boy had been the active partner, and the uncertainty could be exploited in the bawdy and defamatory literature, as shown by the previously mentioned anecdote involving a man and a boy each insisting that they had been the active partner. An anonymous line of poetry spelled out this latent uncertainty:

> He who is civil in *liwāṭ* is not assumed to involve a third party, and if he is alone with his boy, only God knows who does the fucking.[96]

Such poems and anecdotes are clearly "parasitical" in the sense that they consciously break with the dominant, stereotypical representation of pederastic relationships. Yet they do suggest that these dominant depictions were not always adequate to the actual behavior of individuals, and that there was some awareness of this at the time. Not only does there exist the odd indication that boys could sometimes assume the "active" role, but there are also indications that some men had sex with other adult men. Thus the effeminate adult men portrayed in the bawdy literature do not seem to have had particular difficulties in finding other adult men willing to have sex with them. It is also likely that some pederastic relationships continued long after the "passive" partner could reasonably be passed off as a "boy." Yūsuf al-Shirbīnī claimed that this was precisely what some heretical Egyptian dervishes tended to do, and saw therein a confirmation of their rustic, unrefined character.[97] It is doubtful whether such men were thought to actually prefer adult men to boys or women. It seems more likely that the assumption was that they were helping themselves to whatever orifice happened to be at hand. The assumption that rough and masculine men will behave in this manner is one that is still very much alive, as evinced by the stereotype that contemporary Latin American or Arab men, though they may actually prefer to have sex with women, will readily resort to effeminate men or Western homosexual tourists as the second-best thing.[98] The tendency to bugger men of all ages was also denounced by the above-mentioned Iraqi scholar Muḥammad Amīn al-ʿUmarī as "an abomination (*fāḥishah*) which is not perpetrated except by someone with a coarse character and a malicious soul."[99]

The Social Context of Pederasty

The homosexuality represented in the texts of the early Ottoman period was, on the whole, of the pederastic, "transgenerational" or "age-structured" type well known from classical Greece and Rome. It is not that this was the only type that was thought to exist; nor was it the only type that was acceptable—it was not acceptable to many—but it was the type that was conceived as being usual. Even those religious scholars who inveighed the most strongly against sodomy and its antecedents warned against gazing at *boys,* against being alone with a *boy* in a private place, against composing love poetry of *boys,* and so on. That an adult man who was not a *ma'būn* or *mukhannath* should actually prefer fully developed adult men to teenage boys is an idea that seems not to have been seriously entertained.

Rather than desiring and having intercourse with each other, pederasts competed and sometimes fought amongst themselves for boys. The Damascene poet Darwīsh al-Ṭālawī (d. 1606) alluded in verse to one such conflict between a chief judge of Damascus and a footman (*çuhadār*), and was himself deprived of a young, handsome slave whom he loved by the Druze Emir of Mt. Lebanon, Fakhr al-Dīn al-Maʿnī (d. 1635), while passing through the city of Sidon.[100] The above-mentioned Muṣṭafā ʿĀlī, in his description of

Egypt in 1599, noted that the cavalrymen there often quarreled amongst themselves, usually about boys or horses—this in contrast to soldiers in the Turkish regions of the Empire, among whom he claimed "nobody covets another person's possessions or horse or boy."[101]

In the modern West, sexual relations between men tend to be perceived as essentially relations between two persons of the same gender who, because of a psychological orientation or the unavailability of members of the opposite sex, have intercourse with one another. Such liaisons are therefore thought to be especially common in all-male environments: the military, boarding schools, saunas, monasteries, prisons, etc. In the early Ottoman Arab East, *liwāṭ* was usually thought to involve a man and a boy, and it thus tended to be associated, at least in the popular imagination, with social contexts in which the mixing of generations was especially marked. This is not to say that *liwāṭ* was, or was believed to be, confined to such contexts. The generations were not segregated in the way the genders were, and the opportunities for pederastic courtship were correspondingly diffuse. However, it seems clear that certain social environments were thought to be especially suspect (or promising) precisely to the extent that, in them, the mixing of men and boys was particularly intense, or could occur hidden from the public eye. This applies first and foremost to the following realms: education; mystic orders; slavery and servitude; coffeehouses and public baths.

Education

Education in the premodern Arab-Islamic world was a highly personalized affair, and speaking of an educational "institution" or "system" can easily be misleading. A student studied, free of charge, at the hands of individual teachers, and it was from these, rather than from any school, that he derived his certificate (*ijāzah*) and prestige.[102] Biographical notices of a scholar almost always indicate his teachers, and almost never the names of the schools he might have attended. The latter might constitute the physical setting for conducting a class, but was of little further significance; a mosque or private home could do as well. A student would typically acquire certificates from several scholars, but would also normally have one to whom he was especially close, and who was singled out in the biographical literature by phrases such as "he was attached to" (*intamā ilā, ikhtaṣṣa bi*), "he accompanied" (*saḥaba, lāzama*), "he served" (*khadama*). As indicated by such expressions, the professional and the personal—to use an anachronistic distinction—were inextricably merged in such a relationship. The teacher was simultaneously a mentor and a patron, the student a client, disciple, and servant. The educational relationship's strongly personalized character, together with the fact that a student would be attached to a teacher at an age in which he was widely regarded—even by staunch moralists—to be attractive to adult men, explains why it featured prominently in discourses, both apologetic and hostile, on pederastic love. According to the Persian philosopher Mullā Ṣadr al-Dīn al-Shīrāzī (d. 1640/1), the divine purpose behind the existence of refined pederastic attraction was precisely to induce men to frequent and care for boys, thereby ensuring that the arts and sciences of civilization would be transmitted from generation to generation. This kind of attraction was therefore absent among "primitive" peoples such as the Bedouins, Kurds, Turcomans, and Black Africans. Brute heterosexual desire, by contrast, served to perpetuate the species, and was universal among mankind.[103] The argument is hardly original with Mullā Ṣadrā; it was propounded, in much the same words, by the Neoplatonist "Brethren of Purity" (*Ikhwān al-Ṣafā*) in the tenth century, and is strikingly reminiscent of the Platonic conception of adult men procreating physically with attractive women, and intellectually with attractive boys.[104] From a very different perspective, the Meccan scholar and jurist Ibn Ḥajar al-Haytamī (d. 1566) stressed that

> it is imperative for a teacher to safeguard his sight from the handsome beardless boy as much as possible—even though he is allowed [to look at him] in the absence of lust, for the exclusive purpose of teaching—because it might lead to unsettlement or temptation.[105]

In the biographical literature, there are several examples of scholars who went to great lengths to live up to such strictures, for example seating particularly handsome students in such a manner as to avoid facing them.[106] That many scholars also succumbed to the temptation is also abundantly attested: the brother of the biographer and scholar Aḥmad al-Khālidī (d. 1624/5), resident in Ṣafad in Palestine, was charged with sexually assaulting one of his students; the Damascene scholar Aḥmad al-Ṭībī al-Ṣaghīr (d. 1586) was rumored to have had an affair with his student ʿAbd al-Latīf ibn al-Jābī (d. 1617); the Damascene poet ʿAbd al-Ḥayy Ṭarrazalrayḥān (d. 1688) was overcome with remorse when, in disloyalty to a beloved, he took a liking to one of his students; the Iraqi belletrist Muḥammad al-Ghulāmī (d. 1772/3) composed a short elegy when a student he fancied died.[107] The Egyptian scholar and poet ʿAbdallah al-Shabrāwī (d. 1758), the previously mentioned Rector of the Azhar college in Cairo, addressed to a former student a love poem which was unusually earnest and unadorned by the standards of the time:

O gazelle! You whose movements are a snare for mankind.
What have you done to a lover who is anxious and visibly ailing?
Overflowing with cares, love-struck, ill, infatuated with your love.
Who is enraptured with joy if you confer a greeting one day.
And who, if you walk past, cries: "How sweet you are with that bearing!" . . .
Allow me, I implore you, to speak to you; there is nothing less than speaking!
And stay true to a past bond, when you and I were together.
The days you came to me and were not so far from the age of weaning.
The days you came to me to gain elements of culture with diligence.
The days I enjoyed your favor, and fate was smiling at me.
The days happiness was my guest, and my fortune was made.
The days you were called "boy!" (*yā ghulām*)—and the term "boy!" is beneath you . . .[108]

It should be added that, within the educational setting, pederastic relationships were not necessarily confined to those involving teachers and students. The age difference between students could be considerable, and liaisons between the older and the younger of them were not inconceivable. When the scholar and mystic Murād al-Bukhārī (d. 1720) founded the Murādiyyah college in Damascus, he stipulated that it not house beardless boys or married men (who would bring their wives with them), presumably from the fear of tempting the other students on the premises.[109]

Mystic (Sufi) Orders

The Egyptian poet Ḥasan al-Badrī al-Ḥijāzī (d. 1718/9) was known for his biting criticisms of what he perceived to be signs of the moral decay of his times. Some of his most venomous verses were reserved for the "long-haired" (*ulī al-shaʿrah*) mystics:

But they are in depravity the most elevated of men, as you see without doubts.
They have taken beardless boys as their aim unabashedly, thus coveting perdition.
And called them their beginnings (*bidāyātihim*)—of dishonor, evil, and disgrace.[110]

There is reason to think that the poet was thinking of one particular Sufi order active in Egypt, the Muṭāwiʿah. From condemnations of the order by scholars such as Muḥammad Abū al-Fatḥ al-Dajjānī (d. 1660/1) and ʿAlī al-ʿAdawī (d. 1775), it seems that members of the order were notorious for picking especially handsome young novices whom they called *bidāyāt,* and for claiming that it was permitted to be alone with them and to touch their bodies. Adult members of the order apparently had the young, handsome novices sit behind them during their communal rites, and got them to embrace the adult participants, who, as often happened, became ecstatic. This embrace was apparently referred to as "the repose of the dervishes" (*rāḥat al-fuqarā'*).[111] It is not really possible to reconstruct the theoretical justification for these practices from such hostile discussions. The practices may well be related to a line of thinking that is well known to historians of Islamic mysticism. According to a tradition which goes back to Plato, and which has been shown (above all by Helmut Ritter) to have survived in Islamic mysticism, a beautiful human countenance, typically in the form of a handsome beardless youth, could serve as the channel for the manifestation of absolute, divine Beauty.[112] The Syrian mystic Muṣṭafā al-Bakrī (d. 1749) composed a tract condemning certain mystics active in Syria in his time, who were wont to look at "beautiful countenances" (*al-wujūh al-ḥisān*) and who justified their practice by invoking the principle that "all beauty is the beauty of God." Bakrī countered that true mystics adhered strictly to Islamic law, according to which looking at beautiful unrelated women and handsome beardless boys was out of bounds.[113] The biographical entries on Sufis of the period confirm that the practice of contemplating handsome boys was still thought to be a living tradition: "he would on occasion appreciate a beautiful form, and urge his companions to look at it"; "he was accused of liking to look at boys"; "as to his inclination to beautiful forms, that has been confirmed beyond doubt"; "he threw off the reins in loving awe-inspiring beauty, and so became exposed to malicious gossip."[114]

The theoretical justification for the practice of contemplating handsome youths in some mystical circles will be dealt with at greater length in the following chapter. However, it is worth emphasizing at this point that relations with beardless boys within Sufi orders were not always thought by outsiders, as is evident from the cited condemnations, to conform to the Platonic ideal. A couplet by the Meccan judge Aḥmad al-Murshidī (d. 1638) also associated the Sufis of his age with gluttony, drinking wine, sodomy, and the playing of musical instruments:

> The Sufis of the age and time; the Sufis of the wine-press and the eating-tray.
> They have outdone the people of Lot by adding the beating of drums to fornication.[115]

A proverb quoted in Yūsuf al-Shirbīnī's satirical *Hazz al-quḥūf,* dating from the late seventeenth century, is more straightforward: "A youth's chastity is safeguarded in his father's home, and if he becomes a dervish, the buggers (*al-nā'ikūn*) will queue up behind him." In this connection, Shirbīnī related anecdotes involving heretical dervishes in Egypt who get their way with youths by pretending to be saints willing to transmit their powers by means of "a beam of light," "the water of life," or "the miraculous drop." These turn out to be references to the semen of the "saints," as the desired boys eventually discover.[116] A similar story was related by the (intensely anti-Sufi) Shīʿi scholar Niʿmatallah al-Jazā'irī (d. 1702) as having occurred in Isfahan (in Persia) during his lifetime: a man supposedly entrusted his handsome son to a Sufi master, who went on to sodomize the boy, using as pretext the desire to transmit some of his "light" to the new novice.[117] The purpose of such anecdotes is of course satirical or defamatory rather than descriptive, and they should accordingly be handled with caution. Yet it is interesting to note that the Finnish anthropologist Edward Westermarck observed a widespread belief in early twentieth-century Morocco that the blessings (*barakah*) of a saint could be transmitted through hetero- or homosexual intercourse.[118] It is possible that related ideas circulated in some circles in the Arab East in the early Ottoman period. Writing in Egypt in the 1830s, E. W. Lane specifically stated, while speaking of the "holy fools" (*majādhīb*) widely venerated in the premodern Arab-Islamic world, that "the women, instead of avoiding them, sometimes suffer these wretches to take any liberty with them in the public street; and, by the lower orders, are not considered disgraced by such actions."[119] One sixteenth-century Egyptian saint would, according to a contemporary (and sympathetic) source, make advances to beardless boys he met and fondle their behinds, "in front of the boy's father and others," apparently without impairing his saintly reputation.[120]

Worries about the nature of relationships between men and boys in Sufi orders were expressed by many religious scholars, who often pointed out the proprieties that had to be maintained and denounced the orders, such as the Muṭāwiʿah, which flouted them. For example, the prominent Palestinian jurist Khayr al-Dīn al-Ramlī (d. 1671), when asked about the religious-legal status of Sufi gatherings for listening to music (*samāʿ*), answered that such gatherings were permissible, but only if certain conditions were met, and gave as the first such condition the absence from these sessions of beardless boys.[121] On the other hand, several Sufi writers of the period were themselves eager to warn their fellows against the dangers posed by regular mixing with boys. The Egyptian Sufi ʿAbd al-Wahhāb al-Shaʿrānī (d. 1565), for example, quoted his own mentor as warning disciples against frequenting beardless boys or sharing cells in a convent (*zāwiyah*) with them "as much as possible," and to avoid looking at them when participating in the communal rites of the order.

Shaʿrānī also described how another of his Sufi progenitors would not allow handsome beardless boys to reside in his convent, and he exhorted his (fellow Sufi) readers to defer to their master or his lieutenant should he decide on a similar policy.[122] Shaʿrānī's remarks are a testimony both to the rich possibilities for intergenerational contact within convents, and to the anxiety caused by such possibilities.

Given such warnings by prominent legal scholars and Sufi authors, one might suppose that the mystical contemplation of boys was confined to more "unorthodox" or "antinomian" Sufis. Nevertheless, such a judgment has to be qualified. As has been pointed out by for example Michael Winter, the distinction between so-called orthodox and unorthodox Sufis was not always clear-cut.[123] Moreover, speaking of "unorthodox" or "antinomian" Sufis in this context tends to conceal the fact that there was a certain amount of disagreement regarding what the "orthodox" or "nomian" position was. As will be shown in the next chapter, there were defenders of the mystical practice of adoring handsome boys in the early Ottoman Arab East, and some of these were well-versed in religious law, and belonged to orders that are usually regarded as thoroughly "orthodox."

Slavery and Servitude

Many jurists of the period, when discussing sodomy, took pains to emphasize that it was prohibited even with one's male slave, a specification that should be seen in light of the permissibility of concubinage with a female slave in Islamic law. Again, the Meccan scholar Ibn Ḥajar al-Haytamī provides a—somewhat strongly worded—example of this concern:

> The community has reached a consensus (*ijmāʿ*) that he of the criminal, depraved, and accursed sodomites who commits sodomy with his male slave, upon him is the curse of God . . . and this has become common among the merchants and the affluent, who acquire handsome male slaves, black and white, for this [purpose]. So may the most severe, everlasting, and manifest curse befall them, and the greatest shame, ruin, and torment be their lot in this world and the next, as long as they persist in these vile, repugnant, and abominable acts.[124]

A. Russell, an English physician in mid-eighteenth-century Aleppo, who in general was a careful and sympathetic observer of the customs of the inhabitants of the city, noted in his *Natural History of Aleppo* that "the beauty of a male slave enhances the value as much as it does that of a female, occasioned by the frequency among them of a crime not to be mentioned."[125] Russell's remarks about the effect of physical beauty on the price of a slave is supported by evidence from native writers. For instance, the Damascene scholar and mystic ʿAbd al-Ghanī al-Nābulusī noted that the notables of his city "seek to buy handsome slaves (*al-mamālīk al-ḥisān*) and purchase them at high prices (*yatghālawna fīhim bi-al-athmān*), and dress them up in various clothes, and make them stand before them as brides (*ka-al-ʿarāʾis*)."[126] The above-mentioned Egyptian scholar and mystic ʿAbd al-Wahhāb al-Shaʿrānī urged his readers not to think ill of the political rulers and judges "for spending large sums in buying male slaves of handsome countenance . . . for it is the habit of rulers to love beauty and derive pleasure from looking at it in their houses and clothes and servants, without this leading to committing sins."[127] Shaʿrānī's urgings suggest, however, that his contemporaries often *were* suspicious of the habit. He himself wrote that he would indirectly admonish those amongst the political elite (*min ḥāshiyat al-wulāt*) who were rumored to be "debauching" their male slaves, telling them:

> No one should act in accordance with those scholars who have been led astray from the Holy Law and permitted the carnal penetration of a woman in her anus or carnal penetration of a male slave on the basis of ownership, for that is contrary to clear, sacred precepts and to the agreement of the great majority of scholars, ancient and recent.[128]

The biographical literature offers several examples of rumored pederastic relations between notables and their slaves or servants.[129] As suggested by Shaʿrānī's remarks, the political elite—which typically would have the largest number of slaves or servants—seems to have had an especially notorious reputation in this regard. Thus, the Aleppine scholar and biographer Abū al-Wafāʾ al-ʿUrḍī (d. 1660) praised a prominent Turkish scholar—later to become Grand Mufti of the Ottoman Empire—in the following terms: "He likes neither pomp nor ostentatious clothes, nor does he employ beardless boys [as servants], contrary to the practice of most *Mawālī* [i.e., members of the Ottoman ruling establishment]."[130] Similarly, the Damascene chronicler Ibn Ayyūb al-Anṣārī, speaking of a local leader of the Janissary corps, said: "He does not have an inclination to boys as is usual among his kind."[131] The Syrian mystic ʿAlwān al-Ḥamawī (d. 1530), in a work on the religious-juridical provisions of looking or gazing (*aḥkām al-naẓar*), warned his readers of the dangers of watching the processions of the political rulers, partly because they are accompanied by beardless slaves whom they "dress in the finest clothes and adorn with the most beautiful adornments, so that looking at them becomes a temptation for women and men alike."[132] One may compare this testimony with that of the English traveler Henry Blount, who was in the Balkans in the 1630s and accompanied the Ottoman army on part of its journey toward the Polish border: "Besides these [ten to fifteen] wives [*sic*—perhaps concubines], each Basha hath as many, or likely more Catamites . . . usually clad in Velvet, or Scarlet, with guilt Scymitars, and bravely mounted, with Sumptuous furniture."[133] The above-mentioned Palestinian scholar Muḥammad al-Saffārīnī noted that *liwāṭ* in his time was especially widespread among "the Turks" (*al-atrāk*), and since there is no evidence that Saffārīnī traveled to the Turkish-speaking parts of the Ottoman Empire, it is likely that "the Turks" he encountered and passed judgment on were mostly members of the political, military, and judicial elite.[134]

A person who was rumored to have sex with his slaves could find that he was suspected of assuming the passive-receptive role, especially if his slaves looked suspiciously masculine. For instance, the Aleppine poet Ḥusayn al-Jazarī composed several poems accusing a contemporary named Niʿmatallah of being a *ma'būn*. Niʿmatallah apparently owned male black African slaves, and since black African men were stereotypically associated with virility and large sexual organs, Jazarī could easily use the fact to support his accusation:

> Strange that fortune is generous, but to those who do not deserve generosity.
> It withholds what the free man wants, and gives God's blessings (*niʿmat Allah*) to black slaves.[135]

Coffeehouses and Baths

In his biographical dictionary of the notables of the tenth Muslim century (1494–1591), the Damascene scholar Muḥammad Najm al-Dīn al-Ghazzī (d. 1651) touched more than once upon the great controversy concerning the religious status of coffee which marked that age but had subsided by the time he was writing. At one point he commented:

> Consensus has now been reached that it [coffee] is permissible in itself. As for passing it around like an alcoholic beverage, and playing musical instruments in association with it, and taking it from handsome beardless boys while looking at them and pinching their behinds, there is no doubt as to its prohibition.[136]

The context necessary for a full understanding of Ghazzī's remark is probably supplied by two European travelers who were in the Near East at approximately the time in which Ghazzī was writing. Both the Portuguese Pedro Teixeira and the British George Sandys, speaking of Baghdad and Constantinople respectively, noted that coffeehouses employed handsome boys to serve their clientele.[137] The rationale behind such a practice is not difficult to discern. Of course, the boundary between "looking" and "pinching," on the one hand, and making serious advances, on the other, is fluid at best. Likewise, the employment of boys to attract customers could degenerate into outright solicitation. In some instances, legal action was taken against more disreputable establishments on the basis of their association with immorality and prostitution.[138] Incidentally, the image of the cup-bearer (*sāqī*) was a conventional one in the love and wine poetry of the time. The fact that coffeehouses often employed handsome boys to serve the drink suggests that the image, often thought to be a mere literary stereotype (which it undoubtedly often was), may nevertheless have had some connection to social reality. For example, the Damascene poet Aḥmad al-ʿInāyātī was said to have had the habit of going every morning to a coffeehouse "with running water and handsome cup-bearer (*al-malīḥ al-sāqī*) . . . and drink numerous cups of coffee."[139] The *Dīwān* of ʿInāyātī's poetry, still in manuscript form, contains a couple of poems praising the beauty of a particular coffeehouse waiter called Ibrāhīm al-Suyūrī. One of these poems opens with the following lines:

> Come, let us polish our rusty souls with the Ibrāhīmic visage.
> Come, let us gaze at the luminous moon which puts the bright sun to shame.
> Come, let us look at the tender branch, swaying in radiant garments.
> Come, let us take the cup from that lavish hand . . .[140]

Most of the remarks made in connection with coffeehouses apply equally to bathhouses. We have the testimony of the previously mentioned E. W. Lane to the effect that "it is generally a boy, or beardless young man, who attends the bather while he undresses [in the antechamber of the hot room], and while he puts on his towel."[141] The Egyptian Yūsuf al-Shirbīnī indicated in addition that it was often beardless boys who stood for the scrubbing and massaging (*takyīs* and *taḥsīs*) which would occur in relatively secluded chambers.[142] Again, it is likely that such conditions were conducive to prostitution. The Egyptian scholar ʿAbd al-Raʾūf al-Munāwī (d. 1622) inveighed against men making use of beardless boys as masseurs when they visited the baths. He also urged the owner of a bath not to employ beardless boys, and not to allow them to strip in the bathhouse, since such practices lead to improprieties that are "as clear as the sun." Otherwise, warned al-Munāwī, the bath owner may very well be classed with pimps and procurers on Judgment Day.[143] In a more carefree vein, the Yemeni belletrist Aḥmad al-Ḥaymī al-Kawkabānī (d. 1738/9) opined that those who served the clientele in bathhouses should be of amiable character and handsome looks.[144] "How quaint," he added, "are the verses of our friend Ṣarīm al-Dīn Ibrāhīm ibn Ṣāliḥ al-Hindī—may he rest in peace—said of a handsome servant at the baths":

With water the addax of our bathhouse was generous,
And he poured it pouringly on the adorer.
And he said to me, "Do you care for cool [water]?"
"Yes," I replied, "from your fresh mouth."

"He also said," al-Kawkabānī continued, "on an occasion in which he had entered a bath and was massaged by an older, gray-haired associate of the owner, whereas he had hoped to be massaged by a handsome youth named Ṣalāḥ":

I went to the bathhouse to remove the rust (*al-ṣadā*),
And succeed in being with my beloved.
But my hopes were belied; an old man massaged me,
And I had hoped that it would be Ṣalāḥ.[145]

The foregoing quotations are from a work by al-Kawkabānī devoted to advice, stories, and poems relating to baths and their use. In one section of that work, the author reproduced dated invitations to baths that he sent to, or received from, friends. Almost all of these include references to handsome young bath attendants as one of the attractions awaiting the invitee.[146] In a spirit similar to that of al-Kawkabānī, the Meccan scholar ʿAbbās al-Mūsawī (fl. 1736) gave the following advice in a poem:

Do not shave except at the hands of someone willowy, who belittles branches with his figure and stature.
For if you shave at the hands of a bearded fellow—he is as a butcher coming at you with his knife.
And take your cup from someone from whose lips flows the water of life,
Not from one whose hands are like snakes with visible poison [hair?], and at whose sight you'll choke.
And ensure that he who serves you during your bath is lithe, and puts to shame the moon with his appearance . . .[147]

Homosexual Acts and Selves

The British sociologist Mary McIntosh, in an influential article first published in 1968, emphasized the distinction between homosexual behavior and the way a society conceives of those who indulge in such behavior. She argued that while practically all societies recognize that some individuals indulge in homosexual behavior, there was something peculiarly modern about the idea that only individuals of a certain type or constitution will willingly do so. Homosexuality is usually seen in the modern West as an innate and abnormal condition of a minority of humans which reveals itself in a regular desire to have homosexual intercourse, but also in various other ways. For example, a "homosexual" is widely assumed to be effeminate, promiscuous, and sexually uninterested in members of the other sex. McIntosh argued that such a homosexual "role" or stereotype only emerged in England in the late seventeenth century. Prior to that time, and in most contemporary non-Western societies, "there may be much homosexual behavior, but there are no 'homosexuals.'"[148]

McIntosh's thesis has been elaborated and defended by Alan Bray in his widely acclaimed study *Homosexuality in Renaissance England* (first published in 1982). Bray tried to show that there occurred a dramatic change in the homosexual stereotype toward the end of the seventeenth century. During the sixteenth and early seventeenth centuries, those who indulged in homosexual activity were conceived in primarily religious and moralistic terms, as rakes and libertines who committed the heinous sin of sodomy. In the late seventeenth and eighteenth centuries, this conception gave way to the stereotype of the effeminate "molly," a peculiar kind of man who consorted with others of his kind in certain "molly houses," and had his own subcultural mannerisms and jargon. The sixteenth- and early seventeenth-century "sodomite" or "bugger" had been someone who had given in to "a temptation to which all, in principle at least, were subject."[149] The late seventeenth- and eighteenth-century "molly" was perceived as a distinct type of person whose deviance was not confined to sexual acts but to his entire demeanor, his tone of voice, his gestures, his jargon.

> "[M]olly," unlike "bugger" or "sodomite," involved more than sexuality in the most immediate sense alone. In it we can see encapsulated the expansion of the meaning of homosexuality . . . to encompass behavior that was not intrinsically sexual at all, to be the basis for a particular social identity.[150]

Other historical studies have claimed that similar changes in the conception of those who engaged in homosexual intercourse occurred in early eighteenth-century France and the Netherlands.[151]

Independently of McIntosh, the French philosopher Michel Foucault, in the first volume of his *Histoire de la sexualité* (published in 1976), drew attention to the difference between the traditional religious and legal concept of "sodomy" and the late nineteenth-century concepts of "homosexuality" and "inversion" developed by the emerging science of psychology. "Sodomy" was a sinful act that anyone could commit, whereas "homosexuality" and "inversion" referred to a psychological state possessed by a distinct type of person. In a memorable and much-quoted passage, he stated:

> As defined by the ancient civil or canonical codes, sodomy was a category of forbidden acts; their perpetrator was nothing more than the juridical subject of them. The nineteenth-century homosexual became a personage, a past, a case history, and a childhood . . . The sodomite had been a temporary aberration; the homosexual was now a species.[152]

The conceptual break is dated by Foucault to the late nineteenth century. In this respect he differs from McIntosh and Bray, who place the break two centuries earlier. However, both agree that a conceptual break did occur. At some point, whether the late seventeenth or the late nineteenth century, the view that homosexual intercourse was a sin, akin to theft or adultery, gave way to the view that homosexual intercourse revealed the possession of an abnormal psychological or physiological make-up.

The McIntosh-Foucault thesis has elicited much interest and support, but is still controversial. Especially the idea that premodern sodomites were conceived as individuals who merely committed a certain act, and that there was no developed concept of the perpetrator as a peculiar type of person, has come in for criticism.[153] The premodern Arab-Islamic sources may lend some support to this criticism. As has been shown above, the *ma'būn* was not just someone who happened to commit a prohibited act, but an abnormal type of person, whose deviant behavior invited explanations that appealed to his psychological or physiological constitution.[154] As has also been shown above, the criteria for being a *ma'būn* did not necessarily involve actually having been involved in sexual intercourse. It was enough to want to be anally penetrated, as is shown by the example of the *ma'būn* who locked himself up in his room and satisfied his lust with a wooden dildo. Similarly, Abū Jahl, the infamous archrival of the Prophet Muḥammad, was reputed to have had *ubnah,* but would not countenance being "topped" by another man and satisfied his craving with stones instead.[155] Arabic collections of erotic anecdotes, such as *Nuzhat al-albāb* by Aḥmad al-Tīfāshī (d. 1253), provide evidence—long before the eighteenth or nineteenth century—for the existence of a developed *ma'būn* stereotype or role involving effeminacy and sexual voraciousness, and for the existence of a belief that such individuals formed an almost guild-like subculture.[156]

Once the distinction between perceptions of the passive and active sodomite is taken into account, the discontinuity between premodern and modern conceptualizations appears much less sharp. There may indeed be significant differences between the premodern Arabic concept of the *ma'būn* or *mukhannath* and the eighteenth-century English concept of the "molly" or the nineteenth-century psychological concept of the "invert" or "homosexual." However, all these concepts marked out persons with what was thought to be an odd or pathological internal constitution that was reflected primarily in sexual behavior but often also in overall demeanor. In this respect, at least, there seems to have been no dramatic conceptual discontinuity.

It is when one focuses on the active sodomite or pederast that the contrast drawn by McIntosh and Foucault seems defensible. In the premodern Arab-Islamic Middle East, active sodomy was indeed conceived as primarily a moral-religious vice, akin to adultery, theft, and drinking alcohol, rather than the predicament of a peculiar type of person. It is important to point out that the claim here is not that all individuals were thought to be equally likely to commit sodomy. After all, one has to search hard for a society which thinks that all people are equally likely to steal or commit adultery. Some critics seem to believe that any evidence for a perceived link between sodomy and the character of the sodomite before the seventeenth or nineteenth century will falsify the McIntosh-Foucault thesis. However, despite Foucault's claim that the premodern sodomite was "nothing more than the juridical subject" of sodomy (and one ought to remember that Foucault is speaking specifically of legal or canonical codes), it seems very uncharitable to understand him as postulating a purely coincidental link between sin and sinner in pre-nineteenth-century mentalities, so that he would claim that someone who had committed sodomy regularly was thought to be no more likely to commit it again than a person of hitherto impeccable moral conduct. It seems unnecessary to saddle Foucault with such an implausible claim.[157] All that is needed to establish the contrast he postulates is the claim that the connection envisaged in pre-nineteenth-century mentalities between sodomy and its perpetrator was analogous to the connection envisaged between, say, adultery or theft or—in the case of Islamic culture—drinking alcohol and its perpetrator. All these acts could be seen as the consequence of a certain "vile" or "depraved" character, and hence would not be expected from someone who was thought to be "upright" or "pious." However, there appears to have been no sustained or influential effort to delimit those who had the potential for committing such acts in terms of their psychological or physiological constitution. Rather, the criteria for being an adulterer, a thief, or an active sodomite remained closely tied to actually committing or trying to commit the acts in question.

In the remaining part of this chapter I shall discuss textual evidence from physiognomic and biographical works that at first sight may seem to contradict the conclusion just reached. In a sixteenth-century Egyptian work on physiognomy (*firāsah*) it is stated, for example, that a very tall stature with sparse beard growth indicates an active sodomite. A snub nose, too, is supposed to be an indication of being an active sodomite. It could be argued that this offers a clear and decisive refutation of the McIntosh-Foucault thesis, even if we focus exclusively on the active sodomite. Such physiognomic statements seem, at least at first sight, to mark off a certain type of person who is likely to commit sodomy, and hence to be an example of a premodern conception of the sodomite as a distinct and peculiar type of person. However, if one looks carefully at the passages in question, it seems clear that, far from refuting the McIntosh-Foucault thesis, the physiognomic work actually offers additional support for it. The relevant passages are as follows:

> [1] A very tall man with sparse beard is a deceiving scoundrel (*makkār khaddāʿ*), or feeble-minded and sly (*khafīf al-ʿaql rawwāgh*), or a lover of frivolity (*muḥibb al-lahū*) and sodomizing males (*ityān al-dhukūr*). And the very short man is courageous and crafty, and of a deceptive, ignoble mind.[158]

> [2] A snub nose is an indication of lewdness (*shabaq*) and coarseness (*ghalāẓat al-ṭabʿ*). And Rāzī [Fakhr al-Dīn (d. 1209)] has said: it is an indication of sodomizing males (*ityān al-dhukūr*). A high-bridged, straight nose is an indication of good wits. Our Imām al-Shāfiʿī [d. 820] has said: a long nose with a thin tip is an indication of fickleness and stupidity and irascibility.[159]

Thus stated, it is clear that the physiognomic traits betray, not the possession of abnormal desires, but a certain kind of behavior, namely committing sodomy (as an active partner). This is even clearer when we consider the following passages from the same work, in which certain visible traits are said to indicate fornicators:

> [3] The blue [eye] whose blueness is mixed with white indicates something even more evil than the preceding [the yellowish-greenish eye]. And Aristotle has said: it indicates a lack of [*lacuna*] and the love of fornication (*ḥubb al-zinā*). And that which is mixed with yellow indicates very base morals (*radāʾat al-akhlāq*), because the blueness indicates apathy and laziness, and the yellow indicates fear and cowardice.

> [4] The large, thin ear indicates a defective intellect (*naqṣ al-fahm*) and fornication (*zinā*), and if in addition the hair of the ear is apparent this indicates ignorance (*jahl*) and lassitude (*futūr*).[160]

The passages seem to presuppose that the tendency to commit sodomy is comparable to the tendency to commit fornication. People who commit the latter act are clearly succumbing to a moral failing, rather than to peculiar or pathological desires. It would hardly be plausible to insist that passages stating that certain facial features may reveal a person to be an adulterer somehow shows that adulterers were believed to constitute a special category of people—"adulterosexuals"—with a distinct physical or psychic constitution that somehow explains their anomalous behavior. And the physiognomic passages do not give any grounds for thinking that the tendency to commit sodomy was considered to be any different. On the contrary, the genre clearly assumes that committing fornication and (active) sodomy are on a par with being lazy or cowardly or frivolous or irascible. Such characterizations are basically "behaviorist": they *describe* a certain pattern of behavior rather than *explain* it. The terms *ma'būn* or "homosexual" may function in the same way, but they may also be supposed to refer to an inner condition, describable in non-evaluative terms, that causes (and hence explains) outward behavior. This distinction between the use of the terms *lūṭī* and *ma'būn* has already been discussed in connection with Islamic jurists' opinions on terms of abuse that amounted to accusations of illegal intercourse. Despite appearances, the physiognomic literature does not offer any reason to give up this distinction.

The biographical literature too may at first sight offer evidence that some men were singled out as constitutionally peculiar simply by virtue of their sexually desiring boys. The phrase "he is inclined to" (*yamīl ilā*) or "he likes" (*yuḥibb*) boys occurs regularly in biographical entries from the period, and individuals are often said to be inclined to boys, and yet chaste.[161] Nevertheless, several factors suggest that the "inclination to boys" refers, not to a psychosexual orientation, but to a somewhat disreputable behavioral pattern.

First, such phrases are invariably negative characterizations; something one is accused of, which detracts from other positive traits one might have, and which warrant additional remarks attesting to chastity: "he was on occasion accused of loving boys"; "he has intelligence, prudence, and valor, but is inclined to boys"; "he likes handsome youths . . . being content to look at them."[162] However, taking steps to avoid being tempted by an attractive boy is presented in the same genre as illustrative of a laudable character: "if a youth sat at his hands, he would not look at him or teach him in ascetic self-denial (*zuhdan minhu*)"; "they sent him some coffee with a beardless youth from among them, so he did not take it from him but ordered one of his mature-aged associates to hand it over."[163] Jurists who warned against looking at boys assumed that any man was in danger of being tempted. They accordingly buttressed their counsels by referring to the behavior of eminent religious dignitaries of the early centuries of Islam like Sufyān al-Thawrī (d. 778) and Aḥmad ibn Ḥanbal (d. 855), whose exemplary moral character was a given for Sunnī Muslim scholars of the early Ottoman age. According to the Palestinian jurist Khayr al-Dīn al-Ramlī (d. 1671), the venerable Abū Ḥanīfah (d. 767), founder of the school of law to which Ramlī himself belonged, had seated a handsome student of his in such a manner as not to see him, "from fear of betrayal of the eye."[164] The Meccan jurist Ibn Ḥajar al-Haytamī stated that "there are beardless boys who surpass women in beauty and so are more tempting," while according to the Syrian ascetic ʿAlwān al-Ḥamawī, "there is no doubt and no misgiving that the temptation in looking at him [the beardless boy] is certain (*mutaḥaqqiqah*) [i.e., not merely possible]."[165] Yet, both authors would surely have taken offense at being described as having an "inclination to boys."

Second, other occurrences of the verbs "incline to" or "like" in the biographical literature quite clearly refer to a behavioral pattern rather than a deep-seated psychological orientation. The works of Ibn ʿArabī, poetry, music, bawdy humor, solitude, mystics, buying purebred horses, frequenting drug addicts, tobacco, and luxury are all things that individuals are said to "incline to" or "like."[166] The point is even clearer in the—less than a dozen—cases of men who are described as "inclining" toward women or copulation.[167] Such a phrase is hardly to be understood as implying that such individuals are somehow different from the rest of mankind who are not attracted to either. What is being singled out is a "womanizer" and not a "heterosexual"—that is, a man whose inordinate desire for sex with women leads him to marry and divorce frequently, or to buy many concubines, or take his women with him on even short journeys because he could not be without sex even for a few days. Similarly, someone who is said to "incline toward boys" is being depicted as a "boyizer," and not as someone who is abnormal by virtue of the fact that he is susceptible to being sexually aroused by a boy. Indeed, variants of the phrase "he is inclined to boys" are more unambiguously behaviorist: "he was inclined to looking at youths and sitting with them"; "he was accused of associating with beardless boys"; "he was inclined to loving youths."[168]

If the present interpretation is correct, the phrase "he is inclined to boys" would be another expression for "pederast," and hence equivalent to the ordinary, nonjuridical meaning of the term *lūṭī* discussed earlier in this chapter. Whether someone was a *lūṭī* in the strict legal sense ultimately depended on whether he had indulged in anal intercourse with another man. The more extended meaning of the term *lūṭī* was also act-defined but less specific as to the nature of the act committed. While there were notoriously strict rules for attributing sodomy or fornication to a person (unforced confession or trustworthy witnesses to the anal or vaginal penetration), there were no correspondingly clear-cut and consensual criteria for distinguishing a "boyizer" or "womanizer" from someone who displayed a normal responsiveness to the attractiveness of boys or women. If the case of the poet Abū al-Fatḥ al-Mālikī, who openly frequented boys of "ill-repute," seems clear, what of Sinān Pāshā (d. 1666), a military notable of Damascus, who at the age of eighty, and for the first time in his life, fell in love with one of his young male servants?[169] The lack of clear-cut and consensual criteria regarding whether a particular behavioral pattern merited the description "he inclines to boys" left considerable scope to individual judgment as well as individual idiosyncrasy and bias. The Aleppine scholar Abū al-Wafā' al-ʿUrḍī (d. 1660), commenting critically on the biographical dictionary of his fellow Aleppine Ibn al-Ḥanbalī (d. 1563), said that "he took every opportunity to diminish the standing of his enemies . . . and discredited [them] by means of invectives such as saying: so-and-so, though chaste, likes youths."[170] It is also noticeable that the phrase "he inclines to youths," used regularly by some biographical compilers, such as Ibn al-Ḥanbalī, Najm al-Dīn al-Ghazzī, and Ibn Ayyūb al-Anṣārī, seems to have been consciously avoided by others. The phrase does not occur in, for example, the biographical dictionaries of Ḥasan al-Būrīnī, Muḥammad Amīn al-Muḥibbī, and Muḥammad Khalīl al-Murādī. One possible explanation for this might be in terms of compliance with the established ideal of "thinking well" (*ḥusn al-ẓann*) of one's fellow Muslims and avoiding slander and calumny (*ghībah*). The Yemeni scholar Muḥammad al-Shawkānī (d. 1834), for instance, after mentioning that one of his acquaintances was "inclined to those of handsome countenance," assured the reader that he had received the consent of the person in question to mention this fact about him. He would not have mentioned this fact, Shawkānī insisted, if the person had minded, since he wanted to keep his biographical dictionary free from slanderous remarks.[171] It is also important to keep in mind that biographical entries were written within a social setting marked by rivalries, enmity, and alliances, and were thus charged with "political" significance. Many a quarrel between notable households had its roots in unfavorable mentions in, or exclusions from, biographical works. In such a situation, there would be more mundane reasons for a biographer to be as favorable and circumspect as possible in his characterizations of other notables. A more uncharitable explanation of the avoidance of the phrase "he inclines to boys" would suggest that some authors were eager to avoid a phrase that could easily apply to themselves. After all, Būrīnī was himself said to incline toward boys by his contemporary Ibn Ayyūb al-Anṣārī (who—by coincidence?—is not mentioned in Būrīnī's later biographical dictionary of the notables of his age).[172] And, as will be seen in the following chapter, both Muḥibbī and Murādī seem in fact to have had a more sympathetic opinion of chaste pederastic affection than, for example, Ghazzī or Ibn Ayyūb. The more important point, however, is that such authors, though avoiding the disapproving phrase, were not thereby reduced to silence; their works include several anecdotes and poems whose subject is pederastic attraction. Rather, they resorted to a different vocabulary, a different way of speaking, to describe what other scholars dismissed as an "inclination to boys."

CHAPTER TWO

Aesthetes

Aestheticism and Cultural Refinement

The Damascene poet Abū Bakr al-ʿUmarī (d. 1638) was, according to a near-contemporary anthology of poets by Yūsuf al-Badīʿī (d. 1662/3), inclined toward the "turbaned" (male) rather than the "veiled" (female) beloved, and was once apprehended with a beardless boy "in a state which it would be vile to call by its vile name." The two culprits were subsequently pilloried by being dragged through the market places of the city. In his great biographical dictionary of the notables of the eleventh century of the Muslim era (1591–1688), the Damascene scholar Muḥammad Amīn al-Muḥibbī (d. 1699) quoted Badīʿī's passage in his entry on ʿUmarī, only to add:

> I have inquired about this report from among those who knew al-ʿUmarī and did not find any traces of it, and in my opinion it is probably a slander . . . True, al-ʿUmarī had a character that was inclined to beauty (*mayyāl li-al-jamāl*), and an inclination is potentially suspicious to those who vie in the field [i.e., rivals]. In short, a story such as this is related only in order to show it to be groundless . . . The sum of the matter is that al-ʿUmarī was among the accomplished of his age and the outstanding of his time.[1]

In presenting ʿUmarī as an aesthete rather than a pederast, Muḥibbī did not want to imply that the poet would not be attracted to boys. Quite the contrary, many boys were considered to be handsome, and an anecdote that Muḥibbī quoted from ʿUmarī's own collection of poetry has him sitting with a friend in a coffeehouse admiring one of them.[2] However, by recasting the object of ʿUmarī's inclination as beauty rather than boys, Muḥibbī succeeded in presenting him in a more positive light. The phrase "he inclines to boys," being equivalent to the ordinary, nontechnical meaning of the term *lūṭī,* had negative connotations. An inclination to beauty, by contrast, though it might make its possessor vulnerable to malicious rumors circulated by jealous rivals, was perceived as unobjectionable in itself. Muḥibbī attributed it to several other persons, including close friends and relatives, and in contexts that indicate that he did not regard it as a negative trait: "gentle-mannered, of much beneficence to his students, a sincere, guiding teacher . . . an elementary student would make a trite point and he would oblige him and listen to it as if he had not heard it before, and he was an aesthete (*jamālī*) in all his affairs, by character in love with beauty (*yuḥibb al-jamāl*), and he was diligent in conveying kindness and goodness to everyone in need"; "he would mention original witticisms and refined poetry, and mastered the Turkish language, and was enamored of beauty (*mughram bi-al-jamāl*) and spent his whole life in sprightfulness and joy and so was never seen except happy and smiling, and he was munificent and pious, fasting on most days."[3] Other occurrences of the phrase in the biographical literature are usually equally devoid of negative connotations.[4] Indeed, Muḥibbī's distinction between a commendable aesthetic sense and a reprehensible sexual interest was conventional rather than idiosyncratic. One of the most influential Islamic theologians, Abū Ḥāmid al-Ghazālī (d. 1111), in his seminal work *Iḥyā' 'ulūm al-dīn*, which was widely read, quoted, and commented upon in the period under study, insisted on the distinction between the appreciation of beauty and carnal lust:

> Do not think that the love of beautiful forms (*ḥubb al-ṣuwar al-jamīlah*) is only conceivable with an eye toward satisfying carnal desire, for satisfying carnal desire is a distinct pleasure that *may* be associated with the love of beautiful forms, but the perception of beauty in itself is also pleasurable and so may be loved for its own sake. How can this be denied, when greenery and flowing water are loved, not with an eye toward drinking the water or eating the greenery or to obtain anything else besides the looking itself?[5]

The chaste love of beauty is a recurrent theme in the collection of poetry of the Egyptian scholar and Rector of the Azhar, 'Abdallah al-Shabrāwī (d. 1758). At one point, for example, he said:

> I fancy you, you handsome thing, but God knows it is with no ulterior motive.
> I have a chaste conscience, and my soul abhors in love any trait which would displease God . . .
> My creed is to love beauty, and whenever a gazelle appears I fancy him at first sight.[6]

The same contrast between love of beauty and lust is presupposed in the following lines of verse, in which the scholar Ismā'īl al-Nābulusī (d. 1585), who was mentioned in the previous chapter in connection with an accusation of sodomy, denounced a contemporary:

> Judge ʿAlī is but a person who inclines to nothing but *liwāṭ*.
> So he does not love an upright physique, nor is he captivated by a dark-lashed eye.
> But he who has a behind and presents it, is for him the handsome and beautiful.[7]

The literature of the period clearly shows that boys as well as girls could be described as having "an upright physique" (*qadd qawīm*) and "dark-lashed eyes" (*ṭarf kaḥīl*).[8] The poem, in denouncing *liwāṭ,* is therefore not condemning those who would be attracted to these qualities in either sex, but asserts that the judge, because of his lewdness, does not belong to their rank. Scholars who did not mince their words in condemning *liwāṭ* could very well express their own fascination with the beauty of a particular beardless boy. For example, Ḥasan al-Būrīnī condemned the above-mentioned mercenary *Sakbān* in the following terms: "Most of them commit the act of the people of Lot, ever falling [in merit] to the lowest levels of Hell." He also indignantly rejected the rumor according to which an acquaintance of his was inclined to "the males of humanity (*al-dhukrān min al-ʿālamīn*)," an expression used by the Qur'an of the people of Lot.[9] Yet, on several occasions in his biographical dictionary, he dwelled on the attractiveness of certain youths: "upon my life! the beloved was [as] a succulent twig, and a full, radiant moon"; "he was extremely beautiful, like the full moon on the night of the fourteenth [of the Muslim lunar month], and as to his physique, it eclipses a tender branch"; "he was of a beauty that exceeds the moon in its radiance, and the garden as it flourishes in its bloom."[10] Such venting of aesthetic appreciation abounds in the literature and could, in contradistinction to the "inclination to boys," hardly have been regarded as discreditable by their authors. Aḥmad ibn al-Mullā (d. 1594/5), Aleppine scholar and historian, apparently had no compunctions in expressing his enthrallment with a boy he happened to see in the vicinity of the town of Shayzar: "a gazelle fawn, my heart flew toward him only to find a predator between his eye-lids; a beauty who shone like the moon in its fullness, and who smiled, revealing teeth as ordered pearls; he was followed by a group of pretty young women, and he was playing among them as if they were houris, and he one of the boys of paradise."[11] The Damascene poet Darwīsh al-Ṭālawī (d. 1606) was equally unreserved in his praise of a youth who accompanied him and a number of friends on an outing to one of the popular garden-resorts surrounding Damascus: ". . . and with us was a youth in his prime, with a graceful physique and comely cheeks, a lovable fellow called ʿAbd al-Nabī, his jasmine beauty was embellished by a rosy bloom, and its whiteness brought out the blackness of his beauty-spot."[12]

The Iraqi scholar ʿAbdallah al-Suwaydī (d. 1761), spending some time in Damascus on his way to and from Mecca, mentioned that he had taught a youth named Muḥammad some grammar during his sojourn in the city, and that the youth, who was the beloved of one of his local friends, was "in truth and by common consent, the most handsome of the handsome of Damascus; indeed I have never set eyes upon anything more handsome; he has a dazzling beauty and a radiant and bloomy countenance . . . so glory be to Him who created him and formed him in the most excellent fashion."[13]

The difference in terms of actual behavior between "the inclination to boys" and "the inclination to beauty" need not have been particularly great, and it is clear that the two terms were often alternative ways of describing the same behavioral pattern. The Iraqi scholar ʿAbd al-Raḥmān al-Suwaydī (d. 1786), son of the above-mentioned ʿAbdallah, advised chaste lovers of handsome boys not to flaunt their inclinations, since they were liable to be perceived as *lūṭīs* by less sympathetic observers. He added as a case in point: "I have seen people slander a man from among the seekers of learning, despite his piety and asceticism, and ascribe sodomy (*al-liwāṭah*) to him, because he used to say: I love beauty and adore the gazelle [i.e., the beloved]."[14] Two notables whose pederastic love affairs were the topic of several anecdotes were described in the following terms in the biographical work of the Aleppine scholar Abū al-Wafā' al-ʿUrḍī (d. 1660): the poet Aḥmad al-ʿInāyātī was "chaste in love, proverbial in excellence, resplendent in manners, covetous of those with a handsome countenance"; Ibrāhīm al-Batrūnī (d. 1642/3), a student of ʿUrḍī's father, "took beauty as his creed" and was nicknamed "the amorous (*al-gharāmī*)."[15] Yet, as underlined by such passages, the effect of the shift in terminology was to ameliorate, if not to remove completely, the negative connotations associated with the phrase "he inclines toward boys." Ordinary life supplies numerous parallel cases in which divergent descriptions of the same behavioral pattern reveals divergent evaluations. An example was encountered in the previous chapter while discussing the different attitudes toward "screwing" and "committing sodomy." In both instances, the cultural ambiguity tends to betray the coexistence of potentially conflicting ideals in a society. On the one hand, the behavior designated by the phrase "he loves beauty" was not readily assimilable to some widely held ideals, such as piety, asceticism, and dignified sobriety (*waqār*). There is an inkling of such a realization even among those who saw it as, on the whole, a positive trait. In the poetic anthologies and biographical dictionaries, the pursuit of beauty was conventionally attributed to the days of youth, before graying hair served as a reminder of mortality and divine judgment.[16] On the other hand, aesthetic sensitivity was implicated by a complex of ideals whose influence is abundantly attested in the writings of the period. Whether in the biographical or the belletrist literature, one constantly comes across expressions praising a character (*ṭabʿ, ḥāshiyah, mazāj, dhāt*) that is "refined," "delicate," or "elegant" (*laṭīf, raqīq, ẓarīf*).[17] A refined or delicate character was of course recognizable by the traits exhibited by its possessor. The more important of these seem to have been urbanity, affability, wit, emotional sensibility, a taste for belles-lettres, especially poetry, and an appreciation of beauty, particularly human and floral.[18] The same evaluative ambiguity mentioned in connection with the inclination to beauty obtained in the case of the other traits belonging to the same complex. Urbanity, affability, and wit might have been regarded as positive attributes, but so were an otherworldly inclination to asceticism, solitude, austere piety, and religious moralism ("commanding the good and forbidding the bad"). Similarly, the profusion of poetry in the literature of the period leaves no doubt as to its popularity, and biographical works confirm that poetic abilities were highly prized. Yet, it was generally recognized that the Prophet—usually the model of behavior for the believers—had not said any poetry, and some of the sayings attributed to him are indeed hostile to the art. Religious jurists discussed whether secular poetry should be considered reprehensible (*makrūh*), and ascetics often abandoned the genre as part of their turning away from the transitory world.[19] The conflict of ideals was sometimes sought resolved by resorting to the idea of the mean between extremes. After mentioning one of the Prophet's sayings which seem hostile to the art of poetry, the Damascene jurist Ibn ʿĀbidīn (d. 1836) opined that this should be understood as applying to an inordinate attachment. There was no problem with a little poetry, "if it aims at displaying witticisms, subtleties, excellent comparisons, or superior expressions, even if it is of physiques and cheeks [i.e., love poetry]."[20] In the same spirit, a person could be praised for being of a temperate (*muʿtadil*) character, neither a shameless profligate nor a "cold" recluse.[21]

The connection between refined character and the sensitivity to human beauty is apparent in the previously mentioned discussion of human love by Mullā Ṣadr al-Dīn al-Shīrāzī (d. 1640/1). The Persian philosopher explicitly attributed the refined love of handsome youths to *al-ẓurafāʾ* (the "genteel" or "elegant"), and asserted that

> we do not find anyone of those who have a refined heart and a delicate character . . . to be void of this love at one time or the other in their life, but we find all coarse souls, harsh hearts, and dry characters . . . devoid of this type of love, most of them restricting themselves to the love of men for women and the love of women for men with the aim of mating and cohabitation, as

is in the nature of all animals in which is implanted the love of mating and cohabitation.[22]

ʿAbd al-Ghanī al-Nābulusī (d. 1731), the prominent Damascene scholar and mystic, pursued the analogy between insensitivity to beauty and animal behavior in the following lines of verse:

And he for whom there is no difference between the hirsute face (*al-wajh al-shaʿir*) and the comely (*al-ṣabīḥ*),
He is an animal, and has no mind . . .[23]

Notwithstanding such explicit passages by some of the intellectually towering figures of the age, the connection between refinement and aestheticism is more often encountered as an implicit assumption than an articulated proposition. It is revealed, for instance, in the way that certain anecdotes dealing with pederastic attraction are presented in the literature. The following example is found in the biographical work of Muḥibbī: The poet Aḥmad al-ʿInāyātī is sitting in front of one of the shops of Damascus admiring a handsome youth by the name of Aṣlān. The grandfather of Muḥibbī, a close friend of ʿInāyātī, passes by and asks why he is sitting there. The poet replies: "My lord, it has its basis (*aṣl*)," whereupon Muḥibbī's grandfather, hinting at the name of the youth, puns: "Rather, two bases (*aṣlān*)."[24] Another example, which served as the inspiration for several poetic compositions, is the following: The Turkish judge and poet Bāqī (d. 1600) composes lines praising the beauty of a certain youth. The youth in question hears the lines, is impressed by them, and resolves to kiss the feet of the poet. But when attempting to do so, Bāqī reminds him that he had composed the poem with his mouth, not his feet.[25] A third example was related to the Damascene scholar Ramaḍān al-ʿUṭayfī (d. 1684) during his trip to Tripoli by the deputy governor of the town, ʿAlī Sayfā: ʿAlī is sitting with a handsome youth at an elevated place at the outskirts of the town. The youth comments on the beautiful view—the red sand, the green meadow, and the blue sea. The governor subsequently asks the youth why he left unmentioned the white dune (*kathīb*) behind him—thereby alluding to the boy's rear.[26] Common to such stories is that they are introduced as *laṭāʾif*—that is, as humorous and entertaining stories that illustrate the sensibility and wit of its main characters. Sure enough, there would be those who disapproved of such stories. One searches in vain for similar anecdotes in the biographical works of, say, Najm al-Dīn Muḥammad al-Ghazzī (d. 1651). But there was obviously a considerable and vocal proportion of the educated and articulate elite who, though not necessarily irreligious, considered such disapproval to be an expression of narrow moralism and humorless boorishness. It bears emphasizing that the contradiction was not between a "religious" and a "nonreligious" outlook. Religiosity does not necessarily imply asceticism. The proponents of an enjoyment of life within the bounds of the permissible could support their position by drawing on several aspects of the Islamic religious tradition. According to traditions that were widely accepted as authentic, the Prophet himself had said that "God is beautiful and loves beauty" and that "three things refresh the eyes: looking at greenery, flowing water, and the handsome face." He also reportedly exhorted his followers to "seek the good from handsome countenances."[27] The anecdotes cited did not imply a breach of religious law as interpreted by the majority of the jurists of the age. It was thus possible for the non-ascetically inclined to turn the tables on their opponents, and accuse them of prohibiting what is permissible and of ascribing bad intentions to others, both religiously proscribed acts. Thus ʿAbd al-Ghanī al-Nābulusī could say the following of those who censure the contemplation of human beauty:

> They disapprove of looking at the handsome and, in equating the wolf and the gazelle, annul the difference.
> And they would abolish mankind's seeing any difference between the stale and the tender.
> All from the coarseness of their character, and the deficiency of a malignant and impaired mind.
> And they think ill of others, which tomorrow will lead them to torment.[28]

The moralists and ascetics were also liable, then as now, to be accused of hypocrisy, of not being nearly as pure as they pretended to be. The Iraqi poet Jirjis ibn Darwīsh al-Adīb (d. 1727/8), who was reputed to be fond of wine and beardless boys, struck precisely that note in the following lines of verse:

> You blame me for my youthful amusements! You are not my adviser, and I am not listening!
> I am someone who does not give up his pleasures, whether you like it or not, blame or let be!
> And what have I to do with he who claims asceticism as his station? Leave me be, for I have my place among my boon-companions.
> I have rubbed shoulders with ascetics for a time, and did not encounter anything but snakes that bite.
> And I came to know their true nature, so follow your every wish and you will still be more pious than them.[29]

The ideal of refinement and elegance was partly defined in opposition to the coarse, the uncouth, and the vulgar. As such, it was probably particularly relevant to the more comfortable and educated segments of society. Yet, the urban population as a whole—with the possible exception of the poorest inhabitants and the most recent rural immigrants—seem to have been conscious and proud of the cultural distance separating them from the more rustic peasant or nomad.[30] The Egyptian scholar ʿAbd al-Wahhāb al-Shaʿrānī (d. 1565) thus thanked God for bringing him from his rural birthplace, "the land of coarseness (*jafāʾ*) and ignorance," to Cairo, "the town of refinement (*luṭf*) and knowledge."[31] The seventeenth-century work *Hazz al-quḥūf* by Yūsuf al-Shirbīnī may be regarded as one long satire at the expense of the Egyptian peasant, who is portrayed as irredeemably lacking in *luṭf* by comparison with the inhabitants of the towns.[32] The social parameters of the ideal were therefore not likely to have been sharp or narrow. However, its specifically aesthetic dimension seems to have been especially cultivated by two groups: on the one hand, poets and belletrists and, on the other, mystics influenced by a monist, Neoplatonic worldview.

Love of Boys in Belles-Lettres

Arabic poetry between the sack of Baghdad by the Mongols in 1258 and the so-called cultural revival (*nahḍah*) of the nineteenth century has often been dismissed by modern scholars, both Western and Arab, as being of a mediocre, "decadent" quality.[33] Even if one supposes this sweeping judgment to be accurate, the mediocrity can hardly be ascribed to a lack of interest in the art. The literature of the period reveals the extent to which Arab-Islamic high culture was permeated with poetry. A myriad of occasions provided subjects and opportunities for poetic diction: birth, death, circumcision, the attainment of puberty and the appearance of a beard, marriage, return from travel, appointments to posts, the arrival of dignitaries from abroad, major political events, and so on. The educated classes used the medium to praise, condole, congratulate, or to lampoon; to express friendly or amorous feelings; and merely to amuse or display their eloquence (*faṣāḥa*) to their fellows. The volume of poetry committed to writing was remarkable: to the countless collections of an individual's poetry (*dīwān*), one should add numerous books of poetic exchanges (*muṭāraḥāt*), as well as the poetic anthologies, a classical genre which seems to have experienced a renaissance in the early Ottoman period. The taste for poetry also meant that it tended to spill over into other fields. Handbooks on jurisprudence, logic, grammar, and theology were often composed in verse, presumably to facilitate memorization, as were many works of a devotional or mystical nature. Much of the travel literature and historical writing of the period also contain extensive quotations of verse, often introduced at the slightest pretence and leading by association to lengthy digressions. Knowledge and appreciation of poetry was widely thought to be one of the hallmarks of the cultivated, refined person. It was also from the ranks of the cultivated and refined that the composition of high-quality poetry was expected. This is shown by the use of terms like "delicate" (*raqīq*) or "refined" (*laṭīf*) or "polished" (*maṣqūl*) to characterize praiseworthy examples of the art. It was of course assumed that it took a delicate, refined, and polished character to produce delicate, refined, and polished verse. Good poetry was said to be *maṭbūʿ*—that is, to flow from the author's person in a way that was natural and unaffected, and was to that extent considered to mirror his character: "he has poetry that indicates his sensitive character"; "his poetry is, like his character, polished"; "I have mentioned of his poetry what . . . bespeaks a sensitive character"; "I mention a short poem that indicates his refined nature and fine character"; "one may infer his coarse character from the poor and uncouth quality of his poetry."[34] The corollary of this belief was that sensibility and refinement was thought especially characteristic of poets (*shuʿarāʾ*) and belletrists (*udabāʾ*). Darwīsh al-Ṭālawī, for example, said of a jurist (*faqīh*) that "he has a character like that of a belletrist (*adīb*) in refinement."[35]

By far the most commonly cited genre in the poetic anthologies of the period was love poetry (*ghazal*).[36] That this genre was especially popular is also apparent from a remark such as the following by Muḥibbī on the Damascene poet Ismāʿīl al-Ḥijāzī (d. 1592/3): "He has a lot of poetry cast in the mold of delicacy, describing longing and affection and mentioning ardent love and infatuation, and for this reason it stuck to hearts and was deemed attractive by most people, and they inclined toward it, memorized it, and circulated it amongst themselves."[37]

When speaking of the beloved, the poets in most cases, but by no means all, used the masculine gender.[38] It should be emphasized that this does not automatically imply that the beloved was a male. In classical Arabic it is legitimate to use the masculine form of the word "beloved" (*maḥbūb, ḥabīb*) to refer to a female. In addition, the conventional metaphors for the beloved in Arabic love poetry—gazelle (*ghazāl, shādin, ẓaby, rīm, rashaʾ*) and moon (*badr, qamar*)—are of masculine gender. Many a modern scholar would like to conclude therefrom that the love celebrated in *ghazal* was, despite appearances, invariably or at least as a rule "heterosexual." Edward Lane, the great nineteenth-century Arabist, after translating some Arabic love poetry in his *Manners and Customs of the Modern Egyptians,* confidently asserted: "I have substituted the feminine for the masculine pronoun; for in the original, the former is meant, though the latter is used, as is commonly the case in similar compositions of the Egyptians."[39] Perhaps the best retort is to quote again the remark of the Egyptian scholar Rifāʿah al-Ṭahṭāwī (d. 1873), who was in Paris around the same time that Lane was in Egypt, and commented on the unacceptability of pederasty in that country:

> One of the positive aspects of their language and poetry is that it does not permit the saying of *ghazal* of someone of the same sex, so in the French language a man cannot say: I loved a boy (*ghulām*), for that would be an unacceptable and awkward wording, so therefore if one of them translates one of our books he avoids this by changing the wording, so saying in the translation: I loved a young girl (*ghulāmah*) or a person (*dhātan*).[40]

Many modern Arab literary historians likewise seem to assume that premodern *ghazal* is as a rule "heterosexual," and sometimes preface their discussions of the genre with reflections on what they consider to be the universal, timeless character of love between men and women.[41] ʿUmar Mūsā Bāshā, author of one of the very few modern Arabic monographs on the poetry and belles-lettres of the period, consistently assumes that poets are singing the praises of their beloved women, even though he could hardly have been unaware that many of the poets he discussed were interested in boys. At one point, for instance, Bāshā indicates briefly that a large number of short verses by the Syrian poet Amīn al-Jundī (d. 1841) are of a "bawdy" (*mājin*) character. The verses he refers to in the footnotes, which are not "bawdy" at all, were all reportedly inspired by handsome boys. Bāshā pointedly does not mention this fact, nor does he explain by what right he then assumes that the love poetry of the age was "heterosexual."[42] Oussama Anouti, the author of an otherwise useful and pioneering work on Syrian literature in the eighteenth century, even permits himself to say that *ghazal* in which the object of love (and not merely the gender used) was masculine was rare, referring to four such examples from the biographical dictionary of Muḥammad Khalīl al-Murādī (d. 1791).[43] Such a statement is simply and utterly false. Verses in which poets mentioned the beard-down (*ʿidhār* or *ʿāriḍ*) of their beloved abound in this work—the number is much more than ten times that mentioned by Anouti—and these should be understood as describing a young male beloved. The terms *ʿidhār* and *ʿāriḍ* can both denote "cheek" as well as "beard-down," but in the overwhelming number of occurrences the context clearly indicates which of the meanings is intended. The following lines of verse are a case in point:

> ʿUthmān al-ʿUmarī (d. 1770/1): I was infatuated with the honey-lipped when he was beardless, until the myrtle of interlocked *ʿidhār* became apparent.

Aḥmad al-Kaywānī (d. 1760): A boy, as *ʿidhār* spread on his cheeks, it adorned his roses.

Aḥmad ibn Shāhīn (d. 1644): I was in doubt as to [whether he was] female or male, then his *ʿidhār* imparted certainty.[44]

The following examples—among many others—are from the above-mentioned work of Murādī:

Ibrāhīm al-Safarjalānī (d. 1705): When his cheeks became striped with his *ʿidhār* and his lover's passion increased.

Aḥmad ibn Jaddī (d. 1714): For the roses of his cheek he fears a searing touch, so he veiled himself with the basil of *ʿidhār*.

Aḥmad al-Falāqunsī (d. 1759–60): They say [to me]: Can there be dissoluteness after *ʿidhār?*

Ismāʿīl al-Manīnī (d. 1780): Do not think that the basil of *ʿidhār* has appeared on the cheek of he who excels in beauty and splendor.

Aḥmad al-Bahnasī (d. 1735): There he is with the night of the face's *ʿidhār* when it darkened.

ʿAbd al-Ḥayy al-Khāl (d. 1705): I used to say that my heart would forget [you] when *ʿāriḍ* appeared on your cheeks.

ʿAbd al-Raḥmān al-Mawṣilī (d. 1706): (I) Is it sprouting *ʿidhār* or anemones in a garden on which ants have walked with ink on their feet? (II) *ʿidhār* flowed down a cheek, as if it were interlocked pieces of musk on sheets of gold.

ʿAlī al-ʿImādī (d. 1706): I should not have thought before the sprouting of his *ʿidhār* that *ʿidhār* would confirm his beauty.

Muṣṭafā al-Ṣumādī (d. 1725): They looked at the gardens of your cheek, the roses being surrounded by the myrtle of *ʿidhār*.

Muṣṭafā ibn Bīrī (d. 1735/6): Is it *ʿidhār* that has appeared on this your cheeks, or have snares appeared for the catching of hearts?

Muḥammad Amīn al-Muḥibbī (d. 1699): Beauty has protected his cheeks with *ʿawāriḍ* [pl. of *ʿāriḍ*], with which he has killed souls and revivified eyes.

Yūsuf al-Naqīb al-Ḥalabī (d. 1740/1): The sprouting *ʿidhār* on his cheek was a blackbird arriving in an enchanting garden.[45]

These lines provide a sample of the conventional similes used of *ʿidhār* which leave no doubt that what was meant was "down," not "cheeks": myrtle (*ās*), basil (*rayḥān*), ambergris (*ʿanbar*), musk (*misk*), night (*layl*), netting (*shirk*), writing (*khaṭṭ*), tendrils of smoke (*dukhkhān*).

Descriptions of the beard-down of the beloved are common in Arabic poetry from the ninth century and remain very frequent in the poetry of the period under study.[46] Less often, the poets of the early Ottoman period directly spoke of the beloved as a male youth:

Muḥammad al-Maḥāsinī (d. 1662): I fancy him, a lithesome boy of paradise.
Aḥmad al-Jawharī al-Makkī (d. 1669): The eye was wounded by the beauty-spot on a boy's cheek.
Aḥmad al-Bahnasī (d. 1735): I say to the censurer when he in ignorance reprimanded: Should you not turn away from loving this boy?
Muḥammad al-Kanjī (d. 1740): I was taught passionate love and the nature of infatuation [by] the love of a boy whose glance is more than a match for me.
Muḥammad ibn al-Darā (d. 1655): A boy whose cheeks God has clothed in a cover of roses gilded by his shyness.
Muḥammad al-Ghulāmī (d. 1772/3): A boy (*ghulām*) swelled my infatuation and unhappiness, so excuse me for crying over al-Ghulāmī.
ʿAbdallah al-Shabrāwī (d. 1758): I said: Don't censure me, for I'm an old man who has regained his youth by loving a boy.
ʿAbd al-Ghanī al-Nābulusī (d. 1731): Or are you beauty that has appeared in the form of a boy?[47]

The Aleppine scholar Aḥmad ibn al-Mullā (d. 1594/5) devoted an entire work to the description of handsome boys, *ʿUqūd al-jummān fī waṣf nubdhah min al-ghilmān.*[48] This work seems not to have come down to us, but it is presumably modeled on earlier works that have: *Jannat al-wildān fī al-ḥisān min al-ghilmān,* by Aḥmad al-Ḥijāzī (d. 1471); *Marātiʿ al-ghizlān fī al-ḥisān min al-ghilmān,* by Muḥammad al-Nawājī (d. 1455); *al-Ḥusn al-ṣarīḥ fī miʾat malīḥ,* by Khalīl ibn Aybak al-Ṣafadī (d. 1363); and *al-Kalām ʿalā miʾat ghulām,* by ʿUmar ibn al-Wardī (d. 1349).[49]

One may also legitimately conclude that a poem is pederastic when the beloved's male name is indicated in the poem, or he is described as a craftsman, or as entering a mosque or a public bath. Conversely, bracelets, anklets, veils, red-tipped fingers, earrings, or pigtails would usually indicate that a female is being eulogized.[50] However, in terms of frequency of occurrence, mention of beard-down remains the major indicator of the gender of the beloved in love poetry.[51] This implies that the poems that are clearly pederastic outnumber the ones that are clearly "heterosexual" since the absence of references to beard-down usually leaves it undetermined whether a woman or a beardless boy is being praised. In many, perhaps most, cases the gender of the beloved cannot be ascertained, and this is a significant fact in itself. Whether the beloved was a woman or a boy was obviously not a pressing issue at the time, and as will be seen shortly, there was often no real beloved at all. Furthermore, the difficulty of determining the gender of the beloved is partly due to the fact that the poetic imagery remained—on the whole—the same in both cases: dark-lashed eyes that, like swords, cause havoc among admirers; beauty-spots compared to pieces of musk or to Ethiopians; earlocks that lure or incite to love; slim waists and large posteriors, the latter "oppressing" the former; supple and upright figures compared to a branch or a spear; teeth as pearls; cheeks as roses; faces as the moon; hearts as stone; a gazelle's recalcitrance; skin as smooth and sleek as a mirror or water, etc. Such similes are repeated ad nauseam in the love poetry of the period, with no regard to the gender of the described object. In other words, it was largely the same features that were represented as being attractive in females and in male youths. Being measured by the same yardstick, the beauty of women and youths was fundamentally comparable. "He is more beautiful than you," an Aleppine tailor enamored of his apprentice was reported to have told his jealous wife.[52] The comparability of boyish and female beauty also underlies a somewhat peculiar problem discussed in the juridical literature of the period. Some jurists held that it was forbidden for men to look at youths. At the same time, it was, by common consent, permissible for a man to look at a woman he intends to marry. But if he is unable to do so, could he look instead at her beardless brother or son if he hears that they are as beautiful as she is?[53] In the premodern Arab world, as well as in classical antiquity, an attractive youth could be described as having "feminine limbs" (*khanith al-aʿṭāf*).[54] The Damascene judge Muḥammad Akmal al-Dīn (d. 1603) related at first hand a story that occurred in Damascus in 1545–46: a man loved a beardless bookbinder by the name of ʿAlī. The latter actually turned out to be a hermaphrodite and was judged by physicians to be more of a female than a male. A local judge subsequently declared the bookbinder to be a woman. ʿAlī promptly became ʿAlyā (or ʿAliyyā) and could thus be married to his (or rather her) admirer.[55] The story illustrates the problem of describing the original attraction to the boy as "homosexual." A man was standardly represented as being attracted to the specifically boyish or feminine rather than masculine features of a boy, and hence there was usually no expectation that he would not be attracted to women. The taste for handsome youths and beautiful women was often presented in the poetry as going hand-in-hand:

ʿAlī ibn Maʿṣūm (d. ca. 1708): I love ardently with a heart that remains enamored of both the turbaned [i.e., male] and the veiled [i.e., female].

ʿAbd al-Raḥmān al-ʿImādī (d. 1641): And I was fond of beauty in every form and so was blinded [literally "veiled"] by this turbaned beloved.

ʿAlī al-Gīlānī al-Ḥamawī (d. 1702): He turned me from the love of beautiful virgins, and my rival for them was my love.

ʿAbd al-Raḥmān al-Mallāḥ (d. 1635): Is my love a sun [*fem.*] or else a crescent [*masc.*], of the houris or of the boys of paradise?[56]

The difficulty in ascertaining the gender of the beloved in the love poetry of the period may suggest that a remark of Freud's on pederasty in ancient Greece is equally applicable to the premodern Middle East:

> It is clear that in Greece, where the most masculine men were numbered among the inverts, what excited a man's love was not the masculine character of the boy, but his physical resemblance to a woman as well as his feminine mental qualities—his shyness, his modesty and his need for instruction and assistance.[57]

However, such a conclusion ought to be qualified. The poetic descriptions are highly stylized, and it is risky to draw conclusions regarding actual sexual and aesthetic preferences solely on their basis. Bringing in other kinds of evidence tends to complicate the picture somewhat. For example, the Egyptian belletrist and historian Ibn al-Wakīl al-Mallawī (d. ca. 1719) recorded several stories involving friends and acquaintances who meet very handsome beardless youths who later show themselves also to be courageous and physically strong, and this combination of features was apparently appealing to the author and his informers.[58] There is also some evidence to suggest that women were believed to find beardless teenage youths attractive. The Syrian ascetic ʿAlwān al-Ḥamawī (d. 1530), for instance, believed that the dressed-up beardless slaves who could be seen in the processions of political rulers were "a temptation to men and women alike."[59] Poets could likewise mention the eulogized male youth's attractiveness to women as well as men. A couplet by the Iraqi scholar Khalīl al-Baṣīrī (d. 1762), for instance, stated:

> Women reproached me for loving the dark-lashed deer, whose mouth exudes a musky fragrance.
> So I quoted when they became enchanted with him: "This is he concerning whom ye blamed me."[60]

The quotation is from the Qur'an (12:32), where it is attributed to the wife of "Pharaoh" (the biblical Potiphar). She addressed the words to the Egyptian women who were scandalized by her love for Joseph, after she had arranged for them to see the object of her affection and noted their enchantment with his appearance. In the Islamic religious tradition, Joseph (Yūsuf) was proverbially handsome. A saying attributed to the Prophet Muḥammad even stated that "Joseph has been given the moiety (*shaṭr*) of beauty," in the sense that his beauty equaled—or according to other accounts exceeded—the sum of the beauty of all other people.[61] Love poets of the period regularly compared the beauty of their beloved to that ultimate ideal, and it was an ideal that was believed to appeal to both sexes.

An exclusive focus on the "feminine" features of the beloved boys is not really warranted by the poetic descriptions themselves. The frequent descriptions of beard-down are a case in point. In addition, many poets often chose to contrast, rather than gloss over, the charm of boys and women. Comparing the merits of the love of boys and the love of women was a conventional topic of classical Arabic literature, at least since the time of al-Jāḥiẓ (d. 869), who devoted an epistle to the disputation (*mufākharah*) of the lover of boys and the lover of women.[62] A similar disputation also occurs in the version of *The Arabian Nights* printed in Cairo in 1835.[63] The theme was still pursued by poets and belletrists of the early Ottoman period. The Aleppine scholar ʿAlī ibn Muḥammad al-Ḥaṣkafī (d. 1519) expressed his own preference for women:

> Even if handsome beardless boys enchant the possessors of reason, and murder them with their eyes and brows,
> The love of white, virgin women is my creed, and in love people are of many creeds.[64]

In a more ribald tone, another Aleppine, Fatḥallah al-Baylūnī (d. 1632/3), stated:

> I have no wish for beardless boys and only seek to meet a beautiful woman for stomach-to-stomach [i.e., vaginal] copulation.
> And say to those who dissimulate her love: "It is part of religious belief to love one's place of origin."[65]

The belletrists who expressed a preference for women rather than boys often struck such a bawdy tone. The Damascene belletrist Aḥmad al-Barbīr (d. 1817), for instance, said in verse that pederasts "jostled for shit," a reference to their supposed predilection for playing the "insertive" role in anal intercourse.[66] The Aleppine scholar ʿAlī al-Dabbāgh al-Mīqātī (d. 1760) pointed to the danger that the lover of youths could find himself assuming the receptive rather than insertive position.[67] Those who upheld the contrasting position in the early Ottoman period seem to have been less eager to appeal to such explicitly sexual considerations. Indeed, it was hardly an option to appeal to the one kind of sexual intercourse that could be had with male youths but not with women. The Egyptian scholar and judge Aḥmad al-Khafājī (d. 1659) gave as a justification of the preference for male youths the claim—not obviously relevant to the question of sexual object-choice—that "the man is superior to the woman by common consent."[68] The underlying thought, apparently, was that if males were superior to women, then loving males must be superior to loving women. The "argument" of course invited the retort, made by the defender of the love of women in *The Arabian Nights,* that by the same logic, loving fully mature adult men should be superior to loving adolescent youths—a conclusion clearly regarded as a reductio ad absurdum. Another Egyptian scholar and judge, Taqī al-Dīn Muḥammad al-Fāriskūrī (d. 1647), simply expressed a preference for boys in the following couplet:

> I was called to the religion of love by her long and flowing hair, and my creed is but to love the gazelle fawn [*masc.*],
> A beloved in whom God reveals to us in this age the attributes of the Prophet Joseph in beauty and form.[69]

Another poet who expressed a preference for the love of boys was the abovementioned Iraqi Jirjis al-Adīb. His poem is longer and somewhat more earnest in tone than other contributions to this theme, and is worth quoting in full:

> I looked into the opinion of those who fancy males and those who fancy females, and saw that preference went to the male.
> For your love of beardless boys is bliss, and the distinction between the two is clear to me.
> So fancy boys, I say, for among them are tender-featured lads whose eyes captivate the houris themselves.
> And tell him who rejects my verdict and preference that I am like someone who presents mint-leaves to donkeys.
> How far you are from [appreciating] red cheeks and supple physiques! You confuse hearsay with seeing for yourself.
> The most attractive among them is the mature, whose character and manners have been refined since childhood.
> Amongst them is the adolescent gazelle, whose talk revives the spirit and cures the ill.
> Amongst them is the white-skinned with polished cheeks, in which you see figures as images in a mirror.
> Amongst them is the copper-skinned with a radiant splendor that makes superfluous the glow of the moon.
> Amongst them is the dark-skinned with manifest litheness. How lovely are the supple limbs of the dark-skinned!

Amongst them is the full-fledged, with sprouting cheeks like roses fenced with fresh basil.
So take for yourself what you choose, for becoming intimate with them is the pleasure of a lifetime.
You will be able to be near them and talk to them without segregation, fear or caution.
You will touch them in jest and kiss them in play; that—by my life—is the ultimate satisfaction.
And perhaps one day they enter the baths with you, and how lovely is it to see the beloved without clothes!
The body is visible, and the protrusion of the buttocks, and you may even catch a glimpse of him with the loin-cloth off.
And maybe one night they'll agree to drink wine with you and to spend the night in sweet conversation.
How far is that from the guile of women and behavior of girls? Only a knower knows.
May God not bless the love of women and those who court them from among men.
They are hidden, rarely encountered, and hence their lover dies from lack of sight.
If they let their guard down and he gains access to them and he then hears someone at the door, he'll shit in his pants from fear.
So if you must commit fornication with a woman, do not brandish the arse.[70]

The poem's contrast of the situation of the lover of boys and the lover of women is obviously related to the constraints imposed by gender segregation. As mentioned in the previous chapter, public gender segregation did not make "heterosexual" outlets unavailable to men—most adult men were married and those who were not could resort to prostitutes—but it did pose an obstacle to the kind of ambiguous, jesting courtship of which the poet was apparently so fond. It is of course also unlikely that public gender segregation succeeded in preventing all illicit affairs between men and women. However, one may suspect that the subterfuge and secrecy that would be involved in such affairs did not make for the playful ambiguity described by Jirjis al-Adīb, and that the women involved risked their reputation, even in the eyes of the men who sought their favors. By contrast, a teenage boy could hardly avoid rubbing shoulders with adult men, and could be courted without thereby being stigmatized as cheap. The point may be illustrated by an interesting discussion of the love of women by the above-mentioned Egyptian belletrist Ibn al-Wakīl al-Mallawī. In his work *Bughyat al-musāmir,* he collected classical Arabic stories on various themes such as courage and love, and supplemented these with similar stories from his own period. When dealing with love, he cited the stories of famous love couples from previous ages, both "heterosexual"[71] and pederastic, but he had only stories of pederastic love to add from his own time. He excused himself for not mentioning any contemporary love stories featuring men and women, saying that he knew of no such stories. He did not doubt that there were illicit affairs between men and women, but these, he said, involved libertines (*fussāq*), not lovers (*ʿushshāq*). Women were either of easy virtue, as much interested in fornication as the men who had affairs with them, or virtuous and completely beyond reach.[72] Apparently, neither kind of woman could feature in the stories of refined and chaste love to which the chapter was devoted.

It is worth emphasizing that neither Jirjis al-Adīb nor Ibn al-Wakīl al-Mallawī portrayed women as sexually unattractive. Hence, one should be wary of interpreting their remarks as expressions of "homosexuality" as opposed to "heterosexuality." In general, those who participated in the genre of "disputation" expressed preferences. The preferences could be based on considerations that had little to do with sexual desire, as in the case of Jirjis al-Adīb. Even when the considerations adduced were sexual or aesthetic, it is doubtful whether we are dealing with expressions of sexual orientation in the modern sense. Sexual or aesthetic preferences are not the same thing as sexual orientation. A modern "heterosexual" man may say that he has a weakness for blonde women. This will not normally mean that he never finds non-blondes sexually attractive. Belletrists of the early Ottoman period also engaged in disputations comparing Ethiopian and white women, or beardless and downy-cheeked youths.[73] In such cases, the "disputations" seem clearly to be expressions of preference rather than of sexual orientation. The comparisons between boys and women should, all else being equal, be interpreted in the same way. A good example of how modern sexual categories are inadequate to understanding the genre of *mufākharah* is the following couplet by the Damascene poet Ibrāhīm al-Akramī (d. 1638):

> To the censurer who reproached me for loving boys I professed a noble motto:
> I am but a son of Adam and therefore only ever fancy (*ahwā*) sons of Adam.

The couplet was cited by ʿAbd al-Ghanī al-Nābulusī, who informed his readers that he heard it from the poet's *son* Aḥmad.[74] Nābulusī apparently accepted the lines as sincere expressions of the poet's inclinations. He invoked them in support of his contention that many prominent and respectable scholars, mystics, and poets have expressed their passionate love for handsome beardless youths. Yet he did not seem to find anything odd in the fact that Ibrāhīm al-Akramī had nevertheless fathered a son.

There is another reason for resisting the temptation to bring the modern concept of homosexuality to bear on the positions expressed in belletristic comparisons of the charms of women and boys. The participants in the disputations were adult men who expressed their preferences for either women or *boys*. None of the positions involved adult men being attracted to adult men with masculine features.[75] It was recognized that there were such men (the *ma'būn* or *mukhannath*) but, as in the case of women, their tastes were not articulated in the belles-lettres of the period.

Of the various topics of disputation, the most frequently encountered in the belles-lettres of the period is the comparison of beardless and downy-cheeked youths. As in the case of the comparison of women and boys, one encounters three positions: a preference for one, or the other, or an equal attraction to both. The latter position was expressed by the above-mentioned Aleppine scholar Aḥmad ibn al-Mullā. A friend of his, having noticed that he was inclined to a downy-cheeked youth (*muʿadhdhar*), teasingly challenged him to defend his position:

> What fault lies with the beardless boy of smooth cheeks, who surpasses an anklet-wearer [i.e., a woman]?
> With a countenance like the doe's in beauty, and eyes which put to shame the gazelle's.
> With a polished cheek which in clearness exceeds gorgeous pearls.
> So why do you fancy, instead of him, beards like thorn-bushes? . . .

Ibn al-Mullā replied:

> I am enamored of everyone beautiful, admirable in description and deed.
> Whether he be beardless or a youth with beard-down, surpassing in beauty an anklet-wearer.
> Musk has fenced off his rosy cheeks, afraid that we will strike them with arrows [i.e., glances].
> He appears in a halo of beard-down, his face the radiant and beautiful moon.
> That is my love, my creed, and my opinion . . .[76]

The Damascene poet Muṣṭafā al-Ṣumādī (d. 1725) declared his own preference for the beardless:

> Beard-down appears on the cheeks of the beloved and the turbid marks finish him off.

For this reason you will not find me enthralled by a cheek which beard-down has defamed.
I am enamored of pure, soft cheeks complementing a beauty that is impeccable.[77]

The contrasting position was sometimes referred to as "the opinion of the people of Mosul," at least since the time of Usāmah ibn Munqidh (d. 1138).[78] It was professed by the Aleppine judge ʿAṭāllah al-Ṣādiqī (d. 1680/1) in the following lines:

I kissed a downy-cheeked youth with sweet dark-red lips and looked at that primeval beauty.
And asked for a lover's rendezvous with him, so he answered: The time for my compassion or coquetry is past.
The water of beauty has dried up from my cheeks, and prettiness has disappeared from the branch of my upright physique.
I said: The description of a garden [i.e., the rosy cheeks] only becomes attractive if it is surrounded by sprouting vegetation.
Proceed to obey the motto of Ibn Munqidh and know that I have become the judge of Mosul.[79]

A disputation between the beardless and the downy-cheeked youth was composed by the Damascene belletrist Muḥammad Saʿīd ibn al-Sammān (d. 1759). His tract on the subject, which is extant in a few manuscripts, was written in rhymed prose interspersed with verse. The author reproduced the rival claims of a beardless and a downy-cheeked youth, and then went on to state that their dispute left him bewildered and unable to decide who was in the right. He ended his tract by inviting other belletrists to help him out.[80] Several contemporary scholars/belletrists responded to Ibn al-Sammān's invitation. The prominent Damascene scholar Aḥmad al-Manīnī (d. 1759) wrote a short tract praising Ibn al-Sammān's literary effort, and his skill in presenting both sides of the dispute. However, Manīnī himself expressed his firm conviction in the superiority of the beardless to the downy-cheeked:

It is evident to those of sound disposition and proper judgment that beauty is primarily and essentially an attribute of the smooth-cheeked . . . for the attractive features of the downy-cheeked are also attractive features of the beardless . . . Beard-down veils part of it [the boy's beauty] and after its sprouting he retains some traces of bloom and freshness . . . Do you not see that if the beard-down (*ʿidhār*) becomes a beard (*liḥyah*) his features become devoid of their finery, and his cheeks of their radiance, and darkness descends on light, and grass covers the beautiful face, and the lover and friend obtains respite?[81]

On the other hand, the Aleppine scholar Muḥammad al-Jamālī (d. 1760) expressed his sympathy with Ibn al-Sammān's inability to choose between the two disputants:

> To be fair is to suspend judgment, and to give good advice is to leave the option open, for neither the lily-cheeked nor the smooth- and radiant-cheeked are loved purely for their prettiness, beauty, handsomeness, and coquettishness, since loving those of attractive body but unattractive mind is not commendable. True love is chaste love for someone handsome who combines the many visible attractions and whose character is formed by elegance and molded by grace and refinement . . . and he among the two who has these features unquestionably deserves pride of place, and is suitable for infatuation and worthy of love no matter to which of the two types he belongs.[82]

Another Aleppine scholar, ʿAlī al-Dabbāgh al-Mīqātī (d. 1760), wrote a tract on the issue which is reproduced in its entirety in the published biographical dictionary of Murādī.[83] Following a well-established literary convention, Mīqātī initially stated how the work of Ibn al-Sammān had reminded him of his own days of youth and love, leading him to try his hand at composing a similar tract. He then went on to present the claims of the beardless boy, followed by those of the downy-cheeked. He concluded by defending the view that women were more appropriate objects of love than either the beardless or the downy-cheeked male youth:

> It is not part of perfection to love men, and how apposite is he who said: Love is only for anklet-wearers, and a prominent notable has said: He who confines himself to women finds repose.
>
> I love women and the love of women is a duty on every noble soul.
> Shuʿayb, for his two daughters, received God's spokesman Moses as servant.
>
> And it is evident to those who look into the matter that two men under one bed cover is dangerous, for the active part may be surprised and find himself in the role of the passive agent . . . and the best of advice to follow and heed is [the saying of the Prophet]: "From your world I was enamored of perfume and women."

Mīqātī, who was initiated into the Naqshbandī mystical order, concluded by rejecting the love of humans as such for the love of God.

A summary of the claims advanced on behalf of the beardless or downy-cheeked youth in such tracts is not really possible for the simple reason that they consist of a string of poetic similes and metaphors depicting the charms of one or the other, rather than coherent arguments. The most that can be done is to give a sample of the style. The following are extracts from the tract of Mīqātī:

> [The beardless:] In being free of a beard he is akin to the people of paradise [a reference to a well-known tradition according to which the people of paradise will be beardless] . . . The Creator is pleased with him and so did not bring forth what would disfigure his cheeks, thus the mirror of his face is clear, as the cloudless sky . . . He says: I have a sleek freshness, and am of a tender and smooth cheek, my face is favored, and my beauty is soft, and who would hold thorns and lush silk equal? [The downy-cheeked:] If you see him with his temples wrapped in musk thus bringing out his attractiveness and rousing the eyes of his lovers from their drowsiness, you would say: Is a garden attractive without its vegetation? . . . and the moon is seen at its most attractive when its periphery is enclosed with blackness.

Such uses of similes and metaphors reverberate throughout the poetry of the period. At times, beard-down signals the end of love and the freeing of the lover from captivity, at others it is the lover's reason for "throwing off all restraint" (*khalʿ al-ʿidhār*); it is the blackness that indicates the mourning of bygone beauty, or the halo of the moon that makes it shine all the more brightly; it is compared to a feathered wing which beauty uses to take flight, or chains of musk that keep it bound and prevent it from levitating. Two couplets should suffice to give an impression of the poetry in question; the first is by the Aleppine poet Muṣṭafā ibn Bīrī (d. 1735/6):

> They said: He has become downy-cheeked so abandon him. I said: Stop your reproof, his charms have become all the more attractive.
> For the moon is not luminous except if coupled with the darkness of night.[84]

The second is by another Aleppine poet, Muṣṭafā al-Bābī (d. 1681):

> God has clothed the dawn of his cheeks with night, and painted the whiteness black.
> The sap on the side of his face has dried up, and the ember of beauty has become ashes.[85]

It could perhaps be argued that the search for summarizable arguments beneath the glitter of stylized literary images is fundamentally misguided. The contributions to the genre of *mufākharah* were written in verse or rhymed prose, and were clearly intended as polished, belletristic works rather than straightforward polemics. The tone of most contributions suggests that their authors' aims were not necessarily to voice sincere convictions or advance substantial arguments, but simply to muster an arsenal of similes and metaphors in favor of one position or the other. The same person may even have verses in support of two contrasting positions, and these may appear directly after each other in the poetic anthologies, the anthologist simply announcing, "He has [the following] in praise (*madīḥ*) of beard-down," and then "and he has [the following] in dispraise (*dhamm*) of it."[86] Other disputations were apparently little more than word play. Poets could, for instance, debate such questions as whether "east"—the direction and not any geographical region—was better than "west," adducing such "arguments" as "the sun arises from it" and "the sun seeks toward it."[87] The Iraqi scholar and belletrist ʿUthmān al-ʿUmarī (d. 1770/1) composed a lengthy disputation in rhymed prose consisting of the respective boasts of candle, star, moon, water, and glass.[88] It is perhaps natural to ask whether there are any reasons for believing that the disputations concerning women and boys, or beardless and downy-cheeked youths, should be taken any more seriously. The question is an instance of a more general question about the historical relevance of the belletristic evidence presented in this section. To what extent is it legitimate to regard love poetry and belletristic disputations as historical sources that reveal certain values and tastes within the real-life milieu of belletrists and their audience?

Belles-Lettres: A Source for Real-Life Attitudes?

The love of boys loomed large in the Arabic belles-lettres of the early Ottoman period. Passionate love was by far the most favorite theme in belles-lettres, and the portrayed beloved seems more often than not to have been a teenage boy. The idea—still widespread among modern specialists in Arabic literature—that premodern Arabic love poetry as a rule portrayed a female beloved may be true when it comes to pre- or early Islamic poetry. It is not true of Arabic poetry from the ninth to the nineteenth century.[89] As far as the early Ottoman period is concerned, the gender of the portrayed beloved, when it is indicated by the poem itself or by the supplementary remarks of the anthologist or redactor, is more often male than female.[90] The question remains, however, what one is entitled to conclude from this fact. It may be natural to see the frequent and sympathetic portrayals of boy-love in belles-lettres as reflecting one strand in the culture of belletrists and their audiences. Just as, say, the homiletic and juridical discourse reflects a strand of religiously motivated hostility to fornication and sodomy, so the belletristic literature might be assumed to reveal another cultural strand which idealized and sympathized with the refined and chaste love for women or boys.[91] Such a position is, I believe, ultimately defensible. However, it is important to address a possible objection, according to which love poems and disputations should be understood as time-honored literary exercises which belletrists participated in simply with the aim of displaying their erudition and poetic skills. They should not, according to this view, be seen as particularly revealing of what belletrists and their audience actually thought of the passionate love of boys. Some modern scholars faced with sympathetic portrayals of boy-love in the poetry of Renaissance England or the Judeo-Arabic poetry of medieval Spain have argued as much. Alan Bray, for example, maintains that such poetry in Elizabethan and Jacobean England amounted to little more than "exercises which on analysis turn out to be based on classical models" and reveal nothing about the poets' inclinations or experiences.[92]

Some modern specialists on Arabic literature have made comments which suggest they would indeed be skeptical of the legitimacy of using love poetry of boys as a source for reconstructing cultural attitudes toward boy-love. For instance, J. C. Bürgel, confronted with eleventh- and twelfth-century Arabic love poetry of boys composed by Islamic religious scholars of impeccable repute, argued that such poetry was intended and understood to be fictive.[93] Presumably his position is that one must turn to non-belletristic sources to find out what such religious scholars "really" thought about the phenomenon of boy-love. Franz Rosenthal also concluded his overview of the literary theme of "disputation" between the lover of boys and the lover of women in classical Arabic literature by noting that "true feeling is obviously absent from the genre as such."[94] More generally, Suzanne Enderwitz claimed that after the early Abbasid period (i.e., from the ninth century on), the continuity between "life" and "work" in Arabic love poetry was severed, and the genre developed into "entertainment poetry which made no claims to be authentic."[95] It is not entirely clear just how strong a claim Bürgel, Rosenthal, and Enderwitz are making. It is possible that they are merely emphasizing the point that the love portrayed in poetry was *often* fictive, and that one must therefore be wary of making inferences about the experiences and attitudes of a particular poet on the basis of his poetry alone. That claim is uncontroversial. Hardly anyone would deny that Arab poets—and indeed poets of any culture or period—could compose love poetry without necessarily being in love. It is also possible, however, that they are making the stronger and more controversial claim that love poetry after the early Abbasid period is simply irrelevant for a historical study of attitudes toward boy-love. More specifically, the claim would be that it is not legitimate to suppose that the frequency, openness, and sympathy with which belletrists portrayed the passionate love of boys supports the idea that the passionate love of boys formed a visible and condoned part of the real-life milieu of belletrists and their audience.

Such a wholesale, skeptical dismissal of the historical relevance of the pederastic themes in the belles-lettres of the period would in my opinion be unwarranted. It would be so even if it were true—and I will argue below that it is not—that belletrists hardly ever expressed their own amorous experiences and feelings in their work. The lyrics of modern pop songs are not expected to reflect the real-life experiences of their singers or composers, but this does not imply that there is not an intimate connection between the lyrics and the values and assumptions of contemporary culture. One can hardly imagine a Frank Sinatra or a Tom Jones singing about his love for a downy-cheeked boy of fourteen, and their audience would hardly react positively if they did. The fact that the audience knows that singers and songwriters may not be expressing their own feelings and experiences is simply beside the point. One might at the very least conclude from the profuseness of explicitly pederastic poetry in the premodern Middle East that images of an adult man pining for a teenage youth and begging for a rendezvous or a kiss did not arouse disgust or derision among listeners. One might furthermore presume that the popularity of love poetry, pederastic or "heterosexual," indicates that it sometimes struck a chord among those who listened to it. The Meccan jurist Ibn Ḥajar al-Haytamī (d. 1566) specifically stated that it was forbidden for a person in love with a boy or a woman (other than his wife or concubine) to listen to love poetry since doing so would arouse the listener and cause him to pursue what is prohibited by law.[96] A love poem could, in other words, be related to genuine feelings and aesthetic tastes, even if they were not the poet's. The Yemeni poet Shaʿbān al-Rūmī (d. 1736), who composed many love poems of boys, at one time made a living by selling his services to less articulate people who would commission him to compose "some verses on their beloved."[97] It would indeed be difficult to understand the apparent popularity of love poetry if its portrayals of passionate love were completely unrelated to what its audience thought it was like to fall in love, or if its descriptions of the beloved were completely unrelated to its audience's beauty-ideal or sense of what was a likely object of passionate love. Some of the authors of the period under study took it for granted that there was some overall connection between the themes and imagery of love poetry and the tastes, values, and assumptions of the people who composed or listened to it. For example, the Syrian belletrist Aḥmad al-Barbīr (d. 1817) claimed that the Arabs in pre-Islamic and early Islamic times were not inclined to pederasty, and gave as "evidence" (*dalīl*) for his claim the fact that they did not compose love poetry of boys.[98] The same point was made by the Egyptian scholar Marʿī ibn Yūsuf al-Karmī (d. 1624): "The eloquent among people in the first age did not appreciate boys, and their characters did not incline to loving them, but in our time, they have become infatuated with them to an inordinate degree, and love boys more than women, and they [i.e., boys] are now an existing source of temptation."[99] He went on to cite some of the love poetry said of beardless and downy-cheeked youths, apparently in support of his warning that they are "among the greatest of temptations." He concluded: "In sum, beardless boys are the snares of the devil, and the words of people concerning them, and what they have said in verse and prose is too much to mention."[100] Both Barbīr and Karmī were well aware that individual poems could be literary exercises, and that one cannot infer from the fact that a poet composed a love poem that he actually had a love affair.[101] However, they apparently still felt it was legitimate to use the love poetry of a period as a source of information about aesthetic tastes and amorous inclinations within the milieu to which poets and their intended audiences belonged.

In fact, the extreme skeptical assumption that poets never expressed their own experiences and emotions seems as unsubstantiated as the naive assumption that they always did. Several love poems are cited in the sources with explanatory comments or anecdotes that clearly indicate that they were believed to have been said at a concrete occasion and of a specific boy. The Egyptian scholar Aḥmad al-Khafājī was said to have composed a couplet after being criticized by two companions for stopping to admire a handsome youth in the streets of Damascus.[102] The Aleppine poet Muṣṭafā ibn Bīrī was inspired to compose a poem by an incident that occurred when he was buying some tobacco from a handsome young shop assistant.[103] A couplet by the southern Iraqi poet Ibn Maʿtūq al-Ḥuwayzī (d. 1676) was said to have been composed at the behest of a friend when the friend's beloved boy appeared to them in a white turban and a black robe.[104] Often, genuine amorous feeling was said to underlie the stylized poetic imagery. Ibrāhīm al-Batrūnī composed verse which contemporaries recognized as having been said of his recalcitrant beloved Fatḥallah ibn al-Naḥḥās (d. 1642).[105] The historian ʿAbd al-Raḥmān al-Jabartī (d. 1825/6) identified some of the love poetry of his friend Ismāʿīl al-Khashshāb as having been composed when the poet was enamored of a young scribe employed by the French during their brief rule of Egypt.[106] Some of the love poetry of the Aleppine scholar Muḥammad al-ʿUrḍī (d. 1660) was said to have been elicited by a Christian boy with whom he fell in love during an extended stay in Constantinople.[107]

One could perhaps object that the anecdotes that supposedly indicate the context of a poem were themselves generally recognized to be fictional. Bürgel may be making this point when he questions the authenticity of such anecdotes in the context of discussing the relationship between belles-lettres and reality.[108] However, it is again not clear how strong Bürgel's contention is meant to be. He could merely be emphasizing the uncontroversial point that sometimes the anecdotes were not true, being slanderous or based on unfounded rumors. The stronger claim at issue is rather that the anecdotes were widely understood not to be making any truth-claims at all, and that they thus cannot be seen as intending to anchor poems in real-life incidents or liaisons. In assessing the plausibility of this claim, the crucial question is *why* we ought to view the explicatory anecdotes and stories in this way. Many of the cited stories are recorded in biographical sources that are otherwise dedicated to making claims about past events, and that are a major source for the political history of the Arab lands in the early Ottoman period. It is surely appropriate to ask why the stories involving the pederastic love affairs of poets and scholars should be dismissed as entertaining fictions that were neither intended nor understood to depict actual occurrences, whereas other information contained in these works (about, say, political events or dates of birth and death) should be seen as purporting to be true accounts of past events. Those who want to dismiss the cited stories of pederastic love as fictional should explain on what basis they choose to interpret some passages in a chronicle or biographical work as fictional and other passages in the same work as factual accounts assessable in terms of truth or falsity.

One possible reason for not wanting to take the stories at face value is the desire to avoid a stark contrast between an apparent "tolerance" of homosexuality in belletristic and scholarly circles, and the "intolerance" characteristic of the religion to which the belletrists and scholars were committed.[109] However, such a contrast is largely illusory. As will be shown in detail below, belletrists and scholars simply did not operate with a concept of homosexuality, and thus managed to combine a severe condemnation of sexual intercourse between males with a toleration and even idealization of chaste pederastic love. In any case, the idea that pederastic liaisons were a common and visible part of the culture of the premodern Arab-Islamic East does not rest on the evidence of belles-lettres. It can be established solely on the basis of the biographical, homiletic, and juridical literature, as well as the Western travel literature, of the period. If the idea is independently plausible, then it is difficult to see why we should suppose that the pederastic themes in belles-lettres were simply literary exercises which reveal nothing about the mental and emotional world of the poets and their audiences. For example, one may suspect that poets engaged in describing the beard-down of their beloved were often just following a well-established literary convention, rather than expressing personal aesthetic preferences. However, there is non-belletristic evidence to suggest that this was not always the case. The above-mentioned religious scholar Marʿī ibn Yūsuf al-Karmī confirmed that "many boys' faces become more handsome at the appearance of fluffs of hair, and they thereby exceed beardless boys in handsomeness and beauty, and those who have been captivated by them are many."[110] Aḥmad al-Khafājī mentioned that his friend Muḥammad al-Fāsī "was well known for his carefree amusement, and was preoccupied with, and enamored of, the gazelles of the wild, especially if the roseate cheeks were enveloped in the perianth of *ʿidhār,*" and that "in Egypt he fancied a boy on whose rosy cheeks the shade of *ʿidhār* had crept . . ."[111]

Some of the explicatory comments appended to the poetry are short and do not specify the identity of the beloved boy or the other characters involved, except of course the poet himself. Examples of such comments are: "he said of a boy with a mole on his cheek . . ." or "a boy greeted him with a rose, so he said . . ."[112] In such cases, the suggestion that the comments are themselves fictional, and were not intended by authors (or believed by readers) to depict actual occurrences or liaisons, may not be too outrageous. However, the explicatory comments are often much more detailed and specific than that, and to construe them as literary fictions that made no truth-claims is wildly implausible. It is difficult to believe that Jabartī would have said that his friend Ismāʿīl al-Khashshāb fell in love with and composed love poetry of a young handsome scribe working for the French during the brief Napoleonic rule of Egypt unless he in fact believed, or wanted his readers to believe, that this was true. The biographer Muḥibbī would hardly have specified that the verses of Ibrāhīm al-Batrūnī were said of the handsome young Fatḥallah ibn al-Naḥḥās, or that Khafājī was prompted to compose a couplet when he was criticized for gazing at a handsome youth near the White Bridge in Damascus by the local scholars Aḥmad ibn Shāhīn (d. 1644) and ʿAbd al-Raḥmān al-ʿImādī (d. 1641), unless he believed, or wanted his readers to believe, that this was indeed the case. One may also consider the following three stories:

(1) In his poetic anthology *Nafḥat al-rayḥānah,* Muḥibbī mentioned that his close friend Aḥmad al-Ṣafadī (d. 1689), toward the end of his life, fell madly in love with a youth called Rabāḥ. Muḥibbī then cited a short poem his lovestruck friend said, the last verse of which indicates the youth in question:

> Abandon your occupation, and occupy yourself with a beloved, and perhaps time will grant you Rabāḥ[113]

Muḥibbī then reproduced a letter in rhymed prose he sent to Ṣafadī at the time, stating that he too was caught in the tangles of love. Independently of Muḥibbī, the scholar and mystic ʿAbd al-Ghanī al-Nābulusī mentioned that during a visit to the Darwīshiyyah Mosque in Damascus on the 26th of January 1675, he and Aḥmad al-Ṣafadī jointly—each person contributing lines in turn—composed a love poem of a handsome person who was present with them. Nābulusī added that the beginning of each line of the poem provides "a clue." The first letters of the lines of the poem add up to form "Rabāḥ Çelebī al-Khayyāṭ."[114]

(2) The Baghdadi scholar ʿAbdallah al-Suwaydī (d. 1761), while in the town of Mosul, fell in love with a local youth named Ṣāliḥ. However, the youth vowed not to speak to him unless he composed a formal petition (*ʿarḍḥāl*). Suwaydī duly composed such a petition in rhymed prose, to which he appended a poem. One verse of the poem alludes to the name of the beloved youth:

> Not anyone who unites all charms is suitable (*ṣāliḥ*) for being loved, or becomes worthy of my love.

The belletrist Muḥammad al-Ghulāmī (d. 1772/3), a close friend of Suwaydī, related the story and reproduced the petition in his poetic anthology *Shammāmat al-ʿanbar*. He added that the youth asked him for an independent opinion concerning the literary quality of Suwaydī's petition, and was told that it was indeed of a fine quality.[115]

(3) The above-mentioned ʿAbdallah al-Suwaydī related that while he was in Damascus, a local friend of his, a perfumist by the name of Aḥmad ibn al-Nuqṭah, asked him to write a tract (*maqāmah*) in rhymed prose extolling the beauty of his beloved, Muḥammad ibn Shaykh al-Ḥaram, and pronouncing him to be the "sultan of the handsome," more beautiful than the other handsome youths of the city such as Ḥasan al-Ḥarastī, Muḥammad al-Bakrī, Shākir al-ʿUmarī, ʿAbd al-Raḥmān al-Manīnī, Yūsuf al-Jundī, Murād ibn Rakkāb, ʿAbd al-Raḥmān al-ʿAlamī, Muṣṭafā al-Ṭabbāʿ, ʿAbd al-Raḥmān al-Dayrī, and others. Suwaydī, who had taught the youth in question some grammar, agreed that he was breathtakingly handsome, and complied with his friend's wishes. The tract is reproduced in Suwaydī's travelogue *al-Nafḥah al-miskiyyah*.[116] One of the other youths mentioned, ʿAbd al-Raḥmān al-Manīnī (d. 1758/9), who went on to become a prominent belletrist, appears in independent sources where he was said to be "lovable, of beautiful countenance" and "the magnet of love and fancy; the mirror of his handsome face is polished as the surface of a river is polished by the breeze; he who looks at him enjoys a beautiful and blooming garden."[117] ʿAbd al-Raḥmān al-Manīnī was born in 1730/1 and would have been around 14 years old when ʿAbdallah al-Suwaydī was in Damascus.

In the three cited examples, the poems and tracts in rhymed prose themselves indicate the identity of the beloved youth. Many similar cases can be cited. The Damascene Zakariyyā al-Būsnawī (d. 1662/3) was, according to the biographer Muḥibbī, extremely handsome in his youth, and caught the fancy of many poets and belletrists. One of these was the poet Manjak al-Yūsufī (d. 1669), who expressed his love for the youth in several poems, one of which opened with the line:

> Whenever I proceed to think of Zakariyyā, my heart returns full of ardent passion.[118]

Another Damascene poet, Abū al-Fatḥ al-Mālikī (d. 1567/8), composed a poem eulogizing a handsome youth by the name of Muḥammad ibn Ḥusām in which the opening line was:

> How often has he assailed his lovers with the name of his father [*ḥusām* = sword], oh what sorrows result from his glances![119]

Muḥammad ibn Ḥusām, Zakariyyā al-Būsnawī, ʿAbd al-Raḥmān al-Manīnī, and Muḥammad ibn Shaykh al-Ḥaram are examples of youths who seem to have gained a public reputation on account of their beauty. As pointed out by Kenneth Dover in his path-breaking study of classical Greek homosexuality, in a society that placed great value on keeping women hidden from the eyes of men, the status of "pin-ups" in the male public sphere tended to be associated with handsome youths.[120] The Damascene belletrist Muḥammad al-Kanjī (d. 1740), in an anthology of singers, mentioned two local youths in his time who were admired for their beauty as well as their voices: Muḥammad Abū Kulthūm was described as "a youth cast in the mold of beauty . . . the luster of his youth delights hearts, and the beauty of his countenance is of perfect purity and radiance, and how often has his angelic beauty possessed and captured admirers . . ."; the dark-skinned Aḥmad Qusṭanṭīn al-Lālātī was said to be "the innermost core of every heart, and the beloved of all chests and bosoms . . . God has endowed him with a guileless mind, and beautified his appearance, so if you were to see the blackness of his well-contrived eyebrows, above the night of his striped beard-down, on the duskiness of his dark cheek, you would acclaim the opinion of the overwhelming majority."[121] The Egyptian historian Jabartī mentioned a handsome young beardless preacher of Turkish origin named Muṣṭafā al-Lāzijī (d. 1792/3) who used to attract scores of men to the Muʾayyadī mosque in Cairo "to listen to his sermons and watch his person." Jabartī mentioned one Mamluk notable in particular who fell in love with the young man.[122] The biographer Muḥammad Khalīl al-Murādī (d. 1791) mentioned a handsome youth from Baghdad who, when he came to Damascus, elicited enthusiastic eulogies from some of the prominent poets of the city, including Murādī's personal acquaintance Makkī al-Jūkhī (d. 1778/9).[123] A similar story related by the Damascene belletrist Abū Bakr al-ʿUmarī illustrates the complex relationship between poetry and reality in the period. A group of poets from Aleppo had composed couplets ending with the same hemistich in praise of a handsome local youth, and subsequently asked their Damascene colleagues to participate in the venture.[124] On the one hand, the youth was a real individual (ʿUmarī mentioned that he was the relative of a particular notable whom he named) whom some men had found attractive. On the other hand it was not thought to be strange that several of those who were asked to sing his praises had never seen him.

Genuine emotion on the part of the poet, though not conceived to be a necessity, was still widely thought to add an impressive flavor to his product. Muḥibbī, commenting on an elegy composed by the son of the deceased, stated that it was the most touching of the numerous elegies written at the occasion since it expressed true emotions and lacked affectation.[125] Similarly, when it came to composing love poetry, an amorous and aesthetic disposition were thought to be an advantage. In fact, passionate love was proverbially capable of transforming even the thick-tongued into a poet.[126] The connection between impressive *ghazal* and its author's character is underlined in remarks such as the following: "he would not cease to be enraptured by a gazelle, nor budge from loving an addax, and his poetry . . . expresses his condition as tears express the concealed secrets of love"; "he has a fertile talent, and a nature that is inclined to infatuation, and his poetry is free from affectation"; "[he was] infatuated with beauty, of frequent amorous raptures and passions, and for this reason his poetry became more delicate"; "he was often bawdy, and brazen in love and infatuation, and he has poetry which indicates his sensitive character"; "he was constantly enamored of bathing in the radiant beauty of the handsome . . . and because of this, witty and subtle exchanges of poetry would occur between him and other belletrists."[127] Poets were in fact closely associated with the aesthetic ideal, perhaps even cultivating it consciously as part of their occupational ethos. The scholar Najm al-Dīn al-Ghazzī said of the poet Abū al-Fatḥ al-Mālikī: "He followed the way of the poets (*madhhab al-shuʿarāʾ*) in displaying a love for beautiful forms."[128] The Aleppine scholar Muḥammad al-Jamālī opined that the chaste and refined love of beardless and downy-cheeked youths was the "adornment of the elegant, the belletrists, and the clever and high-minded (*ḥilyat al-ẓurafāʾ wa al-udabāʾ wa al-adhkiyāʾ al-nujabāʾ*)."[129] The Iraqi poet Ḥasan ibn ʿAbd al-Bāqī (d. 1745/6), who was reputed to be an aesthete and a wine-drinker, addressed a poem containing the following lines to the cousin of his patron, praising him while playfully suggesting that he did not have what it takes to become a poet:

> You have not drunk wine, nor seized the day, nor loved passionately.
> Only the rake composes poetry who, when the times permit, sins.[130]

The number of prominent poets in the early Ottoman Arab East who were said to love beauty or featured in anecdotes involving pederastic attraction is striking. A list of the poets of whom this is true is almost identical to the list of the most prominent Egyptian, West Arabian, Syrian, and Iraqi poets of the period 1500–1800: Māmāyah al-Rūmī, Aḥmad al-ʿInāyātī, Darwīsh al-Ṭālawī, Ismāʿīl al-Ḥijāzī (sixteenth century); Abū Bakr al-ʿUmarī, Ibrāhīm al-Akramī, Fatḥallah ibn al-Naḥḥās, Manjak, ʿAbd al-Ḥayy Ṭarrazalrayḥān (seventeenth century); Muṣṭafā ibn Bīrī, Muḥammad Saʿīd ibn al-Sammān, Makkī al-Jūkhī, Jirjis al-Adīb, Ḥasan ibn ʿAbd al-Bāqī, Shaʿbān al-Rūmī, Ismāʿīl al-Khashshāb, Amīn al-Jundī (eighteenth century). Judging from the anthology of Kanjī, those who sang poetry were in this respect similar to those who composed it. There is hardly an entry in the work without the subject being described as having an amorous and aesthetic disposition.

The poets (*shuʿarāʾ*) and belletrists (*udabāʾ*) were as a class distinct from the scholars (*ʿulamāʾ*). In fact, "scholars' poetry" (*shiʿr al-ʿulamāʾ*) was notoriously of a poor and amateurish quality.[131] Yet the boundary between the two groups was not always clear. Most members of the class of scholars specialized in specific disciplines, and in this respect one may distinguish between jurists, scholars of *ḥadīth,* theologians, and even specialists in secular sciences such as mathematics, logic, or astronomy. Several scholars gained a reputation for themselves in the sciences of language: grammar, rhetoric, and prosody. They frequently taught would-be poets the theoretical rudiments necessary for their art, and some of them gained an independent reputation as accomplished belletrists. Describing the Rector of the Azhar college in Cairo at the time of his residency in the city, Edward Lane wrote: "In theology and jurisprudence, he is not so deeply versed as some of his contemporaries . . . but he is eminently accomplished in polite literature."[132] The scholar in question was Ḥasan al-ʿAṭṭār (d. 1834), a close friend of the historian Jabartī and the poet Ismāʿīl al-Khashshāb. Several other scholars belonging to this category have already been mentioned in the present study: Aḥmad ibn al-Mullā, Ḥasan al-Būrīnī, Aḥmad al-Khafājī, Muḥammad al-ʿUrḍī, Muḥammad Amīn al-Muḥibbī, ʿAlī ibn Maʿṣūm, Muḥammad al-Kanjī, ʿAbdallah al-Shabrāwī, Muḥammad al-Ghulāmī, ʿAbdallah al-Suwaydī.[133]

The aesthetic and amorous ideal seems also to have been influential in these circles.

The Ideal of Love

Ardent, passionate love (*ʿishq*) was apparently a topic that many in the early Ottoman Middle East found fascinating. It was directly or indirectly the subject matter of most of the poetry and much of the belletristic prose of the period. Determining its nature, symptoms, and stages was a task that invited the efforts of scholars, poets, lexicographers, mystics, and physicians. Yet it remained (and largely still remains) a somewhat elusive phenomenon. According to the Shiʿite scholar Bahāʾ al-Dīn al-ʿĀmilī (d. 1621):

> *ʿishq* is an attraction of the heart to the magnet of beauty. One cannot hope to know the true nature of this attraction, only to express it in ways that increase its obscurity. It is like beauty and poetic meter in that it can be experienced but not expressed in words, and how apposite is the statement of one of the sages: He who describes love has not known it.[134]

An agnostic position of *ʿishq* was also propounded by the Cairo-based scholar Muḥammad Murtaḍā al-Zabīdī (d. 1791). In his commentary on the dictionary (*Qāmūs*) of al-Fayrūzabādī (d. 1415), he wrote:

> Its meaning cannot be known or discovered, and describing it in words just increases its obscurity. It is like beauty in being unknowable and ineffable, and like poetic meter and other such things that are only discoverable by sound taste and upright character.[135]

In literary representations passionate love often appeared as a mysterious and ineffable force that suddenly and unpredictably took hold of the soul. Both Bahāʾ al-Dīn al-ʿĀmilī and the later Shīʿī scholar Niʿmatallah al-Jazāʾirī (d. 1702) cited the following view:

> Love is a spiritual secret that descends on the heart from the supernatural world, and therefore it is called *hawā*, from the root *hwy* and the verb *yahwā*, meaning "falls." It is also called *ḥubb* since it reaches the core of the heart (*ḥabbat al-qalb*), which is the source of life. If it reaches the heart, it then flows with life in all parts of the body, imprinting on it the image of the beloved.[136]

The Damascene belletrist Muḥyī al-Dīn al-Ṣaltī (d. 1702), author of a tract on love, similarly defined it as "a disposition (*malakah*) that seizes the soul; if it gains ascendancy over the soul, the latter will assume its characteristics, and if the soul gains ascendancy over the power, it will be driven back to its world."[137]

To the extent that *ʿishq* was perceived to be an extrinsic power that overwhelmed the heart and soul, it was considered to be a malady with recognized symptoms: emaciation, paleness, fluttering of the heart, insomnia, complete mental absorption with the beloved, etc. Passionate love was regularly classified as a disease in the medical literature of the period.[138] In its most developed stages, it could be lethal: some of the legendary *ʿudhrī* lovers of the early Islamic period were said to have died from love, and Muḥammad ibn Dāwūd al-Ẓāhirī (d. 909), author of the earliest extant Arabic book on profane love, *Kitab al-zahrah,* supposedly died from his love for a youth named Muḥammad al-Ṣaydalānī. The physician Dāwūd al-Anṭākī (d. 1599), who wrote an influential work on love, asserted that *ʿishq* is an especially problematic disease since it affected the soul, the very part of man that was responsible for administering a regimen. Being itself of an ethereal nature, *ʿishq* initially impressed itself on the most incorporeal part of the person. For this very reason, it only afflicted those whose soul was sufficiently delicate and sensitive: "Passionate love is inconceivable in the case of an ignoramus (*jāhil*) with a coarse character."[139] This seems to have been a widespread assumption, already encountered in a previous quotation from Mullā Ṣadrā. Those who were sympathetic toward profane love often made use of this point, hinting that those who frowned on the phenomenon did so because of a character flaw. Both Anṭākī and ʿAbd al-Ghanī al-Nābulusī quoted sayings according to which only those of a "dry" and "insensitive" character remain impervious to love.[140] The Meccan scholar ʿAbd al-Muʿīn ibn al-Bakkāʾ (d. 1630/1) also stated that "I have not seen a man of eminence and refinement anywhere who is immune to love."[141] The Damascene poet ʿAbd al-Ḥayy Ṭarrazalrayḥān subtly resorted to a similar assumption in the following lines:

> He reproves ardent infatuation who does not see in ardent infatuation and chastity anything but foolishness.
> There is nothing reproachable in love, except the delicacy of character and the resulting sensibility.
> And he who has no share in that is not to be blamed for neglecting it.[142]

Falling in love was thus simultaneously a pathological affliction and a testimony to the possession of a refined and sensitive character. The resulting ambivalence is brought out in the treatise of Anṭākī, who initially cited reasons for praising and encouraging passionate love and then gave an exposition of the tragic, sometimes lethal, consequences of being smitten.[143]

The obscurity concerning passionate love extends to the nature of its relationship to sexual desire. On the one hand, it seems clear that the two are related; on the other, it seems equally commonsensical to insist that they are not identical. Each of these assertions served as a departure point for two opposing evaluations of love. The first could be described as cynical and deflationary, the other as idealizing and sentimental. The coexistence of these two evaluations is clearly not peculiar to the Arab East in the early Ottoman period. It is a recurrent theme in Irving Singer's historical and interpretive study of ideas of love in Western history from classical to modern times, where the positions are termed "realist" and "idealist," respectively.[144] Essentially the same duality has been identified by Lois A. Giffen in her survey of the premodern Arabic literature on profane love.[145]

The cynical or "realist" view of passionate love tended to emphasize its supposedly hidden sexual component. Underneath the effuse and sentimental cloak, the lover's feelings were portrayed as basically identical with lust. The terms *ʿishq* (love), *ʿāshiq* (lover), and *maʿshūq* (beloved) could, in appropriate contexts, have such sexual connotations. For example, the author of *Hazz al-quḥūf* used the word *ʿishq* to denote the far-from-Platonic attraction of the heretical dervishes toward the boys whom they succeeded in seducing by promising to grant them supernatural powers.[146] The "realist" perspective could be utilized by poets who on other occasions contributed to the idealization of refined, unconsummated love. The resulting poetry tends to have a marked deflationary character, and clearly parodies the established discourse of chaste and tragic love. Anṭākī cited a poet as saying:

> They say to me, "By God, what would you do if your beloved visited you?" I said, "Fuck him."[147]

In a similar vein, Aḥmad al-Khafājī composed the following couplet:

> Since he whom I fancy visited me, he offered me drink from a mouth [as intoxicating as] wine.
> And his buttocks said to me from behind him: "Today wine and tomorrow action."[148]

The intended effect of such conscious breaks with the conventions of love poetry was, first and foremost, humorous. The cited verses need not be particularly revealing of the poet's "real" attitudes toward love, and may simply be playful contributions to the established genre of *mujūn*—bawdy poetry.[149] However, in a society whose religion proscribed lust except between husband and wife or master and concubine, the cynical-reductionist perspective tended to be coupled with a general disapproval of *ʿishq*. One of the hallmarks of this position was a rejection of the authenticity of the following tradition attributed to the Prophet: "He who loves and is chaste [variants add: and conceals his secret] and then dies, dies a martyr (*Man ʿashiqa wa ʿaffa [wa katama] thumma māta fa-huwa shahīd*)."[150] The tradition rests on two suppositions: that *ʿishq* could be lethal, and that it overwhelmed a person independently of his will. Together, the suppositions tended to assimilate dying of love with, say, being murdered or dying of plague, and the latter fates were generally believed to confer martyr status on the deceased.[151] Those who rejected the tradition contested the second premise. For such scholars, passionate love was simply the consequence of transgressing the religious prohibition of looking at attractive women and boys, in much the same way that intoxication could be the outcome of flaunting the religious ban on drinking alcohol.[152] According to the Palestinian jurist and scholar Muḥammad al-Saffārīnī (d. 1774): "Giving free rein to the eyes leads to inattention to God and the other world, and brings about the intoxication of *ʿishq* . . . The look is the cup of alcohol, and *ʿishq* is the intoxication of that drink."[153] A deflationary reduction of love is also apparent in the opinion, indignantly rejected by the "idealist" Muḥyī al-Dīn al-Ṣaltī, that *ʿishq* is the effect of the excessive accumulation of semen in the body, and could thus be cured by engaging in copulation with a wife or concubine.[154]

The "idealist" position shared the negative evaluation of illicit lust, but nonetheless maintained a positive evaluation of love. Such a combination of attitudes rested on maintaining a clear distinction between the two. "Love (*al-maḥabbah*) is different from sexual desire (*al-shahwah*), and this everyone knows from himself if he abandons obstinacy," said ʿAbd al-Ghanī al-Nābulusī, one of the most fervent defenders of chaste love in the early Ottoman period.[155] On several occasions, poets expressed the chaste nature of their passion. ʿAbd al-Ḥayy Ṭarrazalrayḥān, purporting to address a beloved, assured:

> Have you not known chastity from an ailing person who does not enter the alleys of vice,
> And by nature disdains any indecency not accepted by the schools of religious law?[156]

Muḥammad Saʿīd ibn al-Sammān (d. 1759) proclaimed:

> Leave me and love, and do not prolong a reproach that shatters solid rock;
> For I have a heart that is persistent, and an ear that is deaf to indecency.[157]

Indeed, the love poetry of the period typically described a love that was tragic, unreciprocated and unconsummated. Criticizing a poem, the Damascene belletrist Abū al-Fatḥ al-Mālikī (d. 1567/8) pointed out that it inappropriately used the word "generous" (*karīm*) of the beloved: "The beloved ought not to be described as such, but as ungenerous (*bakhīl*)."[158] In a poem, the Egyptian scholar Yūsuf al-Ḥafnī (d. 1763) quoted a downy-cheeked beloved as telling him:

> "When did you ever see a lover fulfill his desire for being united with the tender-limbed?"[159]

Scholars who discussed passionate love sometimes pointed out the following paradox: the beloved's wish was not to be with his lover (*al-maḥbūb murīd li-al-firāq; al-firāq murād al-maʿshūq*), and the true lover was supposed to adopt the wishes of the beloved, hence a true lover ought not to wish to be with his beloved.[160] This was indeed a paradoxical conclusion. Composers of love poetry regularly expressed their unhappiness at being separated from the beloved, and their hope for a future "lover's union" (*wiṣāl*). The poet could also allude to such "lover's unions" in the past, by way of contrasting past bliss with present suffering. However, such "unions" were not—in this particular genre of poetry—explicitly portrayed as sexual. Indeed their chaste nature was often emphasized. The Damascene poet Aḥmad al-Kaywānī (d. 1760), for instance, stated:

> For there was no *wiṣāl* except talk, and promises, and kisses.
> Our chastity is by character, not from fear of censor or blame.[161]

The Egyptian scholar ʿAbdallah al-Shabrāwī (d. 1758) urged his beloved boy to:

> Grant him [i.e., the poet] what is not religiously prohibited, for he does not have any desire for the prohibited.
> By God, there is nothing blameworthy in granting a lover's union (*waṣl*) to someone like me.[162]

The Iraqi poet Ḥusayn al-ʿUshārī (d. ca. 1781) composed a poem after having a dream in which he kissed the Prophet Muḥammad. One verse of the poem said:

> I became drunk from being united (*waṣl*) with the beloved (*al-ḥabīb,* i.e., the Prophet) and his nearness, and bliss rendered me disoriented.[163]

It is inconceivable that the poet would have used the term *waṣl* in this particular context if it were likely to evoke the idea of copulation.

Poetry as such was not necessarily chaste; as has been seen on several occasions in the present study, some of it could be positively obscene. Yet this bawdy strand coexisted with a centuries-old tradition in Arabic poetry of depicting, in the words of Andras Hamori, "a faithful, chaste and debilitating passion for unattainable objects."[164] The relationship between lover and beloved as portrayed in this kind of love poetry was structurally incompatible with sex: the lover (the man) was invariably the subordinate partner, humbly kept in awe by the unattainable beauty of the beloved (the boy or woman), abjectly pleading for leniency and gentleness. The scholar ʿAbd al-Qādir al-Baghdādī (d. 1682) spelled out this principle:

> The composer of love poetry (*al-nāsib*) should . . . devote his efforts to [depicting] that which indicates ardent love, and all-powerful passion and rapture, and depletion and impatience, and other such testimonies to meekness and utter infatuation, and he should avoid that which indicates pride and confidence and toughness and endurance.[165]

This stands in sharp contrast to literary descriptions of, or allusions to, sexual intercourse, where the masculine, active partner establishes his domination over the feminine and passive. The inversion of roles extends to the poetic imagery; in love poetry it was the beloved whose eyes were like swords, wreaking havoc with the lover and setting his interior aflame.[166] It is instructive to compare this with the defamatory passages cited in the beginning of chapter 1, in which the penis penetrates and ravishes the receptive partner like a weapon. Sexual roles as a rule mirrored nonsexual relations of power, the sexually dominant (the penetrator) also being the socially dominant (the man, the husband, the master). Love, on the other hand, tended to overturn the established social order, causing a master to be enthralled by his slave, and a prominent Muslim scholar like Muḥammad al-ʿUrḍī (later to become Mufti in Aleppo) to be captivated by a Christian boy working in a wine shop. In the words of the scholar Ḥasan al-Būrīnī:

> Strange affairs result from love, for in it the brave is cowardly, the rational bewildered, the patient anxious, and the hard-hearted tearful; its phases are wondrous and its vicissitudes strange; it does not follow the rules of analogy, nor accord with the expectations of people.[167]

There is abundant evidence to suggest that many individuals actually experienced passionate love as an addictive submission to a beloved who would otherwise occupy a lower status than themselves. The historian Raḍī al-Dīn ibn al-Ḥanbalī related how a merchant from Jerusalem became so enamored of a youth from Aleppo that he would lick up the latter's spittle from the ground and swallow it, saying: "I am afflicted with this and I am sixty years of age; what is this condition?"[168] The poet Abū Bakr al-ʿUmarī reported an incident that took place in Aleppo during his lifetime: a man met his death when his beloved boy asked him to prove his love by jumping into the moat surrounding the citadel of the city.[169] Abū al-Suʿūd ibn al-Kātib (d. 1646/7), the son of a wealthy merchant of Damascus, met an equally tragic end. According to the biographer Muḥibbī, he fell in love with a boy who behaved toward him in a very quarrelsome and accusing manner. The unhappy lover eventually committed suicide by taking an overdose of opium. Muḥibbī added that the story was well known, indeed proverbial, among the people of Damascus in his day, and that it started a trend of similar suicides in the city.[170]

Such stories lent support to the belief that love was a tragic affliction for which an individual could not be held accountable. According to Būrīnī: "A lover is not to be blamed because love is an involuntary matter, and man cannot repel that which is involuntary."[171] Muḥibbī articulated the same conviction in verse:

> You who has no heart [the censurer], leave me be! I am not the one who has chosen this tortuous fate.
>
> If there was a choice in love, you would not find the lion of the jungle [the lover] captivated by a gazelle.[172]

To the "realist" position that love was the consequence of looking at an attractive woman or boy, "idealists" could argue that often an involuntary glance was all it took to fall in love.[173] Idealists could also take a different line, and point out that one might look at many beautiful individuals without falling in love with them. In other words, looking at physical beauty was not in itself sufficient (*mūjib*) for the appearance of love on the part of the beholder.[174] In Arab-Islamic love theory, aesthetic appreciation (*istiḥsān*) usually featured as the first stage in a process that culminates in passionate, ardent infatuation. But the procession from one stage to the other was not necessarily depicted as inexorable or mechanical. It was recognized that love was not simply the function of physical beauty, and could instead cause a person to see as beautiful that which was not so. Those who saw love as sublime and praiseworthy were inclined to reject deflationary explanations that would make it the effect of lustful looking or the excessive accumulation of semen in the body. Instead, they sometimes proposed intricate and supernatural accounts of its origin. The Egyptian mystic Zayn al-ʿĀbidīn al-Bakrī al-Ṣiddīqī (d. 1696), for example, suggested that God originally created a composite, spherical soul from which He derived individual human souls by repeated division. Emotional affinity reflected closeness in this spiritual genealogy.[175] A related explanation was propounded by Muḥyī al-Dīn al-Ṣaltī in his treatise on love. He located the origin of love in that moment, mentioned in the

Qur'an (7:171), when God drew forth from the loins of Adam the whole of humanity and made them attest that He was their Creator. In this scheme of things, looking served as a reminder of a primordial proximity.[176] Both accounts are strongly reminiscent of the theory attributed to "Aristophanes" in Plato's *Symposium:* love is the search for one's other half, severed by Zeus in primordial times. A more sophisticated attempt at explaining love from a thoroughly idealist perspective was made later on in that work by "Socrates"—that is, by Plato himself. Individual beautiful things are, he maintained, instances of the eternal and incorporeal Form of Beauty. A lover captivated by a handsome person—Plato's examples are almost always boys—is therefore captivated by a shadow of the world of Forms, to which his soul originally belonged. As he proceeds to love ever more abstract instances of beauty, he simultaneously draws nearer his own otherworldly origin. As will be shown in the following section, related ideas remained very much alive in the early Ottoman Middle East.

It has hitherto been taken for granted that the adoption of a deflationary or an idealist perspective on love was independent of whether the beloved was a woman or a boy. This seems to have been the rule in the premodern Arab-Islamic Middle East. It was of course not the rule in Europe, where idealization was normally confined to "heterosexual" love. An interesting debate on this issue unfolded in the 1820s between the English traveler James Silk Buckingham and his Iraqi travel companion and guide "Ismael." Buckingham, familiar from his own culture with idealist perceptions of love between unmarried men and women, initially responded with sympathy when his companion told him that he had a Christian beloved in Baghdad. When he found out that the beloved was a *boy,* he "shrunk back from the confession as a man would recoil from a serpent on which he had unexpectedly trodden."[177] However, after further talks with his Iraqi companion, Buckingham came to the conclusion that the fact that the amorous feelings were directed at a boy did not automatically imply that they were not "pure" and "honourable." The point was pressed by Ismael himself during their discussions:

> He contended that if it were possible for a man to be enamored of every thing that is fair, and lovely, and good and beautiful, in a female form, without a reference to the enjoyment of the person, which feeling may most unquestionably exist [on this Buckingham and Ismael agreed], so the same sentiment might be excited toward similar charms united in a youth of the other sex, without reference to impure desires.[178]

Buckingham was helped along to this conclusion by his classical education, which told him that the possibility of a chaste love of boys was countenanced by the ancient Greeks. After drawing the parallel with classical antiquity, he concluded:

> From all this, added to many other examples of a similar kind, related as happening between persons who had often been pointed out to me in Arabia and Persia, I could no longer doubt the existence in the East of an affection for male youths, of as pure and honourable a kind as that which is felt in Europe for those of the other sex.[179]

The position of Buckingham's Iraqi companion enjoyed the support of a centuries-old Arabic belletristic tradition. Love poetry could equally be of a boy or a woman, and works on love could relate, in the same breath, the "heterosexual" loves of the legendary *ʿudhrī* poets, and the pederastic loves of people like Muḥammad ibn Dāwūd al-Ẓāhirī and the famous biographer Ibn Khallikān (d. 1282). The coexistence of a literary idealization of pederastic love with a religious prohibition of sodomy was in principle not more problematic than the coexistence of a literary idealization of "heterosexual" love together with a religious prohibition of fornication. The relatively modern idea that passionate love is a normal prelude to marriage could not have gained much resonance in a culture in which premarital contact between the sexes was forbidden and marriages arranged. In any case, the fascination with love seems in large part to have been dependent on its wild and tragic character, which was difficult to reconcile with the tranquility and orderliness of married life.[180]

There were, to be sure, persons even within Arab-Islamic culture in the period under study who would adopt a cynical and deflationary position as regards the love of one sex, and an idealist position as regards love of the other. For example, Dāwūd al-Anṭākī treated love in general, and the various anecdotes relating to the love of women, with unconcealed sympathy. At the same time his presentation of the anecdotes dealing with pederastic love affairs is prefaced with the reductionist claim that this type of love first emerged among the people of Sodom, and that it should be avoided by means of averting the eyes.[181] On the other hand, the previously mentioned Persian philosopher Mullā Ṣadrā, whose discussion is cited in the miscellaneous anthology of the Ottoman Grand Vizier Rāghib Pāshā (d. 1763), identified noble and sublime love with the love of boys, while reducing the love of women to an animalistic desire to perpetuate the species. Muḥyī al-Dīn al-Ṣaltī, in his own treatise on love, only cited examples of pederastic love, many of them plagiarized from earlier works, to which he added others that he had heard of or witnessed. The Egyptian belletrist Ibn al-Wakīl al-Mallawī also confined his attention to pederastic love couples, explicitly stating that courting women was in his day fit for libertines rather than lovers.[182] However, against the background of the dominant literary tradition, such restrictions based on the gender of the beloved appear somewhat idiosyncratic. For example, the Palestinian scholar Muḥammad al-Saffārīnī (d. 1774), who devoted a short tract to denouncing sodomites, divided passionate love into three evaluative categories: (i) praiseworthy, such as the love of a man for his wife; (ii) blameworthy, such as a man's love for a boy; (iii) neither praise- nor blameworthy, such as an involuntary, chaste love of an unrelated woman.[183] However, it seems to have been more usual for religious scholars to allow that the involuntary chaste love of a boy should also be evaluated as neither commendable nor reprehensible. The prominent Damascene scholar Aḥmad al-Manīnī (d. 1759), for example, commented on a risqué poem which said that if the prophet Lot had seen the beauty of the beloved boy, he would not declare him forbidden to mankind. Manīnī argued that this need not be understood in the unacceptable sense that Lot would have permitted sodomizing the boy, but that he would have permitted loving him, "for love is a natural and coercive matter in which the lover does not have any choice . . . and love, if it is not associated with a foul deed, is free from blemish since it does not involve committing what is forbidden by religious law."[184] This was also the position of the Iraqi scholar ʿAbd al-Raḥmān al-Suwaydī (d. 1786). In a short tract on the love of boys (*ʿishq al-fityān*) which he wrote at the request of a friend, he advised caution and discretion, but clearly allowed for the possibility of a chaste and involuntary love of boys that was neither reprehensible nor commendable from a religious point of view. He wrote: "If it is established that passionate love is involuntary and chaste, with no admixture of pretense, one should not reproach those afflicted, neither in word or in thought."[185] The position of Manīnī and Suwaydī was apparently the one sanctioned by Abū Ḥāmid al-Ghazālī's seminal *Iḥyāʾ ʿulūm al-dīn*. To love someone for his beauty and without any carnal lust was, said Ghazālī, possible, since "the beautiful form is pleasurable in itself even if carnal lust is absent." Such a love was not religiously commendable (*maḥmūd*), but it was not blameworthy (*madhmūm*) either. It was simply indifferently permissible (*mubāḥ*).[186] Ghazālī did not explicitly claim that he was speaking of the love of handsome boys, but the principle he defended was general. It is therefore safe to assume that his position was widely understood as allowing for the possibility of a chaste and religiously permissible love of beauty in any form.[187] Indeed, the position of Saffārīnī was liable to the objection that it was arbitrary to allow that the passionate love of an unrelated woman was not reprehensible if it was chaste and involuntary, and yet refuse to allow that the chaste and involuntary love of a boy fell into the same category. Such an objection was made by scholars who discussed whether the above-mentioned saying of the Prophet, "He who loves and is chaste and then dies, dies a martyr," only applied to the love of women. For example, one of the most prominent jurists of the period, the Egyptian Shams al-Dīn Muḥammad al-Ramlī (d. 1596), replied to the position that the martyrs-of-love tradition did not apply to a man's love for a boy in the following way:

> This is plausible in the case of voluntary love which he [the lover] can choose to end but does not. However, if we assume that the love is involuntary in the sense that he cannot choose to end it, then there is nothing to prevent him from gaining martyrdom, since in that case there is no transgression of religious precepts.[188]

As will be shown in the following chapter, the position of Ramlī concerning the martyrs-of-love tradition was the dominant one among religious jurists. What was important was chastity and involuntariness, not the gender of the beloved.

Mystical Aestheticism

In the poetry and prose of the period, eulogies of physical beauty were often combined with exclamations praising its Creator. Such a practice, still widespread in the Arab world today, rested on the theologically unproblematic assumption that God had created all worldly beauty. Far more controversial was a related but more radical conception according to which beauty was, in a deep and intricate sense, divine; to behold it was to behold one of the attributes of God. In the early Ottoman Middle East, such notions tended to be closely associated with mystics influenced by the Andalusian-born mystic Muḥyī al-Dīn ibn ʿArabī (d. 1240), and by his younger contemporary, the Egyptian poet ʿUmar ibn al-Fāriḍ (d. 1235).[189] The central contention of mystics standing in this tradition was that only God is real—an idea sometimes referred to as "the unity of existence" (*waḥdat al-wujūd*). Furthermore, it was believed that this basic metaphysical fact could be experienced by the trained mystic. The mystic could actually perceive the manifestation (*tajallī*) of God, where the uninitiated eye saw only the world of phenomena. This was held to be the true meaning of the Qurʾanic assertion "Wherever ye turn there is God's face" (2:115).

The proponents of this way of thinking were careful to dissociate themselves from crude pantheism. They accepted the idea that God, in essence (*dhāt*), was completely unlike anything that may be sensed or conceived. On the other hand, the Islamic religious tradition sanctioned the use of certain "names" (*asmāʾ*) of God, indicating His attributes (*ṣifāt*) and acts (*afʿāl*), such as the Merciful, the Compassionate, the Glorious, the Knower, the Creator, the Beautiful. The mystics of the Ibn ʿArabī school held that these names are manifested in the phenomenal world in much the same way as the Platonic Forms. For example, all instances of worldly beauty are manifestations of the divine name "the Beautiful."[190] In this sense, it is really impossible to fall in love with anything but God. The uninitiated may think they are enthralled by a beautiful woman or boy, but in reality they are captivated by the Beauty of God. More accurately, since neither lover nor beloved really exists, there is ultimately only God loving Himself. In his famous *al-Tāʾiyyah al-kubrā* (Greater ode rhyming with *T*), Ibn al-Fāriḍ stated:

> For everyone handsome [*masc.*], his loveliness is from Her beauty, and so too the loveliness of everyone pretty [*fem.*].
> For Her, Lubna's Qays became infatuated, and also every lover, like Laylā's Majnūn and ʿAzzah's Kuthayyir.
> So every lover, I am he, and She is the beloved of every lover, and all are names of my guise.
> Names of which I am in truth the named, and it was I who appeared to myself in a soul that has hidden.[191]

Phenomenal beauty is simultaneously a delusory veil and a divine revelation. The uninitiated mistakenly take it for an attribute of a particular, independently existing entity; the trained mystic sees it as a manifestation of the infinite beauty of God. The monist mystics could in certain contexts adopt the language of asceticism, and urge people to turn away from the idolization of phenomenal images. However, such passages should not be taken out of context. The proffered alternative was not to keep one's senses shut to the beauty around, but to see it as the divine epiphany it really is. For example, the Damascene mystic ʿAbd al-Ghanī al-Nābulusī, in the preface to his commentary on the *Dīwān* of Ibn al-Fāriḍ, complained that an earlier commentator, Ḥasan al-Būrīnī (d. 1614), had explained Ibn al-Fāriḍ's poetry as straightforward love poetry. In this way, Būrīnī "made everyone understand that the words of the poet were *ghazal* of gazelles, and avoided the divine meanings and sublime intimations even though it is these that are intended."[192] Against this, Nābulusī protested that the mystical understanding of the poetry was the only legitimate understanding:

> It is clear that it is not permissible to attribute to the people of God [i.e., the Sufis] the amatory meanings that occur to the uninitiated . . . The proper

explanation of the words of the people of God is an explanation in terms of God, as applying to God and nothing else.[193]

Such a passage might lead one to suppose that the love poetry of Ibn al-Fāriḍ is simply allegorical, that the portrayed beloved is simply a fictional character doing duty for the divine beloved. However, further reading reveals that this is not what Nābulusī had in mind. The claim is that Ibn al-Fāriḍ did not compose poetry expressing a love for a woman or youth, but that he instead composed poetry expressing a love for the beauty of God *as manifested in women or boys:*

> All the love poetry which he [Ibn al-Fāriḍ] composes, whether it is for a male or a female . . . he intends therewith the true reality that is apparent, manifesting itself with its eternal face in that ephemeral thing (*al-mutajalliyah bi-wajhihā al-ḥaqq al-bāqī fī dhālika al-shay' al-fānī*). He does not intend that thing which in his considered view is merely an illusory appearance and a suppositious image.[194]

In another part of his commentary, Nābulusī stated:

> It has been related of the poet—may God bless his heart—that he loved a butcher boy in whose form God the Exalted made him see His manifestation (*kāna yuḥibbu ghulāman jazzāran ashhadahu al-Ḥaqqu ta'ālā tajalliyahu bi-ṣūratihi*).[195]

The difference between loving a boy and loving God manifesting his beauty in a boy would probably not have been obvious to the uninitiated onlooker. At one point, Nābulusī wrote that the "censurers" mentioned in one of Ibn al-Fāriḍ's poems referred to the people

> who think that he loves what is other than God, that is, the worldly images, whereas he loves the One who is apparent, manifesting Himself in these images, that is, God.[196]

Not only uninitiated onlookers but also the beloved person might be unable to distinguish mystical from profane love. On more than one occasion in his commentary, Nābulusī cited the following short poem by 'Afīf al-Dīn al-Tilimsānī (d. 1289), a second-generation disciple of Ibn 'Arabī:

> I looked at Her, and the handsome person thinks I look at him. No, by Her dark-lipped smile!
> Rather, She who is lovely has lent him the attribute of beauty which he unjustly claims as his own.[197]

The collection of poems entitled *Tarjumān al-ashwāq* by Ibn ʿArabī is perhaps the most well known example of a mystic composing poetry which was both a celebration of the love of God and yet inspired by human beauty. In the preface to the work, Ibn ʿArabī informed the reader that the work was inspired by his affection for a young woman named Niẓām, the daughter of a Persian friend he met in Mecca, and that "whenever I mention a name in this book I allude to her." Yet, when someone dared suggest that he had simply composed worldly love poetry he indignantly wrote a detailed mystical commentary on the poems.[198]

Of the varieties of phenomenal beauty appreciated by the mystical aesthete, pride of place went to instances of human beauty. According to a perfectly orthodox tradition, the Prophet Muḥammad had said: "God created Adam in his image." Some commentators tried to explain away this saying by claiming that the possessive pronoun "his" referred to Adam, so that the intended meaning is "God created Adam in Adam's image."[199] However, many mystics were prepared to accept the saying at face value. They held that Man was unique among all creatures in displaying all the divine names, and was thus the most perfect locus of divine manifestation. This thesis was elaborated into somewhat recondite theories of the Perfect Man (*al-insān al-kāmil*), in whose image the world is created, and who is the "spirit (*Rūḥ*) of the world."[200]

The English Orientalist and traveler Richard Burton, writing in the late nineteenth century, became acquainted with the line of thinking which has been sketched so far. His description is especially interesting since it is presumably derived from oral sources:

> We must not forget that the love of boys has its noble, sentimental side. The Platonists and the pupils of the academy, followed by the Sufis or Moslem Gnostics, held such affection, pure and ardent, to be the *beau idéal* which united in a man's soul the creature with the Creator. Professing to regard youths as the most cleanly and beautiful objects in this phenomenal world, they declared that by loving and extolling the *chef-d'œuvre,* corporeal and intellectual, of the Demiurgus, disinterestedly and without any admixture of carnal sensuality, they are paying the most fervent adoration to the *Causa causans.* They add that such affection, passing as it does the love of women, is far less selfish than fondness for and admiration of the other sex which, however innocent, always suggests sexuality.[201]

The major modern study of the contemplation of human beauty in Islamic mysticism remains the relevant chapter of Helmut Ritter's magisterial study, going back to 1955, of the Persian mystical poet Farīd al-Dīn ʿAṭṭār (d. 1220).[202] Ritter showed that this "religious love of beautiful people" is attested in Islamic history at least as far back as the tenth century. Though he emphasized the importance of the theories of Ibn ʿArabī in providing a sophisticated theoretical justification for the (pre-existing) practice, his chapter focused on the Persian mystical tradition, and traced the theme in the lives and works of such figures as Aḥmad Ghazālī (d. 1126), Rūzbihān Baqlī (d. 1209), and Fakhr al-Dīn ʿIrāqī (d. 1289).[203] There has not, to my knowledge, been any modern study that attempts to trace the theme in the Arabic mystical tradition. In what follows, I will discuss three prominent Arab mystics of the early Ottoman period who may be considered mystical aesthetes.

Ayyūb al-ʿAdawī al-Khalwatī (1586–1660)

Ayyūb was born in the Ṣāliḥiyyah suburb of Damascus, and studied with several local scholars.[204] As his name indicates, he was initiated into the Khalwatī mystical order, and he eventually gained a reputation as a knowledgeable mystic to whom many ascribed supernatural powers. In fact, Ayyūb's reputation as a living saint seems to have reached the imperial court in Constantinople, and he was asked to come to the capital and extend his blessings to Sultan Ibrāhīm (r. 1640–48). He was described by the Damascene biographer Muḥibbī in the following terms: "He was enamored of absolute beauty, and never tired or wearied of love and infatuation." Some of Ayyūb's poetry, as for instance the following couplet, attests to this characterization:

> I was blamed by mankind for loving beauty, and they do not know my aim, if only they knew!
> By means of it I attained the unbounded, and thus my heart approaches a bounded beauty they avoid.

The Damascene scholar Abū al-Mawāhib al-Ḥanbalī (d. 1714), who was initiated into the Khalwatī order by Ayyūb, confirmed that his master was indeed a somewhat controversial figure, and provided some indication of what Ayyūb's love for "bounded beauty" involved: "People used to criticize him for frequenting beardless boys."[205] One of the miracle stories related of this mystic had him attending a gathering at which there was a very handsome youth. When night came and those present made preparations for sleeping in the living room, he asked to lie next to the youth. One of those present silently disapproved of this, and remained awake through the night to keep the mystic under observation. When the observer left the room, he saw Ayyūb outside praying. Surprised, he went back in, only to find him sleeping. After checking this a couple of times, the doubter repented and became convinced that he had to do with a saint.

As mentioned in the previous chapter, the later Syrian mystic Muṣṭafā al-Bakrī (d. 1749) stated that some mystical groups active in his time used to invoke the dictum that "all beauty is the beauty of God" in defense of their practice of contemplating the beauty of women and boys. Bakrī, who was also a Khalwatī mystic, omitted to mention that the dictum was actually part of a short poem by Ayyūb al-Khalwatī:

> All beauty is the beauty of God, there is no doubt, though the proscribing blamers are in doubt.
> The essence and the attributes are one, without doubt. You who approach the One, consider and you would not doubt![206]

ʿAbd al-Ghanī al-Nābulusī (1640–1731)

Ayyūb al-Khalwatī's writings, some of which are extant, seem all to have dealt with mystical topics. ʿAbd al-Ghanī al-Nābulusī, on the other hand, was one of the most versatile scholars of the early Ottoman Middle East.[207] Himself the son of a prominent Ḥanafī jurist, his voluminous writings contribute to such disparate fields as jurisprudence, tradition, Qurʾanic commentary, dogmatic theology, rhetoric, travel literature, dream interpretation, and agronomy. In his own eyes, and those of his contemporaries, he was perhaps first and foremost a mystic (initiated into the Qādirī and Naqshbandī orders), particularly renowned for his mystical poetry, his sympathetic expositions of the idea of the "unity of existence," and his commentaries on the *Dīwān* of Ibn al-Fāriḍ and the *Fuṣūṣ al-ḥikam* of Ibn ʿArabī.[208] He was also a vigorous defender of controversial Sufi practices such as listening to music and contemplating human beauty.[209] Mystical aestheticism is a recurrent theme in his own *Dīwān* of Sufi poetry:

> We are a people who are fond of handsome countenances, and with them God augments His favors to us.
> From the Preserver we have an eye, which increases our certainty and insight.
> To us has been passed the wine of divine manifestation, and with it our cup has been filled.[210]

To be sure, the mystic does not love the countenances as such. A particular collection of skin and bones is an insubstantial and inert form that only appears beautiful insofar as it is the locus of the manifestation of divine Beauty:

O He who is apparent in His creation, while being hidden; O He who is hidden in Himself while being apparent.
You appeared to me in everything, and I was no one but You, the seen as well as the seer . . .
In everyone handsome [*masc.*], indeed in everyone pretty [*fem.*], you became visible until you were affirmed by hearts.
And it is not my creed to love appearances, but I love what the appearances indicate.[211]

Base, carnal love aims at satisfying the self's desires. By contrast, the mystical love of beauty involves an annihilation of the self—an attempt to become a transparent medium for the outflow of divine love directed at divine beauty:

"O boy," if I regard you as a body, and if I ascend to a higher level I say, "Spirit of essences,"
And if I reduce you and me to nothing I say, "O Lord, in his most comprehensive attribute."[212]

The contemplation of phenomenal beauty is not only permissible but also necessary if one is to transcend the phenomenal world, including one's own self, and experience the omnipresence of God. As Nābulusī wrote in his commentary on the *Dīwān* of Ibn al-Fāriḍ:

> It is not simply by reciting supererogatory prayers and incessant invocations, without applying yourself to perceiving the manifestations of Truth the Exalted, that you raise yourself from the depths of your self and your nature to the peak of being united with the Beloved of unbounded Beauty.[213]

Nābulusī expressed the same idea in verse, alluding to a saying controversially attributed to the Prophet:

He who is lost in love, is the one who in Truth exists,
And he is dead [as a self] and alive [fading away in God's Attributes], the witness and the witnessed,
And every door to God except that is locked . . .
The best of all mankind [the Prophet Muḥammad], the sea of beneficence and munificence, says:
"Have recourse to the handsome countenances and the large-pupiled eyes."[214]

In his valuable study *The Sufi Orders in Islam* (1971), J. S. Trimingham inserted a rather curious footnote in which he claimed that after the fifteenth century, the mystical contemplation of beardless boys "was prohibited altogether in the Arab world, the occasional reference, as in ʿAbd al-Ghanī al-Nābulusī's works, does not mean anything."[215] It is not clear what lies behind Trimingham's cursory dismissal. He possibly believed that a prominent and respectable Islamic scholar like Nābulusī simply could not have condoned such a practice, and that this theme in his mystical poetry was simply a literary convention which should not be taken literally. This would be in line with the more general view that Islamic mystical poetry eventually became fossilized, and continued to make use of the daring images of earlier poets but without any genuine conviction.[216] However, the idea that the theme of the mystical love of boys in Nābulusī's poetry was a mere literary convention is untenable. It is clear from, say, Nābulusī's commentary on the *Dīwān* of Ibn al-Fāriḍ that he wholeheartedly accepted the appropriateness of Ibn al-Fāriḍ falling in love with a butcher boy and regarding the manifestation of divine beauty in that human form. Furthermore, the recently edited tract by Nābulusī entitled *Ghāyat al-maṭlūb fī maḥabbat al-maḥbūb* is a lengthy and esoteric defense (in prose) of the permissibility of loving handsome beardless boys. The thesis of this remarkable work is adumbrated already in the preamble, where he invokes blessings on the Prophet Muḥammad,

> who made it part of his tradition to love comeliness and made it permissible to perceive beauty, so that this becomes part of moral excellence, and he who considers it a defect, and criticizes those who follow and imitate this lead, is an unbeliever.[217]

Nābulusī defends this bold claim by showing that several of the companions of the Prophet were handsome, beardless youths. For instance, Muʿādh ibn Jabal is reported to have converted at the age of eighteen, and was twenty-one when the Prophet died. He was said to be "tall, and of lovely hair, and big eyes, and bright white teeth." Nevertheless, uncontroversial traditions related that the Prophet once said to him, "I love you (*innī la-uḥibbuka*), Muʿādh," and that Muʿādh replied, "And I love you," whereupon the Prophet gave him instructions on what to say at the conclusion of a prayer.[218] Similarly uncontroversial traditions related that Zayd ibn al-Ḥārithah, who at the age of eight was bought and freed from slavery by Muḥammad, was "the love of the Prophet of God (*ḥibb Rasūl Allah*)." Zayd's son Usāmah, who was nineteen when the Prophet died, was—again according to uncontroversial traditions—"the love, son of the love (*al-ḥibb ibn al-ḥibb*)."[219] According to one tradition, the Prophet had also said: "He who loves God, let him love Usāmah ibn Zayd."[220] The Prophet thus "loved" several young male companions, and enjoined his followers to "love" them too. Anyone who finds fault with loving a handsome beardless youth is therefore finding fault with behavior that can be attributed to the Prophet and that was endorsed in his sayings—and this is incompatible with being a believing Muslim. Similarly, the jurists who proclaim that it is not permissible to look at a beardless boy are prohibiting something that it is reasonably certain that the Prophet did, which again is incompatible with being a Muslim.[221] Of course, the love in question was devoid of lust. However, this does not invalidate the major point that Nābulusī was interested in making, namely that those who "look at handsome countenances and like to see beauty in created forms (*yanẓurūna ilā al-wujūh al-ḥisān wa yuḥibbūna ru'yat al-jamāl fī al-ṣuwar*)" are in the right.[222]

Nābulusī was committed to the idea that the "handsome countenances" which reveal divine beauty could be both women and beardless youths. However, in *Ghāyat al-maṭlūb* he was especially eager to show that it is permissible, indeed recommendable, to look at and love handsome male youths. He repeatedly made use of the same argument that Burton encountered in the late nineteenth century, namely that looking at boys is more often devoid of lust, and hence less problematic, than looking at the opposite sex.[223] Furthermore, the elements of religious tradition which Nābulusī adduced in support of mystical aestheticism are especially relevant to the love of boys. Nābulusī traced the ancestry of the mystical contemplation of beauty back to the Qur'anic passages (2:34, 7:11, 17:61, 18:50, 20:116) which describe how God ordered the angels to "bow" or "prostrate" themselves before Adam, and how Satan alone refused to do so, appealing to the baseness of the material from which the first human was created. The relevance of this incident to Nābulusī becomes clear when he, on the basis of several traditions, asserted that Adam was created as a beardless youth.[224] In his view, the angels prostrating themselves before Adam are the archetype of the mystics contemplating the beauty of beardless youths, while Satan's refusal to bow before what he considered a creature made of clay is the archetype of those antimystical scholars who insist that all there is to see in a handsome youth is his tempting flesh:

> You blamer who in ignorance blamed me for loving that precious boy!
> What do we care for the ignorant, seeking us out with baseless words and a vile mind!
> In beauty and masculinity there is a secret unknown except to the sanctified . . .
> If you equate the handsome and the ugly amongst people, your reasoning is fallacious.
> You were told: "Bow yourself to Adam"; you were not told: "Bow yourself to Satan."[225]

Nābulusī also appealed to a widely accepted saying of the Prophet Muḥammad according to which the angel Gabriel often appeared to him in the form of Diḥyah al-Kalbī, a very handsome man from Mecca.[226] The examples adduced by Nābulusī of the Platonic, mystical love that he defends also tend to reveal a preponderance in favor of the love of youths: the love of Muḥammad for Zayd ibn al-Ḥārithah, and Zayd's son Usāmah; Ibn al-Fāriḍ's love for the young butcher; and the love of the great Persian poet and mystic Jalāl al-Dīn al-Rūmī (d. 1273) for his student and successor, Ḥusām al-Dīn Çelebī, to whom he devoted his great *Mathnawī*.[227]

It is tempting to relate the focus on the contemplation of beauty in male youths to Nābulusī's personal history. He was said to have been especially fond of one of his students, Muḥammad al-Dikdikjī (d. 1719), who was thirty years his junior. The Damascene mystic Muṣṭafā al-Bakrī (d. 1749), who was a student of both, described Nābulusī's feelings in terms that imply a strong emotional attachment: "He adopted him from his youth, since he was enraptured and captivated by his love (*tabannāhu fī al-ṣibā lammā hāma fī ṣabbihi wa ṣabā*)." The Damascene biographer Muḥammad Khalīl al-Murādī (d. 1791) also noted that Nābulusī "loved" Muḥammad al-Dikdikjī "intensely" (*kāna shadīd al-maḥabbah lahu*).[228] The following love poem by Nābulusī may well have been elicited by his feelings for his beloved student:

> My heart is tossed high and low by a yearning that knows no bounds!
> Woe! Woe unto me from the languid glance of one so young and delicate!
> He's a radiant moon if he appears; a succulent branch if he sways.
> He looks with a gazelle's eyes, but fills my heart with fear and trembling.
>
> . . . .
>
> By God! By God! Have mercy upon me, O wispy shape!
> Yearning has melted me, and undone the knot of patience.
> What is the fault of my heart that it should be ever in flames?
>
> . . . .
>
> All you people! Is there no one to help me?
> Is fire the deserved lot of he who fancies (*yahwā*) Muḥammad?[229]

The only time that Nābulusī was known to have cried over a deceased was, according to a great-grandchild, when Dikdikjī died.[230]

It would undoubtedly be facile to classify Nābulusī as a "homosexual"—he was married and had children, and was eager to distinguish the mystical love he defended from illicit lust, let alone sodomy. Yet, one may suppose that Nābulusī conceived of the relationship with his student as an instance of the same type as the love of Ibn al-Fāriḍ for the butcher boy, and that he would have empathized with Mullā Ṣadrā's contention—mentioned in the previous chapter—that God had instilled in adult men a sensibility to youthful male beauty so that they would educate and care for youths.

ʿAbd al-Raḥmān al-ʿAydarūsī (1722–1778)

ʿAbd al-Raḥmān ibn Muṣṭafā al-ʿAydarūsī was born in the Yemen, and traveled to India in his youth with his father.[231] He spent most of his adult life moving between the towns of Mecca, Medina, and Ṭāʾif in western Arabia, and the city of Cairo in Egypt, where he died. He was initiated into the ʿAydarūsī and Naqshbandī mystical orders, and became widely recognized as a prominent mystical poet and thinker. While in Cairo, he was lionized by prominent Egyptian scholars such as the Rectors of the Azhar college ʿAbdallah al-Shabrāwī (d. 1758) and Muḥammad al-Ḥafnī (d. 1767).[232] He was also the mystical master of Muḥammad Murtaḍā al-Zabīdī (d. 1791), famous for his commentaries on the Arabic dictionary (*Qāmūs*) of al-Fayrūzabādī (d. 1415) and the *Iḥyāʾ ʿulūm al-dīn* of Abū Ḥāmid al-Ghazālī.

ʿAydarūsī's poetry often evokes the theme of the mystical contemplation of beauty:

> May God guard your beautiful visage! You marvelous form! You medicine for the ill!
> You prevail over all those of lovely splendor; you enthrall everyone with your dark-lashed eye . . .
> I do not want anything from you except to catch a glimpse of the unbounded in that smooth cheek.
> You who ask about our passionate love—our love for beauty is of this kind.[233]

Another example is the following:

> Revive the spirit with cups of wine, and pour it to us and to our noble companions.
> And laud in verse those of loveliness, who are garbed with that most precious beauty.
> And perceive the unbounded in the shapely young, and in every gazelle of dark-red lips.[234]

The reference to wine may again raise the issue of the extent to which such verses should be taken literally. One may presume that ʿAydarūsī, a widely respected religious notable, is not literally asking for wine. If, however, we are to understand the wine (*rāḥ*) symbolically, as commentators of mystical poetry typically did, then it may seem natural to ask why one should not understand "the shapely young" and "every gazelle of dark-red lips" in the same way. However, the analogy between "wine" and "gazelle" is not perfect. Mystical theoreticians did not claim that drinking wine was permissible, nor did they assign any experiential value to the drinking of wine. However, at least some influential mystical theoreticians did claim that contemplating human beauty was permissible, and that such contemplation could afford valuable mystical insight. One of those mystics was ʿAydarūsī himself. In a work recording some of his poetic exchanges with contemporaries, he cited a poem sent to him from a Meccan belletrist named Badr al-Dīn ibn ʿUmar Khūj. In this poem, Badr al-Dīn excuses himself for not having written for some time, and complains that he has been suffering from fervent love for a beautiful but recalcitrant beloved. In reply, ʿAydarūsī wrote:

> If you want the cure which is both distant and near, immerse yourself in love both secretly and openly.
> And let your soul be lowly in love, and say: My lowliness in love has raised me.
> And die in love—you will live happy and strengthened, and say: My death in love has revived me . . .
> Were it not for my absorption in the unreal, I would not on consideration be called "Man."[235]
> Neither would I be dead in the lovers' quarter, nor would He who is living make me forget the dead . . .

ʿAydarūsī then appended some prose to his letter, urging the belletrist to "add the end to the beginning . . . for love for the unreal is the bridge to the Truth (*al-ʿishq al-majāzī qanṭaratu al-ḥaqīqah*)."[236]

The same work by ʿAydarūsī provides evidence that he at some stages in his life conceived a passion for at least one attractive person. For instance, he wrote that he once, while in a garden in Ṭāʾif, composed a short acrostic extolling "one of those of splendid appearance (*baʿḍ dhawī al-ṭalʿāt al-bahiyyah*)." The first letter of each verse reveals the name Jamāl, which is presumably the (male) name of the person extolled.[237] He further related that the above-mentioned Badr al-Dīn ibn ʿUmar Khūj then composed a couplet assuring ʿAydarūsī that all those of beauty ought to be at his service, since he was a descendant of the Prophet and since all worldly beauty is derived from the Light of Muḥammad.[238] The belletrist then added some lines in prose which ʿAydarūsī decided not to cite "out of reverence for God (*tawāḍuʿan li-al-Ḥaqq*)."[239]

In the same work, ʿAydarūsī also reproduced a poetic exchange between him and an unnamed "beloved," and adds at the end of it:

> You who comes across the preceding verses: To think well of one's fellows is appropriate to the trusted and steadfast, so think well of both parties and God will recompense you twice . . . and I had initially decided not to include them in this book, but one of my friends deemed it appropriate, and appealed to the

two lines of poetry attributed to the great scholar, author of *al-Tanbīh* on Shāfiʿī law, Abū Isḥāq al-Shīrāzī [d. 1083], may God be pleased with him:

> I love young women without transgressing the law, and adore the cup without wine.
> And my love is not for anything shameful, but I saw that love is the habit of the noble.[240]

There are no analogous reasons to believe that ʿAydarūsī ever drank wine.

The practice and underlying theory of what I have called "mystical aestheticism" was highly controversial. To many Islamic religious scholars, the idea that only God truly exists, and that the created world is but a manifestation of His attributes, was plain pantheism (*ʿayniyyah*) or "incarnationism" (*ḥulūl* or *ittiḥād*). Throughout the Mamluk era (1250–1517), controversies had erupted concerning the orthodoxy of Ibn ʿArabī and Ibn al-Fāriḍ. Among their more prominent opponents were scholars such as Ibn Taymiyyah (d. 1328), Ismāʿīl ibn al-Muqriʾ (d. 1434), and Ibrāhīm al-Biqāʿī (d. 1480).[241] By the early sixteenth century, the controversy seems to have abated somewhat. Authoritative scholars such as the Egyptians Jalāl al-Dīn al-Suyūṭī (d. 1505) and Zakariyyā al-Anṣārī (d. 1520), and the Ottoman Grand Mufti Kamāl Pāshāzāde (d. 1534) expressed themselves, with varying degrees of caution, in favor of the two mystics.[242] As one of his first acts after conquering Syria and Egypt, the Ottoman Sultan Salīm I (r. 1512–20) paid homage to the tomb of Ibn ʿArabī in Damascus, and ordered a mosque built at the site.[243] Hostility to Ibn ʿArabī continued to be espoused by a few figures, such as Muḥammad ibn Ismāʿīl al-Amīr in Yemen (d. 1768) and Muḥammad ibn ʿAbd al-Wahhāb (d. 1792) in central Arabia, and as the Wahhābī and Salafī movements inspired by these figures gained strength in the nineteenth century, such negative evaluations came to the fore again.[244] However, the dominant tendency amongst Sunnī Muslim scholars within the Ottoman Empire from 1500 to 1800 seems to have been to follow the more positive evaluations of Suyūṭī, Anṣārī, or Kamāl Pāshāzāde.[245] Yet, as has been remarked by Michael Winter, the evaluation was more in favor of the persons than their ideas. The attitude expressed by Suyūṭī and Anṣārī was that the mystics in question were saints whose inspired words should not be judged by those who were strangers to their experiences and terminology. Indeed, Suyūṭī declared that reading the books of Ibn ʿArabī was not permissible, even while he vigorously defended the mystic against the charge of heresy. The idea of the "unity of existence" continued to be the source of widespread anxiety. Nābulusī's writings were often very polemical, which by itself suggests that the views he expressed were controversial. He seems to have been aware that mystical aestheticism was a particularly sensitive issue. In his commentary on the *Dīwān* of Ibn al-Fāriḍ, he referred to the

> ignorant and heedless censurers who despise the people of God [i.e., the Sufis] and rebuke them, and accuse them of indecencies and ignominies of which they are innocent, especially if they are acquainted with whom they love from among the forms of divine manifestations and appearances.[246]

Indeed, the contemplation of human beauty was controversial even within the ranks of Islamic mystics. As was mentioned in the first chapter of the present study, the practice was condemned by several prominent Sufis. For example, the Egyptian ʿAbd al-Wahhāb al-Shaʿrānī (d. 1565), in a handbook for Sufi novices, wrote:

> He [the novice] ought to avert his eyes from attractive forms as much as possible, for looking at them is like an arrow which hits the heart and kills it, especially if he looks with lust, for that is like a poison arrow which melts a man's body instantly . . . And he who raises himself from the condition of mere libertinage and asserts that this love is spiritual rather than bodily, we say to him: that is an interpolation from the self and the devil. The devil may make someone imagine that there is no harm in that [i.e., looking at attractive forms], and that all beauty in existence derives its beauty from the beauty of God the Exalted. To this we say: He whose beauty you claim to be seeing is the one who has prohibited this seeing.[247]

Later in the same work, Shaʿrānī expressed himself even more vehemently:

> No one claims that it is permissible to look at the attractions declared out of bounds by the Lawgiver, except those who are debauched and have abandoned the Way, and disguised themselves for the commoners so that one who does not know the Holy Law thinks they are saints, though they are the most libertine of libertines . . . Satan has insinuated to them to appear ecstatic and listen to music with women and male youths . . . and insinuated to them to incline to sit with them and talk with them, until he succeeded in making them incline to seek debauchery with them.[248]

It is possible that Shaʿrānī's warnings were aimed specifically at novices, and not to more advanced mystics. In other words, it may be that the difference in opinion between Shaʿrānī and, say, Nābulusī is exaggerated when passages from a handbook for novices by one author are juxtaposed to passages from an esoteric work by the other. This said, the vehemence of Shaʿrānī's condemnation seems to indicate sincerity. It is plausible that Shaʿrānī simply represents a different, more ascetic streak in the Sufi tradition than Nābulusī. He defended Ibn ʿArabī against detractors, but did so in a spirit that seems much closer to his teacher Zakariyyā al-Anṣārī than to Nābulusī: he simply insisted that all problematic passages in Ibn ʿArabī's works were later interpolations, and rejected the idea of "the unity of existence."[249] He also advised his readers to shun works which were even bolder in expressing monist ideas, such as the *ʿAyniyyah* (ode rhyming in the letter *ʿAyn*) by ʿAbd al-Karīm al-Jīlī (d. 1428), whereas Nābulusī composed a commentary on the work.[250] In a work enumerating the spiritual virtues conferred on him by God, Shaʿrānī stated:

> One of the blessings conferred on me by God the Exalted is His shielding me constantly from looking at unrelated women and beardless boys, even without lust, ever since I was young . . . My master ʿAlī al-Khawāṣ—may God have mercy on him—used to say: The true reason for the prohibition of looking at what is out of bounds is that it occupies the mind with what is other than God, for God the Exalted has made the heart his home and the locus of His secrets and the believer ought not introduce into it any of the things that souls desire, for the love of God will then depart [from the heart] because He is jealous . . . From this it is clear that the prohibition of looking at women and what is considered analogous to them [i.e., beardless boys] is not based on the fear that this will lead to debauchery, but on this leading to the introduction into the heart of the love of what is other than God, without His permission.[251]

Shaʿrānī's assumption was that the love of God precludes the love of other creatures. For mystical aestheticism, on the other hand, the love of God consists in loving his creatures with the right attitude. According to Nābulusī:

> Some have divided love into two parts, and distinguished between a love that is worldly because its object is a created entity, and a love that is divine because its object is the Creator, and the truth of the matter as I see it is that it [i.e., love] is one thing . . . Its object is in the beginning a created entity which is an act of the Creator. It then takes on God as an object if it is accompanied by Islam and faith (*īmān*) and charity (*iḥsān*) and is devoid of outward or inward disobedience.[252]

To the ascetic claim that loving a created individual is incompatible with exclusive devotion to God, Nābulusī replied:

> To become enamored of a created being insofar as it is created will usually imply lust in the case of handsome forms; to become enamored of it insofar as it is a particular trace of the Possessor of infinite beauty is not to be preoccupied with a created being at all, and thus the Prophet (God bless him and grant him salvation) loved Usāmah ibn Zayd and loved his father Zayd before him . . .

> and ʿĀʾishah [the favorite wife of Muḥammad] was the beloved of the Prophet (God bless him and grant him salvation) and this was not to preoccupy the heart with a created being.[253]

The preceding two quotations are from Nābulusī's above-mentioned tract *Ghāyat al-maṭlūb fī maḥabbat al-maḥbūb*. It is worth reiterating that this was an esoteric tract that Nābulusī—according to a great-grandson—had asked his sons not to show except to the select few.[254] As will become clear in the following chapter, Nābulusī in that work clearly moved beyond what mainstream religious scholars would have accepted.

CHAPTER THREE

Sodomites

The Controversy over Gazing (*Naẓar*)

Descriptions of the physical features of the beloved loomed large in the love poetry of the Arab-Islamic Middle East in the early Ottoman period. Poets typically dwelled on the eyes, skin, cheeks, neck, hair, figure, and gait—among other things—of the portrayed woman or boy. The descriptions, if taken as realistic representations of actual emotions and experiences, presupposed a fair amount of "looking" or "gazing" (*naẓar*). However, such a taking in of the charms of women or beardless youths was deeply problematic from the perspective of Islamic law. To be sure, the love poetry was often *not* taken realistically. The Meccan scholar Ibn Ḥajar al-Haytamī (d. 1566), one of the most prominent jurists of the early Ottoman period, based his conclusion that love poetry was religiously permissible on the following principle:

> Amorous verse is not an indication of having looked with lust; as a rule the poet says it by way of making his poetry more delicate and to exhibit his craftsmanship, not because he is really in love . . . The composition of amorous verse is a craft, and the intention of the poet is to produce attractive discourse, not the verisimilitude of what is mentioned.[1]

The idea that "poets say what they do not do" thus made room for a peaceful coexistence between the sensual ideals often celebrated in love poetry and the rather more austere ideals upheld by religious jurists. As argued in the previous chapter, poets did not *always* "say what they do not do," but the assumption that they did so "as a rule" allowed them to express a fondness for wine, women, or boys, without compromising themselves.[2] Had it not been for this view of poetry, the coexistence would presumably have been more problematic than it was. The drinking of alcoholic beverages was strictly forbidden by the recognized interpreters of Islamic law, and transgressors were in principle liable to flogging. The visual appreciation (*istiḥsān*) of a "foreign" woman (i.e., a woman who was neither a close relative nor a wife or concubine) was also legally out of bounds. There was broad agreement among the jurists of the period that a man was not allowed to look at a woman who was not his wife, concubine, or close relative, except for specific purposes such as witnessing in a legal case, medical treatment, or teaching.[3] In fact, the jurists of the period tended to agree that young women especially should veil their faces in public, precisely to prevent men from contravening this very principle.[4]

Some jurists held, more controversially, that the same strictures should apply to looking at beardless youths. According to Ibn Ḥajar al-Haytamī, "There are beardless boys who surpass women in beauty and so are more tempting . . . and so more deserving of prohibition."[5] Both women and youths were suspected sources of temptation (*maẓinnat al-fitnah*), and consequently neither looking at (*al-naẓar*), touching (*al-lams*), nor being alone with (*al-khalwah bi*) them was allowed: "The most correct [view is] that all of this is prohibited with a woman or a beardless boy, even if lust is absent and one does not fear temptation, by way of severing the means of vice as much as possible."[6] If youths, in contrast to women, were not ordered to veil themselves, this was merely due to the practical necessity for them to associate with adult men to learn the various sciences and crafts.[7] As to the idea of the Platonic contemplation of handsome youths, Ibn Ḥajar's opinion was unequivocal:

> The claim that there is nothing prohibited in looking at them by way of contemplation (*iʿtibāran*) is a satanic interpolation . . . There are plenty of other and more marvelous things that may be contemplated, but those who are wicked in soul and corrupt in reason and religion, and who do not comply with religious law, Satan suggests this to them in order to make them fall into what is worse than it [i.e., than looking].[8]

A position similar to Ibn Ḥajar's was propounded by the Syrian scholar and mystic ʿAlwān al-Ḥamawī (d. 1530). In a work devoted to the religious-legal provisions of looking, he wrote:

> Looking at the beardless youth is prohibited, whether he is handsome or not, with lust or without it, whether one fears temptation or not . . . Some of them [scholars] qualify [the ruling], and say: It is permissible when one does not fear temptation, and prohibited when one fears it. Other scholars say: If he is handsome it is prohibited to look at him, otherwise it is not. It is more circumspect to block the openings and sever the means [of vice], and to avert the eyes from the beardless boy except for transactions such as teaching a science or a craft, and similar instances of necessity.[9]

Both scholars could adduce several elements of the religious tradition in support of their position. Traditions warning against the temptation posed by beardless youths were numerous, some of them attributed to prominent religious figures of the early Islamic period, others to the Prophet Muḥammad himself. One tradition related that the Prophet prohibited men from gazing at beardless boys, and another that Muḥammad himself had seated a handsome young member of a visiting delegation from the tribe of Qays behind him so as to avoid looking at him.[10] Both traditions were considered to be of dubious authenticity, but they could be buttressed by other traditions, relating how a venerable figure of the early Islamic period such as Sufyān al-Thawrī (d. 778) had fled from a handsome youth in a bath saying that he saw a devil with every woman and seventeen devils with every beardless youth; how Aḥmad ibn Ḥanbal (d. 855), founder of the Ḥanbalī school of law, advised a visiting friend who had brought along a handsome sister's son not to bring him along on future visits and not to walk with him on the streets, lest he expose himself to malicious rumors; and how Abū Ḥanīfah (d. 767), founder of the Ḥanafī school of law, had seated a handsome student of his behind him "for fear of betrayal by the eye."[11] The declared purpose of such appeals to the deeds and sayings of venerable predecessors was to underline that no one ought to consider himself immune to temptation and exempt from the prohibition of looking at boys. According to ʿAlwān al-Ḥamawī: "Perhaps the wicked souls will tell their possessors: Your looking is free from obscenity and lust and you do not have a [tempting] devil; to him is replied: O conceited self-deceiver, do you have more piety than the outstanding Companions [of the Prophet]?"[12] Ibn Ḥajar concurred: "And alike in everything we have mentioned is the look of the righteous, scholars, teachers, and others."[13] The emphasis on the universality of the prohibition should probably be seen against the background of the frankly elitist arguments in defense of practices such as listening to music and contemplating human beauty. Mystics who defended these practices often held that the relevant religious rulings should take into account the spiritual station of the persons involved. Listening to music, for instance, could very well be prohibited (*ḥarām*) to warm-blooded young commoners (for whom it was likely to lead to sin), while being indifferently permitted (*mubāḥ*) to others, and positively recommended (*mandūb*) for the mystic.[14]

The view that looking at youths was prohibited to adult men was a minority opinion within the Shāfiʿī school of law, apparently first formulated by the jurist Yaḥyā al-Nawawī (d. 1277), and hence often referred to as "the way of al-Nawawī" (*ṭarīqat al-Nawawī*). It was a controversial view, and most

Shāfiʿī scholars seem to have followed "the way of al-Rāfiʿī," named after another prominent jurist of the school, ʿAbd al-Karīm al-Rāfiʿī (d. 1226), who, more conventionally, held that looking at youths was permitted in the absence of lust. Ibn Ḥajar al-Haytamī and ʿAlwān al-Ḥamawī were two prominent exponents of the position of Nawawī in the early Ottoman period. They were, however, not unique. The Meccan scholar Muḥammad ʿAlī ibn ʿAllān (d. 1648), for instance, quoted approvingly the verdict of al-Nawawī:

> It is prohibited to look at a beardless boy if he is handsome, whether [the onlooker] fears temptation or not. That is the correct view held by those who examine the question thoroughly . . . because he is as a woman, for he is desired as she is desired, and his beauty is similar to a woman's beauty, and indeed many of them [beardless boys] are more attractive than many women. Indeed they are more worthy of prohibition, since it is easier to gain access to vice in their case than in the case of women.[15]

Similar views were also voiced in the lifetime of ʿAbd al-Ghanī al-Nābulusī (d. 1731), who devoted a virulent polemic to refuting an unnamed contemporary jurist who would prohibit outright looking at beardless youths.[16] Nābulusī insisted that the basic position of religious law as regards looking at humans in general was permission (*ibāḥah*), and that this general principle should be circumscribed only when there were clear indications in the Qur'an or Sunnah (i.e., the sayings and doings of the Prophet Muḥammad) that something was taboo (*ʿawrah*), or when looking was associated with illicit lust. The face of a male youth was, by common consent, not taboo, and hence the proposed prohibition would be based on the second point. The criteria for establishing the presence or absence of lust was, to be sure, a problematic matter, on which jurists themselves did not agree. But, said Nābulusī, in any case no one was in a better position to judge than the onlooker himself, and it was not permissible to claim that one knows whether others look with lust or not. Rather, one was obliged to think well of one's fellow Muslims unless there was weighty evidence to the contrary. Several jurists, Nābulusī added, had taken to the reprehensible practice of issuing general prohibitions—whether on the question of listening to music, of looking at youths, of drinking coffee, or smoking tobacco—that were not based on sound juridical principles, but merely out of a moralistic conviction that wickedness and depravity was widespread. In fact, Nābulusī specifically mentioned both Ibn Ḥajar al-Haytamī and ʿAlwān al-Ḥamawī as examples of this kind of scholar.[17] His opinion of them, though concealed beneath outward manifestations of respect, is apparent from his advice to a student who wanted to study some of the works of ʿAlwān al-Ḥamawī with him. Nābulusī advised the student to study the works of Ibn ʿArabī instead. The works of ʿAlwān al-Ḥamawī, Nābulusī said, with their focus on reprehensible customs and practices, would induce the young student to adopt a disparaging and faultfinding attitude toward his fellow Muslims.[18]

The weakness of the argument of Nābulusī was that it also applied to looking at women. Many jurists held that women's faces were *not* taboo.[19] Hence, the very same argument used by Nābulusī to establish that looking at beardless youths was in principle permissible would also establish that looking at "foreign" women was in principle permissible. To a majority of scholars at the time, such a conclusion would not have been acceptable. Even within Nābulusī's own Ḥanafī school of law, which did not regard a woman's face as taboo, jurists nevertheless asserted that "in the present age," with the prevalence of immorality and depravity, young women especially were obliged to veil themselves in the presence of men.[20] A scholar who wished to maintain the permissibility of looking at youths would have to argue for a basic difference between looking at youths and looking at women. Indeed, Nābulusī alludes to such a difference on more than one occasion: looking at the opposite sex was more likely to give rise to lust than looking at the identical sex; a man's sexual desire for a woman was "natural" (*ṭabīʿī*), whereas his desire for a beardless boy—by implication—was not.[21] Such statements look deceptively like modern assertions to the effect that "homosexuality" is "unnatural," and it ought to be remembered that Nābulusī was an outspoken defender of the passionate love of boys, and obviously did not regard sensitivity to the beauty of beardless youths as abnormal. The appeal to nature should be seen within the context of the overall controversy. As in the case of the realist and idealist perspectives on love, both sides in the juridical dispute were appealing to propositions which separately were regarded as truisms, but which were potentially in conflict with one another. On the one hand, it was widely believed that sexual intercourse, and the attraction leading to it, ought in principle to occur between a male and a female, and that sexual attraction or intercourse between men or between women was at variance with the divinely sanctioned order of things. In the juridical literature, it was repeatedly asserted that neither the anus nor the male was created for the purpose of being sexually penetrated. The (false) supposition that homosexual intercourse is unknown among animals, repeatedly heard in Western history from antiquity to the present, was also not foreign to the premodern Middle East. According to Ibn Ḥajar al-Haytamī: "We do not find a male animal who copulates with his like."[22] On the other hand, there was an equally widespread conviction that beardless youths posed a temptation to adult men as a whole, and not merely to a small minority of deviants.

Perhaps the most striking evidence for this belief is the ruling of the Mālikī school of law concerning minor ritual ablution (*wuḍūʾ*). One of the items that negate the state of ritual purity and necessitate *wuḍūʾ* is, according to authoritative manuals of the school, touching with lust the flesh of that "which is normally the object of lust (*mā yushtahā ʿādatan*)" or that "which normally gives rise to pleasure (*yaltadhdh ṣāḥibuhu bihi ʿādatan*)." Thus, commentators of the manuals explained, a man would negate his state of ritual purity if he touched with lust the skin of an unrelated woman, but not an animal, a child, a corpse, or another bearded man. Mālikī scholars of the early Ottoman period repeatedly confirmed that a man would negate his state of ritual purity if he touched with lust the skin of a beardless or downy-cheeked youth, since they fell under the category of that "which is normally the object of lust."[23]

To be sure, it is not logically inconsistent to hold that a phenomenon is "unnatural" and yet common. But by emphasizing one rather than the other of these claims, diametrically opposed positions could be reached on a specific issue. Scholars who wished to prohibit looking at boys emphasized their feminine attractiveness, thus assimilating their case to that of women: "and that is because he is a suspected source of temptation like women"; "because he is a suspected source of temptation, for he is as women when talk is of the beautiful of face and the tender of body."[24] Alternatively, those who insisted that looking at boys was permitted as long as it was not linked to lust emphasized the masculine gender of the boy and thus assimilated him to the bearded adult: "because he is a male similar to the bearded"; "and a man may look at another man, even a handsome beardless youth, except for what is between the navel and the knees."[25]

Most jurists in the early Ottoman period dissented from the view that looking at youths was prohibited. The dominant position, even among Shāfiʿīs, was to permit it in the absence of lust.[26] To that extent, the beardless youth was to be treated as an adult male. However, traces of anxiety remained, and the permission was often qualified. Ibn ʿĀbidīn, after discussing the issue of looking at youths and concluding that it is permissible in the absence of lust, nevertheless added that "it is clear that it is more circumspect not to look at all."[27] The Egyptian Ḥanbalī jurist Manṣūr al-Buhūtī (d. 1641) cited the ruling of his school that "it is permissible . . . for a man to look at what is not taboo [i.e., what is between the navel and the knees] of another man, even a beardless boy," but almost immediately added: "but if the beardless boy is beautiful and temptation is to be feared from looking at him, it is not allowed to make a habit of looking at him."[28] The qualifications sometimes explicitly ruled out notions of an aestheticist appreciation of boyish beauty. The Egyptian-based Ḥanbalī scholar Marʿī ibn Yūsuf al-Karmī (d. 1624) quoted the prominent and controversial Ibn Taymiyyah (d. 1328) as stating that "he who repeatedly looks or gazes at the beardless boy and says 'I am not looking with lust' is lying."[29] The Egyptian Shāfiʿī scholars Shams al-Dīn Muḥammad al-Ramlī (d. 1596) and Ibrāhīm al-Bājūrī (d. 1860), two representatives of "the way of al-Rāfiʿī," both cited a fourteenth-century jurist of their school as saying: "Many people look at the beautiful beardless boy while delighting in his beauty and loving him, and think that they are free from sin since they confine themselves to looking without desiring fornication (*al-fāḥishah*), and they are not free [from sin]."[30] In the same vein, the Egyptian Mālikī jurist ʿAbd al-Bāqī al-Zurqānī (d. 1688) quoted an authority of his school as saying: "And they [scholars] have agreed upon the prohibition of looking at him [the beardless boy] with the intention of obtaining pleasure and delighting the eye with his charms."[31] Adult men's interaction with boys was the object of juridical restrictions that were absent in the case of interaction between adult men. The prominent Palestinian jurist Khayr al-Dīn al-Ramlī (d. 1671) opined that a father could force his legally mature son to reside with him, and restrict his freedom of movement, if the son was still a handsome youth (*ghulām ṣabīḥ*).[32] Several Ḥanafī scholars deemed that it was disapproved (*makrūh*) for a comely beardless or downy-cheeked youth to function as leader (*imām*) of communal prayer.[33] As has been mentioned, the Mālikī school ruled that touching a beardless or downy-cheeked youth with lust negated a man's state of ritual purity. Shāfiʿī jurists of the period asserted that, even if looking at boys was not prohibited, touching them or being alone with them was, again by analogy with unrelated women. Thus the Egyptian jurist ʿAlī al-Zayyādī (d. 1615) said: "Being alone with him [the beardless boy] or touching a part of his body is prohibited even according to the way of al-Rāfiʿī."[34] Marʿī ibn Yūsuf al-Karmī cited the opinion that "being alone with, and sleeping next to, a handsome beardless youth is [prohibited] as in the case of a woman."[35] Though it seems to have remained a minority view among jurists, the idea that looking at, and being alone with, a beardless boy was prohibited was influential enough to be reflected in the belles-lettres of the period. One of the "arguments" attributed to the downy-cheeked youth in ʿAlī al-Dabbāgh al-Mīqātī's literary disputation—discussed in the previous chapter—is that "looking at him [the beardless boy] is prohibited while looking at me is permitted . . . being alone with him is prohibited as in the case of the unrelated woman."[36] Indeed, the controversy over looking seems to have been echoed outside scholarly circles. The Aleppine biographer Ibn al-Ḥanbalī mentioned a local maker of *sanbūsak* (i.e., small meat pies) who was "inclined to loving youths, so if it was said to him: Are you a Rāfiʿī or a Nawawī? he would answer: Rāfiʿī."[37]

Liwāṭ in Islamic Law

The apprehensions concerning looking at, touching, or being alone with women or youths was in large part due to these acts being considered "preliminaries" (*muqaddimāt*) of what was, by common agreement, one of the "major sins" (*kabāʾir*). Fornication (*zinā*) was indeed considered to be inferior only to unbelief (*kufr* or *shirk*) and murder (*qatl*) in gravity. Islamic law treats it as a transgression against "a right of God" (*ḥaqq Allāh*)—as opposed to transgressions against the rights of other humans (*ḥaqq ādamī*)—for which a prescribed punishment, a *ḥadd,* had been revealed in the Qurʾan or the Sunnah.[38] In juridical works on positive law (*furūʿ*), anal intercourse between men (*liwāṭ*) was invariably discussed within this context. The four acknowledged schools of law in the Ottoman Empire differed somewhat in their assessment of the penalty for *liwāṭ,* and it is therefore appropriate to discuss each of them separately.

Ḥanafī

The Ḥanafī school of law occupied a special position by virtue of being the official school of the Ottoman Empire.[39] Predominant in Turkey, the school also had adherents among the Arabic-speaking Sunnī Muslims of the Empire, the majority of whom, however, were Shāfiʿī. Of the four Sunnī schools of law, the Ḥanafī was unique in that it did not consider *liwāṭ* to be a variety of fornication, and thus not liable to *ḥadd* at all. The rationale behind the ruling was in part definitional: the school simply defined *zinā* as vaginal intercourse between two persons legally forbidden to each other. Anal intercourse, between two men or between a man and a woman, was different, argued the jurists of the school, both in that the desire leading to it (usually) came only from the active party, and in that it did not have the same consequences for which *zinā* had been forbidden. Furthermore, the punishment for *zinā* was specified by revelation, while the punishment meted out to *lūṭīs* by the Companions of the Prophet varied: some burned them alive, others threw them off the highest building in the city, others demolished a wall above them, etc. Though such examples suggest a more severe punishment for *liwāṭ* than for *zinā,* the somewhat scholastic conclusion of Ḥanafī jurists was that *liwāṭ* should then be punished by discretionary chastisement (*taʿzīr*), and this was usually less severe than *ḥadd.* For instance, if chastisement took the form of whipping, the number of lashes should not exceed thirty-nine, which is one less than the lowest number of lashes in a case of *ḥadd.* The form of chastisement was in principle left to the discretion of the presiding judge. The punishment most often suggested by the jurists of the period was whipping and/or imprisonment, with the proviso that repeat offenders could—and according to others should—be put to death. In the various Ottoman codes of law (*qānūn*), which in theory constituted the basis for the rulings of state-appointed judges within the Empire, the punishment for active sodomy tended to be a fine, the heaviness of which depended on the perpetrator's marital status (married men were punished more severely than unmarried) and his economic condition. Passive sodomy usually merited a discretionary number of whip lashes, and a fine.[40]

Shāfiʿī

Followers of the Shāfiʿī school of law were predominant in Syria, Lower Egypt, Western Arabia (the Hijaz), and amongst the Sunnīs of Iraq.[41] The school considered *liwāṭ* a variant or subtype of *zinā,* but the punishment prescribed was somewhat peculiar. In the case of illicit vaginal intercourse, the offender, if *muḥṣan*—that is, if he or she was in a state of *iḥṣān,* having once consummated a legally valid marriage—was liable to death by stoning. If not *muḥṣan,* the punishment was one hundred lashes (fifty for the slave) and banishment for a year. In the case of anal intercourse, whether between two men or between a man and a woman (who was not his wife or concubine), the punishment was the same, except that the passive, penetrated partner was never liable to stoning. The somewhat peculiar reason given was that the anus is not included in the state of *iḥṣān.* The Egyptian scholar Sulaymān al-Bujayrimī (d. 1806) explained that "the state of *iḥṣān* is irrelevant to he who is penetrated in his anus, since there is no conceivable way of licitly inserting a penis into an anus in order for the state of *iḥṣān* to effect a difference in the punishment prescribed for him [the passive partner]."[42] The implicit reasoning seems to have been the following: the state of *iḥṣān* means that one has had access to licit vaginal intercourse, and this should satisfy the normal "phallic-insertive" urges of the man and the "vaginal-receptive" urges of the woman. A man who is *muḥṣan* and yet assumes the "active" or "insertive" role in an illicit sexual relationship is therefore being particularly willful and merits a harsher punishment than he who is not *muḥṣan.* However, in the case of voluntary subjection to anal intercourse, it is questionable whether being *muḥṣan* similarly makes the transgression any more willful and hence more heinous.

Shāfiʿī jurists of the period sometimes mentioned, but did not adopt, a different ruling based on a tradition attributed to the Prophet: "Those whom you find committing the act of the people of Lot, kill the active and the passive partner." The tradition was considered to be sound (*ṣaḥīḥ*), and was included in three of the six collections of traditions that Sunnī Muslims considered especially authoritative. However, there was no straightforward connection between a particular sound tradition and the ruling of a school of law. Jurists could, for instance, explain away one tradition by appealing to another. They could also press the point that a tradition which would legitimate the execution of Muslims had to be not only sound but also impeccable, and the tradition calling for the execution of the active and passive partner was not included in the two most authoritative collections of *ḥadīth* (by Bukhārī and Muslim).[43] The ruling of the Shāfiʿī school was based partly on analogy with heterosexual fornication, and partly on other traditions. One such tradition had the Prophet Muḥammad say: "If a man has intercourse with a man, the two are [to be considered] fornicators," and another had the third caliph of Islam, ʿUthmān, acting upon the advice of the Prophet's son-in-law ʿAlī, ruling that a *lūṭī* who was not *muḥṣan* was liable to a hundred whip lashes. These latter traditions were, however, not included in a comparably authoritative collection.[44] In the late nineteenth and early twentieth centuries, the Salafī movement in the Islamic world would launch an attack on juridical scholasticism and call for a return to the textual sources of Islamic law. The movement was inspired by earlier scholars such as Ibn Taymiyyah (d. 1328) and his disciple Ibn Qayyim al-Jawziyyah (d. 1350), and the Yemenis Muḥammad ibn Ismāʿīl al-Amīr (d. 1768) and Muḥammad al-Shawkānī (d. 1834). From the perspective of such "purist" critics of legal scholasticism, the explaining away of the *ḥadīth* calling for the killing of both the active and the passive sodomite was wrong-headed.[45]

Ḥanbalī

In the early Ottoman Arab Middle East, the Ḥanbalī school was numerically of less importance than the Shāfiʿī or the Ḥanafī.[46] There were followers of the school in various parts of geographic Syria, such as Baʿalbak, Nablus, and Damascus. However, the major concentration of Ḥanbalīs was in the central Arabian highlands of Najd, which was outside effective Ottoman control and which in the eighteenth century became the center of the revivalist Wahhābī movement. According to the ruling of the school, *liwāṭ* was to be punished as illicit vaginal intercourse: if the offender was a *muḥṣan* the punishment was stoning to death, otherwise one hundred lashes (fifty for a slave). As in the case of the Shāfiʿī school, a more severe punishment based on the above-mentioned tradition was sometimes cited. However, it was again overruled by reference to the same traditions on which the Shāfiʿī ruling rested. All the major Ḥanbalī juridical works produced in the early Ottoman period expounded the rule that *liwāṭ* should be punished as illicit vaginal intercourse. This applies to the works of the Egyptian-based jurists Marʿī ibn Yūsuf al-Karmī (d. 1624), Manṣūr al-Buhūtī (d. 1641), and ʿUthmān al-Najdī (d. 1686), and the Damascene-based Mūsā al-Ḥajjāwī (d. 1560) and ʿAbd al-Qādir al-Taghlibī (d. 1723). The works of these jurists are still considered authoritative by present-day Ḥanbalīs, but some modern scholars of the school, presumably influenced by Ibn Taymiyyah, Ibn Qayyim al-Jawziyyah, and the later Salafī movement, seem to have departed from their ruling concerning *liwāṭ* and to have adopted the more severe punishment, according to which offenders are to be executed regardless of marital status.[47]

Mālikī

The Mālikī school was predominant in North Africa and Upper Egypt.[48] It was unique among the four Sunnī schools in distinguishing between the punishment of anal intercourse between a man and a woman (who is not his wife or concubine) and between two men. The former was to be punished as illicit vaginal intercourse, while the latter made the offenders liable to unconditional stoning. Contrary to the assertions of the article "Liwāṭ" in the *Encyclopaedia of Islam,* it was thus the Mālikī school and not the Ḥanbalī that had the most severe ruling on sodomy between men among the Sunnī schools of law, at least in the early Ottoman period.[49]

Imāmī Shīʿī

The Imāmī or "Twelver" Shīʿī school of law was not recognized within the Ottoman Empire.[50] There were nevertheless followers of the school in Iraq, eastern Arabia, Jabal ʿĀmil in what is today southern Lebanon, and (as a clandestine minority) in the Holy Cities of Mecca and Medina. The Imāmī Shīʿī school of law is more severe than even the Mālikī school when it comes to *liwāṭ*. It prescribes the death penalty (the manner of death is left open) for both partners, regardless of marital status. Non-anal intercourse between men, which all the Sunnī schools regard as a minor sin punishable by discretionary chastisement, is considered a major sin and is punishable by one hundred lashes, and four-time offenders are to be executed. Though this was the considered position, Shīʿī jurists often mentioned and discussed even more severe punishments. It is perhaps natural to ask why the Shīʿī school of law is more severe on this point than the Sunnī schools. It is, however, difficult to answer such a question. Shīʿī jurists, like their Sunnī counterparts, simply appealed to the opinions of previous jurists of their school, and to the traditions they recognized as authoritative. However, simply citing these factors as an explanation of the different rulings is clearly not very satisfying, since this merely invites the further question of why the traditions recognized by the Shīʿī school are more severe than those recognized by the Sunnī schools. In any case, the Shīʿī ruling on *liwāṭ* goes back at least to the thirteenth century, when the scholar al-Muḥaqqiq al-Ḥillī (d. 1277) composed the influential law-manual *Sharāʾiʿ al-Islām.* To pursue the origins of the comparative severity of the rulings is thus well beyond the scope of the present study.

The cited rulings of authoritative Islamic jurists on *liwāṭ* offer a corrective to the view, expressed for instance by V. Bullough in his *Sexual Variance in Society and History,* that "Islam" regards homosexual sodomy as a less serious crime than heterosexual fornication, and that the punishments it lays down for the activity are "ambiguous."[51] Bullough's opinion seems to have been based on a few translated manuals of Ḥanafī law, and he supported it by claiming that the only passage in the Qurʾan which could be interpreted as specifying the punishment for homosexual conduct was: "If two of you commit it, then hurt them both; but if they turn again and amend, leave them alone, verily, God is easily turned, compassionate" (4:16). The phrase "the two of you" translates the Arabic *al-ladhān,* which is the dual masculine form of the relative pronoun. In the immediately preceding verse (4:15), the Qurʾan speaks of "those of your women who commit adultery." This has led some Islamic commentators to interpret Qurʾan 4:15 as referring to sexual intercourse between two women, and Qurʾan 4:16 to sexual intercourse between two men. Bullough pointed out that the stipulated sentence seems to be both ambiguous and mild, repentance on the part of the perpetrators apparently relieving them of punishment. However, the Qurʾanic passage he invoked was simply not considered by Islamic scholars to be the basis for legal opinions on the punishment for sodomy. First, as Bullough himself acknowledged, not all scholars understood the verse as applying to homosexual intercourse. In fact, even Ḥanafī commentators, whom one might expect to have exploited the verse in defense of their school's peculiar ruling on *liwāṭ,* interpreted the verse as applying to fornication between a man and a woman.[52] Second, even the Qurʾanic commentators who did hold that the verse originally applied to *liwāṭ* quickly added that the punishment mentioned had been abrogated (*mansūkh*) by later passages which called for the flogging or stoning of fornicators, including sodomites.[53]

Legal conviction of unlawful intercourse presupposed either voluntary confession, or witnesses to the act of penetration. The minimum number of witnesses required for conviction of *liwāṭ* was four according to the Shāfiʿī, Ḥanbalī, Mālikī, and Imāmī Shīʿī schools, and two according to the Ḥanafī school (since it did not regard *liwāṭ* as a case requiring *ḥadd*). The witnesses were to be *ʿadl* ("of good character"—that is, not to have committed major sins themselves, or persevered in minor ones), free (as opposed to slaves), male, and Muslim. They had to testify to having seen the genital contact; having seen the couple together under a blanket, for instance, is not enough. It has often been remarked that the stipulated preconditions make conviction for unlawful intercourse practically impossible. However, this was not regarded by jurists as regrettable. According to the Medinese-based scholar ʿAlī al-Qāriʾ al-Harawī (d. 1614): "It is a condition that the witnesses [necessary for a conviction of fornication] are four . . . and this is because God the Exalted likes [the vices of] his servants to remain concealed, and this is realized by demanding four witnesses, since it is very rare for four people to observe this vice."[54] Far from encouraging people to denounce their fellows, the jurists explicitly upheld the ideal of "overlooking" or "concealing" (*satr*) the vices of others, except in cases of repeated and unabashed transgressions. The Egyptian scholar and mystic ʿAbd al-Wahhāb al-Shaʿrānī (d. 1565), for example, thanked God that he was able to fulfill his obligation to regularly "conceal" the vices of his fellow Muslims who were not ostentatious in their transgressions of divine law.[55] It was thus generally agreed that witnessing in a case of *zinā* was "contrary to what is most appropriate" (*khilāf al-awlā*).[56] The same applied to confession; it was best for the offender to refrain from publicizing his misdeed, and to repent in silence.[57]

The Islamic jurists also operated with the principle that the scope of *ḥadd* punishments should be reduced as much as possible by evoking the possibility of unintentional transgression caused by a confusing "resemblance" (*shubhah*). The principle was based on a saying attributed to the Prophet: "Ward off *ḥadd* punishments as much as you can," or according to a different version, "Ward off *ḥadd* punishments with resemblances (*shubuhāt*)."[58] *Shubhah* could arise, for example, if a slave claimed that he or she had been forced to commit fornication by his or her master; when a recent convert to Islam or a Muslim from an isolated or outlying area claimed that he was unaware of the prohibition; or if a man had sexual intercourse with his father's female slave, or anal intercourse with his own wife or concubine. A few jurists even held that prostitution constituted a *shubhah,* since paying a woman for sex might be taken to "resemble" the dowry paid by the groom to his bride.[59]

Ḥanafī jurists, who were well aware that the other schools held *ḥadd* punishments to be applicable to *liwāṭ,* nevertheless claimed that there existed a consensus to the effect that discretionary chastisement (*ta'zīr*) rather than *ḥadd* was applicable in case a man had anal intercourse with his male slave, because of a mitigating *shubhah.*[60] Thus, the Ḥanafī Mufti of Aleppo Muḥammad al-Kawākibī (d. 1685) wrote:

> If, however, he commits *liwāṭ* with his male slave, or female slave, or wife, then he is by consensus (*ijmā'*) not liable to *ḥadd,* since there are those who deem it is permissible [to do so] on the basis of the saying of the Exalted [Qur'an 23:6 and 70:30]: "Except for their wives or what their right hands possess."[61]

This was contradicted, however, by the jurists of the other schools who asserted that *shubhah* did not apply to male slaves. *Liwāṭ* with a male slave was consequently to be considered as equivalent to *liwāṭ* with any other man.[62] It was often underlined that there was a binding consensus (*ijmā'*) among scholars that the Qur'anic verses that allow a man to have sexual intercourse with his slaves only applied to female slaves.[63] The very fact that the jurists were eager to point this out suggests that the interpretation that they wished to disallow had, at one time or other, been voiced, and was possibly still advanced outside of scholarly circles. The Ḥanafī jurist Ḥaṣkafī asserted that a person who interprets the relevant Qur'anic verses as legitimizing *liwāṭ* with a male slave was to be regarded as an apostate (*murtadd*). Yet, other jurists of the same school, such as Ibn 'Ābidīn, stated that a person who claims that *liwāṭ* with a male slave is permissible is not thereby to be considered an unbeliever.[64] This would make *liwāṭ* with a male slave equivalent, from a Sunnī point of view, to "temporary" (*mut'ah*) marriage (which is allowed by the Shī'ī school of law): both were prohibited, but a person who upholds its permissibility is not an unbeliever. Other Ḥanafī jurists specified that it is anal intercourse with a female slave or wife that could be claimed to be permitted without falling into unbelief.[65] In any case, this whole line of thought was said to be one of the things that are "known [by scholars] but should not be made known [to people in general]" (*yu'lam wa lā yu'lam*).

The condemnation of *liwāṭ,* and most probably the word itself, may be traced to the Qur'an.[66] On several occasions, the Qur'an refers to the peculiar vice of the people of Sodom to whom the Prophet Lot (*Lūṭ*) had been sent (translations by E. H. Palmer):

> 7:81–82—and Lot, when he said unto his folk, "Will ye commit abomination such as no creature ever did before you? Lo, ye come with lust unto men instead of women. Nay, but ye are wanton folk."

26 : 165—when their brother Lot said to them . . . "Do ye approach males of all the world and leave what God your Lord has created for you of your wives? nay, but ye are people who transgress."

27 : 55—And Lot when he said to his people, "Do ye approach an abominable sin while ye can see? do ye indeed approach men lustfully rather than women? nay! ye are a people who are ignorant."

29 : 29—And Lot when he said to his people, "Verily, ye approach an abomination which no one in all the world anticipated you in! What! do ye approach men? and stop folks on the highway? and approach in your assembly sin?"

The Qur'an (11 : 77ff.; 15 : 61ff.) also relates that God sent "messengers" (traditionally interpreted as angels in human form) to Lot, and that the inhabitants of the town "hurried" to the host, presumably to rape his guests. Lot offered his own daughters to the aggressive townsmen instead but was rebuffed. Thereafter God destroyed the people of Lot with a rain of "stones of baked clay," and by "making their high parts their low parts"; the latter was usually interpreted to mean that their land had been raised up to the sky and then turned upside down. Both forms of divine punishment were reflected in the otherwise peculiar above-mentioned penalties for *liwāṭ:* burning the perpetrators alive, throwing them down from the highest part of a city, or demolishing a wall over them. Interestingly, the relevant passages of the Qur'an do not specify which sexual acts had been committed by the people of Lot. Nevertheless, from an early period, Muslim jurists identified "the act of the people of Lot" (*fiʿl qawm Lūṭ*) with anal intercourse, to the extent that in juridical terminology *liwāṭ* could be used to refer to anal intercourse between a man and a woman.

Several sayings (*ḥadīth*) attributed to the Prophet Muḥammad are also severely condemnatory of *liwāṭ*. Two of these have already been mentioned, one demanding the death penalty for both partners and the other classifying *liwāṭ* as *zinā*. In addition, one may cite the following:[67]

That which I fear most for my people (*ummatī*) is the act of the people of Lot [variants of this tradition ascribe this status to other vices such as fornication or drinking wine].

If sodomites (*al-lūṭiyyah*) become common, God, the Glorious and Exalted, will wash his hand of mankind and not care in which abyss they perish.

May God curse he who commits the act of the people of Lot.

God, the Glorious and Exalted, has no regard for a man who has intercourse with a man or a woman in her anus.

> Four will face the anger of God and witness the wrath of God: men who adopt the antics of women; women who adopt the antics of men; he who commits bestiality; and he who sodomizes men.

As regards the last tradition, it is noteworthy that "men who adopt the antics of women" and "he who sodomizes men" (*al-ladhī ya'tī al-rijāl*) are assumed to belong to different categories. The vices that tradition ascribed to the people of Lot were numerous, and a few sources did include the vice of "using henna and adorning themselves like women."[68] Yet their dominant image as presented by commentators of the Qur'an was not one of effeminacy but rather of aggressive masculinity. The objects of the Sodomites' desires were, on one account, said to be strangers passing through their areas. In the popular fifteenth-century commentary of "the two Jalāls" (Jalāl al-Dīn al-Maḥallī and Jalāl al-Dīn al-Suyūṭī), the phrase "stop folks on the highway" (*taqṭaʿūn al-sabīl*) was interpreted as sexual assault on travelers.[69] Some commentators explicitly stated that the people of Lot only sodomized strangers (*kānū lā yafʿalūna dhālika illā bi-al-ghurabā'*).[70] According to other traditions, the people of Lot were pederasts. Qur'anic commentators of the period apparently agreed that the angels who visited Lot and whom the Sodomites wanted to rape had assumed the form of handsome, beardless youths.[71] Abū al-Suʿūd Efendī (d. 1574), the Ottoman Grand Mufti, explained that the Qur'an spoke of the people of Lot having intercourse with "men" (*rijāl*) rather than "youths" (*ghilmān*) by way of emphasizing the despicable nature of their deed, and not—one may infer—because the sodomized were actually adults.[72] The traditions according to which "the people of Lot" raped strangers and sodomized boys were, of course, not irreconcilable. According to one much-cited tradition, they started to sodomize strangers as a way of driving visitors and immigrants from their prosperous land, and then started to become addicted to the vice after having raped handsome, beardless youths. Some accounts had Satan assume the form of a wise old man recommending sodomy as a way of getting rid of strangers; other accounts had him assume the form of a very handsome youth who was the first "victim" of the policy and who thereby corrupted the tastes of the Sodomites; and yet other accounts had him play both roles.[73]

The jurists' discussion of *liwāṭ* sometimes included brief considerations on whether it was more or less grave a sin than *zinā* between a man and a woman. Given the rulings of their school, the opinion of Mālikī and Imāmī Shīʿī jurists could not be in doubt. To jurists of the other schools the question was in principle open, though most of them seem to have agreed that *liwāṭ* was the more abominable of the two. It should be emphasized that what was being compared was not "homosexuality" and "heterosexuality," but "anal intercourse between men" and "illicit vaginal intercourse between men and women." Non-anal intercourse between men was, at least for all the Sunnī schools of law, not as grave a sin as illicit vaginal intercourse between a man and a woman. The arguments adduced in discussions of the relative gravity of the two acts tend to fall into the following three types:

(i) Appeal to religious tradition: The Egyptian scholars ʿAbd al-Wahhāb al-Shaʿrānī (d. 1565) and ʿAlī al-ʿAzīzī al-Būlāqī (d. 1658) both emphasized that the Qurʾanic verses and the sayings of the Prophet which condemn *liwāṭ* are, on the whole, more severe in tone than those which condemn *zinā*.[74] The Ḥanbalī Marʿī ibn Yūsuf al-Karmī also considered *liwāṭ* more reprehensible than *zinā*, and based his judgment on the fact that "some" scholars held that the former should be punished more severely than the latter.[75] A tradition related by the Shīʿī scholar Muḥammad al-Ḥurr al-ʿĀmilī (d. 1693) said: "The inviolability (*ḥurmah*) of the anus is greater than the inviolability of the vagina, and God destroyed a people because of the inviolability of the anus and did not destroy anyone because of the inviolability of the vagina."[76]

(ii) Appeal to the repulsiveness of *liwāṭ:* Several scholars asserted that *liwāṭ* is "contrary to natural disposition" (*muḥarram ṭabʿan*), in the sense that it is repulsive to people of "sound character" (*al-ṭabʿ al-salīm*), whereas *zinā* is not.[77] The same belief would seem to be presupposed by several commentators of the Qurʾan when they stated that the act pioneered by the people of Lot was something that was so abominable that it had not occurred to humans before that time. Abū al-Suʿūd Efendī explained the absence of *liwāṭ* in the pre-Sodomite era in terms of its "completely abominable character, for the agreement of all individuals of mankind in shunning it [until then] is only because it is what disgusts dispositions and repels inclinations."[78] Again, it bears emphasizing that it is *liwāṭ* and not "homosexuality" that was said to be contrary to "sound character." In accordance with juridical terminology, *liwāṭ* would not include instances of non-anal intercourse between men, but could easily apply to anal intercourse between a man and a woman. The statement that *liwāṭ* is repulsive to someone of "sound character" is therefore most safely interpreted to mean that anal intercourse is repulsive to those of "sound character," regardless of whether two men or a man and a woman were involved. Such an assumption does not, however, by itself imply that the people who committed the act were thought to be pathologically abnormal. The term "sound character" is hardly a purely descriptive medical term. Like the term *dāʾ* discussed in chapter 1, it can often be used in an almost purely evaluative sense. The Egyptian scholar ʿAbd al-Raʾūf al-Munāwī (d. 1622) explicated the claim that *liwāṭ* is contrary to sound character in the following manner: for the passive partner the inducement to commit the act was either effeminacy or a pathological itch in the rectum; for the active agent, it was the rational faculty's subservience to animal desires.[79] In the latter case, the failing was thus clearly of a moral rather than pathological character. The idea that the people of Lot behaved "animalistically" (*bahīmiyyah*) in pursuing sexual pleasure with no regard to the divinely sanctioned purpose behind intercourse—progeny and "fortification" against fornication—was repeatedly asserted in the Qur'anic commentaries of the period.[80] To be sure, there was a potential tension in condemning an act as unnatural and hence absent from the animal kingdom, and condemning its perpetrators as "animalistic." Presumably, we are dealing with another expression of the above-mentioned tension between believing that *liwāṭ* is contrary to the natural order of things, and that *liwāṭ* is a common temptation to be kept in check by reason and religion (which animals lack).

(iii) Appeal to consequences: The Egyptian Shāfiʿī jurist ʿAlī al-Shabrāmallisī (d. 1676) judged *liwāṭ* to be less reprehensible than *zinā,* since it did not result in the confusion of lineages.[81] The Ḥanbalī scholar Muḥammad al-Saffārīnī (d. 1774) considered *liwāṭ* to be more heinous than *zinā* if the two acts were compared in isolation, but added that *zinā* was the graver sin in respect of the consequences, since it led to the confusion of lineages.[82] Ḥanafī jurists also referred to this difference between *liwāṭ* and *zinā* in their arguments for their school's position that the former sin was to be punished by discretionary chastisement rather than *ḥadd.* The same point was cited by Shaʿrānī as a possible argument in favor of the superior gravity of *zinā,* though he himself adopted the contrary conclusion. Another remark by Shaʿrānī is interesting in that it allows a glimpse of a more concrete difference in the respective consequences of *liwāṭ* and *zinā:* "People are not as zealously protective of the male, and do not venture to kill the one who sodomizes him, as they are zealously protective of free women if someone commits fornication with them."[83] Sodomy might have been considered more reprehensible than fornication by a majority of jurists, but it could very well have been both easier and safer in a premodern, gender-segregated society in which private vengeance was possibly a more immediate threat than state action.

Liwāṭ in Paradise?

The discussion of the comparative gravity of *liwāṭ* and *zinā* was related to the question of the rationale behind their prohibition by God. As regards illicit vaginal intercourse, the reason adduced was invariably the danger of a confusion of lineages (*ikhtilāṭ al-ansāb*). It was often remarked by jurists that *zinā* was thus prohibited by all communities (*milal*), and not just the Islamic.[84] To the extent that rational arguments were given for the prohibition of *liwāṭ*, these appealed to the aforementioned belief that the divinely sanctioned purpose of sexual intercourse was to propagate the species. According to the Egyptian scholar ʿAbd al-Raʾūf al-Munāwī (d. 1622):

> Everything created by God in this world He has made suitable for a specific function and so is not suitable for anything else, and He has made the male for [sexual] activity and the female for [sexual] passivity and has instilled in both of them the desire for procreation and the continuity of the species, so the person who reverses [this order of things] counteracts this divine wisdom.[85]

The Egyptian scholar Sulaymān al-Jamal (d. 1790) cited the following opinion:

> God, the Blessed and Exalted, created man and instilled in him the desire for intercourse to ensure the continuity of the species and the peopling and prosperity of the world, and made women the object of sexual desire and the source of offspring; so if man abandons them and turns instead to other men, he dissipates and exceeds and contravenes because he puts something beside the proper place and locality for which it has been created, because the anus of men is not a place for childbirth, which is the purpose of this desire in man.[86]

According to the Egyptian-based scholar Muḥammad Murtaḍā al-Zabīdī (d. 1791):

> It [i.e., *liwāṭ*] is worse than *zinā* because *zinā* is the placing of the seed in a fertile recipient in an improper way and is like planting in someone else's land . . . and in the case of *liwāṭ* the seed is destroyed, and its perpetrator is like those of whom God has said that they "destroy the tillage and the stock" [Qur'an 2:205], and for this reason He has condemned the people of Lot for "dissipation" (*isrāf*), saying, "Lo, ye come unto men instead of women. Nay, but ye are wanton folk (*musrifūn*)."[87]

Muḥammad al-Ḥurr al-ʿĀmilī related a Shīʿī tradition according to which ʿAlī ibn Abī Ṭālib had been asked by a heretic (*zindīq*) for the reason behind the prohibition of *liwāṭ*. ʿAlī supposedly answered: "If carnal penetration of a boy (*ityān al-ghulām*) were permitted, men would dispense with women, and this would lead to the disruption of procreation and the inoperativeness of vaginas (*taʿṭīl al-furūj*), and from allowing this much evil would arise."[88]

The proposed justification for the prohibition of *liwāṭ* would of course not hold in a world in which there was sexual intercourse but no childbirth. Such a world was, according to premodern Islamic tradition, paradise. While the

Qur'an speaks somewhat vaguely of the (male) believers being "wed" to houris who were beautiful, loving, and virginal, the religious tradition elaborated on the sexual nature of this wedlock to an extent that many modern Muslims find distasteful: each man would receive dozens, perhaps even hundreds, of beautiful maidens; he would receive the potency of a hundred men; each maiden would be passionately fond of copulation and her hymen would be reconstituted after each intercourse.[89] Several scholars also discussed the issue of whether sodomy could be present in paradise. The issue was raised by one of the most prominent Ḥanafī jurists of the early Ottoman period, the Egyptian Zayn al-ʿĀbidīn ibn Nujaym (d. 1563) in his *al-Ashbāh wa al-naẓā'ir.* With laconic brevity, he sketched three possibilities:

> [1] The prohibition of *liwāṭ* is established by reason and so it will not be found in heaven; [2] and it has been said, [the prohibition is established solely] by revelation and so it will be found in it; [3] and it has been said, God the Exalted will create a group whose upper half will be like males and whose lower half will be like females; and the correct [position] is the first.[90]

It is not clear what is meant by the assertion that *liwāṭ* will not be found in heaven if its proscription is established by reason. As later commentators of this passage pointed out, the dominant theological position amongst Sunnī Muslims held that nothing can be religiously proscribed by reason alone. At most, human reason may comprehend the rationale behind some of the prohibitions established by divine revelation.[91] This is precisely what was attempted by the scholars who cited God's purpose behind instilling sexual desire in mankind, and their arguments do not imply that *liwāṭ* would be absent in heaven. In any case, the grounds that Ibn Nujaym gave in other works for preferring the first conclusion have nothing to do with *liwāṭ* being prohibited by reason independently of revelation. In his *al-Baḥr al-rā'iq,* an authoritative commentary on a compendium of Ḥanafī law, he appealed to the fact that the Qur'an deplored *liwāṭ* and indirectly called it a "foul deed" (*khabīthah*).[92] The problem with this argument, as pointed out by the Egyptian scholar Aḥmad al-Ḥamawī (d. 1687) in his commentary on Ibn Nujaym's *al-Ashbāh wa al-naẓā'ir,* is that it does not follow from a thing being denounced in such terms that it would not be found in heaven. Wine is called a satanic "filth" (*rijs*) in the Qur'an, but is nevertheless promised the believers in paradise. Ḥamawī himself grounded the absence of *liwāṭ* from paradise in the thesis that people will not have anuses in the hereafter, since they will not defecate. A similar resolution of the issue was offered by a prominent pupil of Ibn Nujaym, Muḥammad al-Tumurtāshī (d. 1595).[93] The fact that such a conclusion was regarded as satisfactory suggests that what was at issue was anal, rather than homosexual, intercourse. This may also be inferred from the remark of Ibn ʿĀbidīn to the third of the alternatives mentioned by Ibn Nujaym; the idea that God would create beings who were male from the waist up, but with female sexual organs: "This has nothing to do with the issue since the dispute concerns anal intercourse (*al-ityān fī al-dubur*)."[94] Ibn ʿĀbidīn here seems to identify *liwāṭ* with anal intercourse and to dismiss the question of the gender of the penetrated partner as irrelevant. This was in accordance with especially Ḥanafī usage: Ibn Nujaym spelled out the principle that "anal intercourse with the unrelated woman is also *liwāṭ*."[95] However, the jurists' use of the term was not entirely consistent. Ibn ʿĀbidīn himself commented thus on Ḥaṣkafī's assertion that *liwāṭ* is to be considered more reprehensible than *zinā:* "Intercourse with males cannot be made permissible, in contrast to intercourse with females, which becomes legal through marriage or procurement [of a concubine]."[96] The implication here is clearly that *liwāṭ* is something a man commits with another man. On this account, the *lūṭī* is someone who commits sodomy with men, not women. Commenting on the perceived irrelevance of the third alternative of Ibn Nujaym, the Egyptian Ḥanafī scholar Aḥmad al-Ṭahṭāwī (d. 1816) stated that "the interest of the *lūṭī* is in the lower half and if it is like a female his interest will not be met."[97] In juridical texts, the meaning of *liwāṭ* constantly oscillates in this way between the two senses of "*anal intercourse* between men" and "anal intercourse *between men*." An emphasis on the bodily organs involved implied that the term could be extended to cover anal intercourse between a man and a woman; an emphasis on the gender of the people involved suggested that other forms of sexual intercourse between men could be termed *liwāṭ*. A similar ambiguity seems to have been characteristic of the medieval European concept of "sodomy," which could even (in contrast to *liwāṭ*) be applied to cases of bestiality or oral intercourse.[98]

Another *locus classicus* for the question of whether *liwāṭ* could be among the pleasures of paradise is the following passage describing an eleventh-century debate on the issue:

> There occurred a discussion between Abū ʿAlī ibn al-Walīd al-Muʿtazilī and Abū Yūsuf al-Qazwīnī concerning the permissibility of intercourse with the boys of paradise (*al-wildān*). Ibn al-Walīd said, "It is not precluded that this should be part of the pleasures of paradise because of the cessation of its evil consequences, since it has been prohibited in this world because it involves the disruption of procreaction and because it [the anus] is the outlet of noxiousness (*adhā*), and these [procreation and excrement] are not to be found in paradise; for the same reason drinking wine will be permitted since it will not

> involve intoxication, boisterousness (*ʿarbadah*), and the paralysis of reason, and so there is nothing to preclude the permissibility of taking pleasure in it." So Abū Yūsuf said, "The inclination to males is a flaw (*ʿāhah*) and is vile (*qabīḥ*) in itself because it [the anus] is a place that has not been created for intercourse, and for this it [*liwāṭ*] is, in contrast to wine, not permitted by any law, and it [the anus] is the outlet of impurity (*ḥadath*), and paradise is free from flaws." So Ibn al-Walīd said, "The flaw is [to want] to be polluted with noxiousness (*adhā*), and if that is absent nothing remains but taking pleasure."[99]

Ibn al-Walīd al-Muʿtazilī (d. 1086) initially put forth the reasons for thinking that the prohibition of *liwāṭ* will not carry over into the next world: the prohibition is based partly on the this-worldly end of sexual intercourse, namely procreation, and partly on the "uncleanliness" of the anus. Neither factor would be relevant to a world in which sexual intercourse was for pleasure only, and in which there was neither procreation nor excrement. In the attempt to counter this argument, Abū Yūsuf al-Qazwīnī (d. 1095) made a claim that may look like a "modern" disqualification of homosexuality as perverse: "The inclination to males is a flaw, and is vile in itself." Such an understanding of the claim is, on closer consideration, questionable. Abū Yūsuf stated that "the inclination to males is a flaw" *because* the anus has not been created for being sexually penetrated and is the outlet of noxious excrement. What appears at first sight as a disqualification of "homosexuality" is actually a disqualification of the desire to phallically penetrate the anus. This is indeed the way in which the statement is understood by the opponent who protests that the inclination to males is only a flaw to the extent that it involves polluting oneself with "noxiousness," a clear reference to the excrement that a person would normally not want to touch with any part of his body. Both Abū Yūsuf's argument and Ibn al-Walīd's rejoinder apply equally to the desire to sodomize a woman. The desire to sodomize men is thus a "flaw" in the same sense as the desire to sodomize women. By contrast, the whole discussion presupposes that the desire to sodomize is not a "flaw" in the same sense as the desire to be sodomized. It would without doubt have seemed very outlandish to hold a serious discussion on whether the pleasures awaiting male believers in paradise could include being sodomized by beings especially created for that purpose.

The Iraqi scholar Maḥmūd al-Alūsī (d. 1854) took issue with the position of Ibn al-Walīd al-Muʿtazilī, and did so in terms that make it clear that the desire to sodomize was not regarded as a "flaw" in the same sense as the desire to be sodomized. Alūsī took Ibn al-Walīd al-Muʿtazilī to be denying that *liwāṭ* is "contrary to natural disposition," and countered by wondering whether Ibn al-Walīd would want to be anally penetrated in paradise. "If he wants today to be anally penetrated tomorrow, then the man is quite likely a *ma'būn*," that is, he would suffer from a pathological condition that it is safe to assume would not be present in paradise. Alūsī continued by pointing out that it would not help Ibn al-Walīd to "invoke the distinction between the active and the passive partner, as cannot but be clear to the clear-minded."[100] Alūsī could hardly be claiming that someone who wants to sodomize boys in the future is also a *ma'būn* now. Given the meaning of the term *ma'būn* explicated in the first chapter of this study, such a claim would make no sense. His point is rather that once it is established that a passive sodomite has an unsound character and that paradise is free from character flaws, then it follows that there will be no passive sodomites, and hence no sodomy, in paradise. The whole issue of why the desire to sodomize should be regarded as a "flaw" is neatly sidestepped.

Maḥmūd al-Alūsī's rejection of the idea that sodomy might be allowed in paradise seems to have been the most common verdict of scholars of the period who debated the issue. His opinion was, as has been seen, shared by Ibn Nujaym, Muḥammad al-Tumurtāshī, and Aḥmad al-Ḥamawī, and the verdict of these scholars was cited by others such as Muḥammad ʿAlāʾ al-Dīn al-Ḥaṣkafī, ʿAbd al-Ghanī al-Nābulusī, and Aḥmad al-Ṭahṭāwī.[101] It should be mentioned, however, that some scholars were not as eager to preclude the possibility. The following words by the prominent Egyptian scholar Muḥammad al-Ḥafnī (d. 1767), who was Rector (*Shaykh*) of the Azhar from 1758 to his death, must have given the reader the impression that the question was open:

> It has been said: *liwāṭ* is not permissible in paradise because of its filthiness; and it has been said: it is permissible, and the mentioned reason has been countered by pointing out that there is no filth or reproduction in paradise.[102]

At least one scholar of the period was prepared to defend the thesis that *liwāṭ* with boys would be part of the pleasures available to believers in paradise. The Turkish scholar Muḥammad Zīrekzāde (d. 1601) invoked the following two Qur'anic verses in support of the position:

> 76 : 19—And there shall go round about them eternal boys; when thou seest them thou wilt think them scattered pearls.
>
> 41 : 31—And ye shall have therein what ye call for.

Taken together, Zīrekzāde argued, the two verses suggested that boys would be sexually available to men in paradise: "The verse [76 : 19] implies that there will be handsome beardless boys in paradise, and it is implausible (*baʿīd*) that they will not be sexually desired."[103] However, Zīrekzāde's position was far from being the standard one, and it was cited by the later Turkish scholar Ismāʿīl Ḥaqqī al-Būrsawī (d. 1724) with the rejoinder that the conclusion is "not acceptable to those of sound heart and right-thinking mind." Būrsawī argued that the phrase "go round about them" in the first Qurʾanic verse suggested that the boys were servants rather than catamites, and that the people of paradise would simply enjoy looking at "their beauty and radiance." The second verse promised believers whatever they desired in paradise, but it was possible (*yajūz*) that *liwāṭ* would not be desired by the people of paradise.[104]

The discussion concerning whether *liwāṭ* could exist in heaven was linked to the somewhat enigmatic figure of the boys of paradise (*wildān*). These are referred to in the following passages of the Qurʾan, describing the blissful condition of the believers in the hereafter:

> 52:24—And round them shall go boys of theirs, as though they were hidden pearls.
>
> 56:17—Around them shall go eternal youths, with goblets and ewers and a cup of flowing wine.
>
> 76:19—And there shall go round about them eternal boys; when thou seest them thou wilt think them scattered pearls.

Muslim commentators of the period mentioned different suggestions as to who these boys of paradise were. They could be the sons of the believers, or possibly the children of the unbelievers who died before puberty. The dominant interpretation, however, was that the boys were specially created by God, like the houris, to serve the believers. In the case of the boys, the service was, as has been seen, usually not thought to be of a sexual nature. Yet the commentators did not shy away from the fact that the verses seem to present the physical beauty of the boys as one of the attractions of paradise. In the Qurʾanic commentary of "the two Jalāls," the verses, which have been bracketed in what follows, are explained thus:

> (And around them) for service (shall go) slave (boys of theirs, as though they were) in handsomeness and delicateness (hidden pearls). (And there shall go round about them eternal boys) in the form of boys who never grow old; (when thou seest them thou wilt think them) because of their handsomeness and dispersal in service (scattered pearls).

Sulaymān al-Jamal, in a supercommentary on the mentioned work, explicated what is to be understood by "eternal":

> That which is meant by their being eternal is not changing from the condition of boys in respect of their tenderness (*ṭarāwah*) and handsome physique (*ḥusn qadd*), in contrast to the boys of the world who change as they grow older.[105]

In the Qurʾanic commentary of Abū al-Suʿūd Efendī, the relevant verse is explained in the same spirit:

> (And there shall go round about them eternal boys,) that is, forever persevering in their tenderness and beauty; (when thou seest them thou wilt think them scattered pearls) because of their handsomeness, clear complexion, and radiant countenances.[106]

According to some commentators, the term *mukhalladūn,* which is usually understood to mean "eternal" or "never-changing," could also be understood to mean "bearing earrings (*khild*)," so that the phrase *wildān mukhalladūn* may be translated either as "eternal boys" or as "boys with earrings."[107] Of course, the first—more usual—reading did not preclude that the ever-youthful boys would be "adorned with rings, bracelets, earrings, and beautiful clothes."[108]

The boys of paradise were widely assimilated to the beauty-ideal celebrated in the belles-lettres of the period. As has already been indicated on more than one occasion in the foregoing chapter, love poetry sometimes compared the beauty of the beloved to that of the paradisiacal youths. The *wildan* were also represented as one of the attractions that a believer could look forward to in the hereafter. The Shīʿī scholar Niʿmatallah al-Jazāʾirī (d. 1702), reminding his reader how earthly pleasures pale in comparison with the pleasures awaiting in paradise, wrote:

> If you are among those who are slaves to their sexual organs, then [keep in mind the Qurʾanic verse (44:54)]: "We shall wed them to bright and large-eyed maids"; and if you are among those who gaze, then [keep in mind the Qurʾanic verse (76:19)]: "And there shall go round about them eternal boys; when thou seest them thou wilt think them scattered pearls."[109]

According to the Damascene scholar Ḥasan al-Būrīnī (d. 1615), who was said by a contemporary to have "an inclination to boys," "The attractions available in paradise are of many forms, including boys and houris."[110] The biographer Muḥammad Khalīl al-Murādī (d. 1791) mentioned a poetic eulogy of the Prophet Muḥammad composed jointly by three eighteenth-century scholars, in which one of the lines is as follows:

> So I do not ask except for an intercessor [i.e., the Prophet] who will lead me
> to the boys of paradise by his guidance.[111]

A verse in a poetic elegy by the Aleppine scholar ʿAbd al-Raḥmān al-Baʿlī (d. 1778/9) likewise stated:

> And around him [the deceased] are boys and youths (*al-ghilmān wa al-wildān*)
> adorned like hidden and scattered pearls.[112]

The Qurʾan was thus understood as simultaneously condemning sexual intercourse between men in the severest terms and depicting handsome youths as one of the otherworldly rewards awaiting the male believers. This could hardly have failed to appear to aesthetically inclined scholars as a confirmation of their own sympathies for the chaste love of beauty.

The Meaning of *Liwāṭ*

On the basis of the severe religious-legal rulings on *liwāṭ,* it would appear reasonable to claim that "Islam" prohibits "homosexuality." Having established this, the profuseness of homoerotic poetry and anecdotes in Arab-Islamic literature may be seen as an indication that "in practice" homosexuality was nevertheless indulged or tolerated in Arab-Islamic societies. Yet, as stated at the outset of this study, such an interpretation seems to simplify a more complex picture. None of the schools of law operate with a concept of "homosexuality." From a juridical perspective, a *lūṭī* is someone who commits a specific act. His desires or inclinations are in principle irrelevant; he does not become less of a *lūṭī* if he commits the act for payment, or merely to satisfy a curiosity rather than out of desire. Even a victim of heterosexual or homosexual rape could, in a strict sense, be regarded as a fornicator or sodomite, though duress qualified as a "resemblance" (*shubhah*) that removed legal liability for the act. Thus, the Ḥanbalī jurist Buhūtī asserted that "there is no *ḥadd* punishment if a legally mature woman is forced to commit fornication, or a passive sodomite is forced to commit sodomy."[113] The same point would seem to be presupposed when Shāfiʿī jurists claimed that duress does not make fornication permissible; it simply removes legal liability, apparently in the same way that a minor cannot be prosecuted for fornication though he or she is not permitted to commit it.[114] According to the Damascene Ḥanafī jurist Ibn ʿĀbidīn, accusing a victim of rape of being a fornicator does not amount to a false accusation of unlawful intercourse (*qadhf*), because "duress obviates the sinful nature of the act, but not its being fornication."[115] Not all contemporary jurists would have agreed with Ibn ʿĀbidīn. Jurists of the Mālikī school included consent in their definition of *liwāṭ,* and accusing a victim of rape of being a *lūṭī* was thus deemed libelous.[116] However, the disagreement was based on a scholastic quibble about whether voluntariness should be included in the formal definition of *liwāṭ,* and not on any fundamental difference in the concept. There was agreement on all sides that a person who commits *liwāṭ* for pecuniary reasons is as much of a *lūṭī* as someone who commits it for pleasure. There was also agreement among the jurists that a person who experiences recurrent desires to commit *liwāṭ* but does not act on them, or who intends to commit it but never gets the chance, is not a *lūṭī.*

Liwāṭ is narrower than homosexuality in another sense. In the four Sunnī schools of law, it referred specifically to anal intercourse rather than to "homosexual" acts in general. Kissing, caressing, and intercrural intercourse between males were considered reprehensible acts that merited chastisement, but were not cases of *liwāṭ.*[117] The standard manuals on Islamic law were quite explicit about this point. An authoritative Shāfiʿī manual thus defined fornication (*zinā*) as "the illicit insertion of the penis into a vagina" (*īlāj al-dhakar bi-farj muḥarram*), and added that inserting the penis into "the male or female anus is as [inserting it into] the vagina, according to the school" (*wa dubur dhakar wa unthā ka-qubul ʿalā al-madhhab*). It went on to state that *ḥadd* punishments did not apply in the case of intercrural intercourse (*mufākhadhah*) and other things that do not involve penetration (*mimmā lā īlāj fīhi*) such as intercourse between women.[118] A standard Ḥanbalī manual also defined fornication as "committing the abomination in the vagina or anus" (*fiʿl al-fāḥishah fī qubul aw dubur*), and went on to specify that it is a precondition for the application of *ḥadd* punishments that the glans is inserted (*taghyīb al-ḥashafah*) into either orifice.[119] A standard Mālikī manual defined fornication as a "legally mature Muslim's insertion of the penis into a human vagina that is not allowed to him," thus explicitly excluding cases of nonpenetrative sex such as intercourse between the thighs (*lā ghayr farj ka-bayn fakhdhayn*). The manual specified that "insertion" (*īlāj*) meant the introduction of the glans (*taghyīb ḥashafah*) into the orifice, and sodomy (*liwāṭ*) was then specified to be the introduction of the glans into the anus of a male (*idkhālihā fī dubur dhakar*). *Ḥadd* punishments were stated not to apply to sexual intercourse between women "since there is no penetration" (*li-ʿadam al-īlāj*).[120]

Ordinary, nontechnical usage was, as has been seen in the first chapter, not as strict. Juridically, however, a person who accused another of being a *lūṭī* on the grounds that he had kissed, caressed, or had intercrural intercourse with a boy would be liable to eighty lashes for false accusation of unlawful intercourse. According to the Ḥanafī, Shāfiʿī and Ḥanbalī schools, anal intercourse between a man and a woman (other than a wife or concubine) and anal intercourse between two men were instances of the same type of transgression, and merited the same punishment. By contrast, sexual intercourse between women (*siḥāq*) was considered an independent transgression and was not assimilated terminologically, or in terms of punishment, to anal intercourse between men.

In assessing the gravity of a sexual sin, the mode of intercourse was more important than the genders of the partners. Illicit vaginal intercourse between a man and a woman was a graver sin, and was punished more severely, than kissing, caressing, or intercrural intercourse between men, or sexual intercourse between women. The latter acts, which did not involve phallic penetration of the vagina or anus, were apparently not considered by Sunnī jurists to be "major sins" (*kabāʾir*) at all.[121] The Egyptian Shāfiʿī jurist Sulaymān al-Bujayrimī (d. 1806), after expounding the rulings of his school on *zinā* and *liwāṭ,* added that nonpenetrative sexual intercourse such as "intercrural intercourse (*mufākhadhah*) or hugging or kissing" were not major sins unless done repeatedly, and should be punished by discretionary chastisement, which ought to be milder than the least severe *ḥadd* punishment.[122] The Shāfiʿī jurist Muḥammad al-Khaṭīb al-Shirbīnī (d. 1570) likewise stated that discretionary chastisement, and not *ḥadd,* applied to cases of intercrural intercourse, inserting the penis in orifices other than the anus or vagina such as the navel [*sic!*], the "preliminaries" of intercourse (which in light of the preceding presumably refers to kissing and fondling), or intercourse between two women.[123] Even the otherwise severe Ibn Ḥajar al-Haytamī conceded that "kissing, fondling, and intercrural intercourse (*mufākhadhah*) are minor sins (*ṣaghāʾir*)," but added that they became major sins if done with the wife of a neighbor, illustrating the general principle that a minor sin, such as nonpenetrative sex, becomes a major sin in conjunction with another minor sin such as abusing the trust of a neighbor.[124] He went on to assert that looking with lust at a boy did not contravene the juridical status of being "of good character" (*ʿadl*), which made one eligible to be a witness in a court of law.[125] The Egyptian Mālikī scholar Muḥammad al-Dasūqī (d. 1815) made the same point: isolated instances of looking with lust at a woman or beardless boy did not disqualify one from being a witness in a court, though making a regular habit of it (*al-idmān*) did. The principle applied in general to the antecedents of fornication—in other words to all nonpenetrative sexual acts (*wa hiya mā ʿadā al-īlāj*).[126] Another Egyptian Mālikī scholar, ʿAbd al-Bāqī al-Zurqānī (d. 1688), likewise asserted, in the context of discussing the issue of looking at beardless boys, that "the transgression of the eye is a minor sin which is atoned for by overall obedience to the law."[127] The underlying principle assumed by Zurqānī was that major sins required repentance to be wiped off the sinner's debit side on the Final Reckoning, while minor sins did not. The latter would be compensated for by simply avoiding major sins. Even if the minor sins were committed repeatedly and willfully (*maʿ al-iṣrār*), they would be compensated for by supererogatory works, even if the perpetrator did not repent.[128] It was in this spirit that scholars tended to understand the Qur'anic dictum that "good works remove evil works" (11:114).[129] Some scholars believed that the "venial faults" (*lamam*) mentioned in the following Qur'anic verse: "Those who shun great sins and iniquities, all but venial faults, verily thy Lord is of ample forgiveness" (53:32), referred specifically to nonpenetrative sexual acts.[130] In accordance with such a scaling of the seriousness of sins, jurists envisaged situations in which one would be religiously obliged to perform a minor sin to ward off a more serious situation. For instance, the Egyptian jurist Shihāb al-Dīn Aḥmad al-Ramlī (d. 1550) was asked whether it was permissible for a lover to kiss an unrelated woman or a boy if, in line with accepted medical theory, he feared that he would die if his passion remained frustrated. Ramlī answered that kissing the object of one's passion in such a situation was not only permissible but actually a duty, and that it was incumbent on the beloved woman or boy to allow this.[131]

Falling in love with a boy was widely considered to be an involuntary act, and as such outside the scope of religious condemnation. Many, perhaps most, religious scholars were prepared to concede that a person who died from unconsummated love for a boy could earn the status of a martyr (*shahīd*), which would guarantee him a place in heaven. The "martyrs-of-love" tradition, mentioned in the previous chapter, though perhaps never completely uncontroversial, seems to have been regarded as respectable by most scholars. In the fifteenth century, its authenticity was upheld by influential experts on *ḥadīth* such as Ibn Ḥajar al-ʿAsqalānī (d. 1449) and Muḥammad al-Sakhāwī (d. 1497), and it found its way into *al-Jāmiʿ al-ṣaghīr,* a very influential compilation of traditions by Jalāl al-Dīn al-Suyūṭī (d. 1505). In the popular topically arranged reworking of Suyūṭī's compilation by the Meccan-based scholar ʿAlī al-Muttaqī al-Hindī (d. 1567/8), entitled *Kanz al-ʿummāl,* the tradition appeared in the section on "laudable character traits and acts."[132] Discussions of the tradition in the early Ottoman period tended to dissent, explicitly or implicitly, from the view of Ibn Qayyim al-Jawziyyah (d. 1350), who dismissed it as an outright fabrication.[133] Scholars who were widely regarded as specialists in the field of *ḥadīth,* such as the Medinese ʿAlī al-Qāri' al-Harawī (d. 1614), the Egyptian Muḥammad al-Zurqānī (d. 1720), the Damascene Ismāʿīl al-ʿAjlūnī (d. 1749), and the Indian-born, Egyptian-based Muḥammad Murtaḍā al-Zabīdī (d. 1791), judged the saying to be authentic, though within that general category there was some uncertainty as to whether its line of transmission should be classified as "good" (*ḥasan*) or "weak" (*ḍaʿīf*).[134] Even scholars who were otherwise influenced by Ibn Qayyim al-Jawziyyah and his teacher Ibn Taymiyyah, such as Muḥammad al-Saffārīnī and Muḥammad al-Shawkānī, seem to have been content to leave the issue of authenticity open, rather than expressly denying it.[135] Authors of works on love, such as Dāwūd al-Anṭākī (d. 1599), the Ḥanbalī jurist Marʿī ibn Yūsuf al-Karmī (d. 1624), and Muḥyī al-Dīn al-Ṣaltī (d. 1702), also accepted the tradition, though in the first two cases, note was taken of the existence of the controversy.[136] It was possible to argue that the tradition applied only to heterosexual love. This was the position of Zabīdī and the Egyptian scholar ʿAbd al-Raʾūf al-Munāwī (d. 1622), who both asserted that the saying only applied to "what could conceivably be the object of licit sexual intercourse," thus excluding a man's love for a boy.[137] However, this seems to have been a minority opinion. The stricture proposed by Munāwī was explicitly rejected by the Rector of the Azhar college Muḥammad al-Ḥafnī (d. 1767), who insisted that the martyrs-of-love tradition applied "even if [the man's love was] for a beardless boy, in accordance with the works on positive law and contrary to the commentator [i.e., Munāwī]."[138] Ḥafnī's reference to the works on positive law (*furūʿ*) reflects the fact that the authoritative works of the Shāfiʿī school to which he belonged regularly included a discussion of the various kinds of death that conferred martyr status on the deceased. Their conclusion was almost invariably that a man who dies from passionate but chaste love should be seen as a martyr, whether his love was for a woman or a boy. Ibn Ḥajar al-Haytamī, one of the most prominent Shāfiʿī jurists of the early Ottoman period, opined as follows:

> If he [a man] looks licitly at the beardless boy, as in the case of the involuntary glance, and passionate love for the boy results, and he is chaste and keeps the love secret, it is not implausible that it should then be said that he is a martyr, since there is no transgression involved.[139]

The equally authoritative Shāfiʿī jurist Shams al-Dīn Muḥammad al-Ramlī (d. 1596) concurred. As mentioned in the previous chapter, he stressed that the martyrs-of-love tradition applied to the love of boys as long as it was involuntary:

> If we assume that the love is involuntary in the sense that he [the lover] cannot choose to end it, then there is nothing to prevent him from gaining martyrdom, since in that case there is no transgression involved.[140]

A student of Ramlī, Sulṭān al-Mazzāḥī (d. 1665), reiterated the opinion in unambiguous terms:

> The considered ruling of our teacher al-Ramlī and others is not to differentiate between beardless boys and others, the premise being chastity and keeping the love secret.[141]

A host of other jurists expressed their opinion that the martyrs-of-love tradition also applied to the love of boys.[142] The following passage by the Rector of the Azhar at the time of the French occupation of Egypt, ʿAbdallah al-Sharqāwī (d. 1811), is representative:

> Among the martyrs . . . [is] one who dies from passionate love if he refrains from transgressions of religious law . . . and keeps the love a secret . . . whether the passionate love is for what could become available for licit intercourse or not, such as a beardless boy, according to authoritative verdicts. And the assertion of some [scholars] that loving him is a transgression and that he can never become available [for licit intercourse] and thus cannot lead to martyrdom should be understood to pertain to voluntary love, whereas if the love is involuntary, chaste, and kept a secret, in cases where he is [involuntarily] led to love a beardless boy, or is [legally] allowed to look, and love takes hold of his heart without willing what is not permitted, and this leads to his death, then there is no disagreement in his obtaining martyrdom. And how appropriate are the words of the poet:
>
> The lovers' torment in this world is enough, by God Hell shall not
> torment them thereafter!
> Rather, eternal paradise shall be their adorned home, to be enjoyed
> by them in reward for their patience.
> How could it be otherwise, and they have loved chastely and kept
> their love secret? Thus attests the tradition . . .[143]

In the literary anthology of the Ottoman Grand Vizier Rāghib Pāshā (d. 1763), a discussion of the martyrs-of-love tradition follows immediately after the extract from Mullā Ṣadrā's sympathetic exposition of the nature of the Platonic love of boys. Scholars who were positively inclined toward chaste pederastic love, such as Ḥasan al-Būrīnī and ʿAbd al-Ghanī al-Nābulusī, also referred to the tradition, and may be assumed to have thought that it applied to the love of boys.[144]

Composing pederastic love poetry, far from being considered to be *liwāṭ,* was actually permitted by most jurists of the period. This was the conclusion of Ḥanafī and Shāfiʿī jurists who discussed the issue.[145] Their verdict was that love poetry of a boy or a woman was permissible, as long as his or her identity was not specified. The following statement is from an authoritative handbook of Shāfiʿī law glossed by the Egyptian scholar Aḥmad al-Qalyūbī (d. 1658):

> It is permissible to say or recite poetry, and to listen to it, except if it involves defamation or obscenity or portraying a specified (*muʿayyanah*) woman, or a

specified (*muʿayyan*) youth [Qalyūbī: i.e., a beardless boy], in which case such things are prohibited . . . in contrast to portraying without specifying [Qalyūbī: the woman or beardless boy] because composing love poetry (*al-tashbīb*) is a craft and the aim of the poet is to produce attractive discourse, not the verisimilitude of what is mentioned.[146]

The Ḥanafī scholar Muḥammad Murtaḍā al-Zabīdī concluded his treatment of the issue with a similar verdict:

> al-Rāfiʿī [i.e., ʿAbd al-Karīm al-Rāfiʿī (d. 1226)] has said: . . . saying love poetry of women and boys (*al-tashbīb bi-al-nisāʾ wa al-ghilmān*) without specifying identity (*min ghayr taʿyīn*) does not contravene the status of being *ʿadl* [i.e., eligible for being a witness in a court of law], since the aim of the poet is to produce attractive discourse, not the verisimilitude of what is mentioned. The author of *al-Imtāʿ* [*fī aḥkām al-samāʿ*—Kamāl al-Dīn al-Udfuwī (d. 1348/9)] has said: This is the position favored by enquiry, and if I were to cite the poetry of exemplary scholars, and examples of their listening to this kind of poetry, it would be plentiful, and God knows best.[147]

The discussions of the Ḥanafī and Shāfiʿī jurists often took note of an alternative opinion, expressed by some older jurists of their schools, which forbids love poetry of boys regardless of whether their identity is specified or not. This latter position was apparently still endorsed by jurists of the Ḥanbalī and Imāmī Shīʿī schools, who constituted a minority within the Arabic-speaking areas of the Ottoman Empire. Such jurists permitted saying love poetry of a woman if she was a wife or concubine, or if her identity was not specified, but held that composing love poetry of a boy was always out of bounds.[148] The Imāmī Shīʿī scholar Zayn al-Dīn al-ʿĀmilī (d. 1558), for instance, commenting on a manual of law which stated that it was prohibited to say love poetry of a specific woman not available for licit intercourse, added:

> And exempted by the phrase "not available for licit intercourse" (*ghayr muḥallalah lahu*) is a wife or concubine, the implication being that saying love poetry of them is permissible . . . and the saying of love poetry of a boy is prohibited absolutely, since the object is prohibited [to the poet].[149]

The Ḥanbalī scholar Muḥammad al-Saffārīnī (d. 1774) also asserted that saying love poetry of a boy is prohibited, "whether the identity of the beardless boy is specified or not."[150] He explicated the term "licit poetry" as "that which is free from the defamation of Muslims, and from descriptions of alcoholic beverages, a beardless boy, or a specified woman not available for licit intercourse."[151]

The Ḥanbalī and Imāmī Shīʿī jurists thus assimilated the case of saying love poetry of a boy to that of saying love poetry of a specified woman who was not a wife or concubine. Both cases were deemed impermissible, since they involved portraying a passionate love for what is not available for licit sexual intercourse. Of course, the position involved a "realist" or "deflationary" reduction of passionate love to lust. In retort, it was possible to claim, as did ʿAbd al-Ghanī al-Nābulusī, that there was nothing reprehensible in loving a boy chastely. In his *Ghāyat al-maṭlūb,* Nābulusī mentioned the permissibility of pederastic love poetry in the context of defending the chaste love of boys, and devoted a chapter of the work to mentioning respectable scholars and saints who fell in love with women or boys and expressed their amorous feelings in verse.[152] Most jurists who argued for the permissibility of pederastic love poetry, however, chose to defend their opinion on other grounds, despite the fact that many of them were committed to the idea that the involuntary love of a boy did not involve a transgression of religious precepts. Instead, they rejected the opinion that pederastic love poetry was prohibited by appealing to the belief that poets need not be referring to real-life boys or to genuine emotions. The proffered justification gave a particular twist to their position. A statement such as "saying love poetry of an unspecified boy is permissible" could be interpreted to mean that it is permissible to say love poetry of a real boy as long as his identity is not revealed. However, the suggested interpretation seems to be ruled out when the permission is grounded on the belief that poetry is usually fictional. Most jurists, while resisting a position which would make much of the poetry of the age illicit, were apparently not willing to fully endorse the view that there was nothing wrong with feasting one's eyes on a handsome beardless boy, or the view that passionate love was entirely different from plain lust.

The position of mainstream Ḥanafī and Shāfiʿī jurists thus seems to have been that saying pederastic love poetry is permissible if it is a display of poetic skills, rather than an expression of genuine amorous inclinations for a particular boy. This position may have been much closer to the position of Ḥanbalī and Imāmī Shīʿī jurists than is apparent at first sight. The latter's stated principle that saying love poetry of a boy is forbidden "whether the boy's identity is specified or not" need not have been incompatible with the position that only love poetry of a real boy is prohibited, whereas love poetry which portrays a fictitious love for an imaginary boy is not. There is reason to believe that some Ḥanbalī jurists understood their school's position in that way. For example, Marʿī ibn Yūsuf al-Karmī (d. 1624) composed the following lines, in which the gender of the portrayed beloved is revealed by the reference to beard-down (*ʿidhār*):

By my soul! He with whom I have so many pending banquets, and for the love of whom I have so many a censurer and critic!
On his cheeks there are two roses, and his beauty-spot is like musk of charming description, and the mouth is smiling.
His locks of hair are as night, and the appearance of his face as day revealed to beaming hearts.
So worthy of praise! On his cheek flows beard-down (*ʿidhāran*) to which my chaste (*ʿudhrī*) love attends.
It is surprising that I've managed to keep his friendship, which to me is necessary in love,
When there is an abyss between me and a lovers' union (*wiṣāl*), and separation from him is my constant companion.[153]

Karmī's juridical verdict was as follows:

> And also not eligible for being a witness in court is a poet who is excessive in praising when paid and in rebuking when not paid, or who says poetry which involves praising alcoholic beverages or beardless boys or a specified woman not available for licit sexual intercourse, and he is thereby a sinner (*fāsiq*), and the relating of such poetry [by others] is not prohibited.[154]

On the face of it, such a verdict should have precluded the verses just cited. It is possible, however, that the proscription was intended to apply to those who routinely composed such poetry, and not to those who made one or two contributions to the genre. The term "poet" (*shāʿir*) in the quotation from Karmī could, in other words, be intended to refer to full-time practitioners, and not to anyone who composed a poem. This would, for instance, be in line with the verdict of the Ḥanafī jurist Ibn ʿĀbidīn, which was that only excessive preoccupation with love poetry was improper. "Small amounts of such poetry is unobjectionable," Ibn ʿĀbidīn added, "if the intent is to display witticisms, subtleties, nice comparisons, and elegant expressions, even if it is of physiques and cheeks."[155] It is also possible that Karmī did not intend his remark to apply to cases where there was no real boy at all, and the poem was just a means of exhibiting a scholar's literary skills. In his tract on love entitled *Munyat al-muḥibbīn wa bughyat al-ʿāshiqīn,* Karmī, after citing many poems said of beardless or downy-cheeked boys, added this comment:

> Eminent scholars and exemplary religious leaders have often indulged in this art of verse and love poetry, as is known to those who are acquainted with their books, and this is not a blemish or fault on their part, for their likes are too dignified for such shortcomings, rather this is part of their noble nature and due to their knowledge that poetry is the art of the eloquent and cures the heart of ailments.[156]

Karmī went on to cite several of his own love poems, which conform to the standards of the time in portraying the unreciprocated, chaste love of a woman or boy.[157] Karmī's understanding of the principle that saying love poetry of a boy is prohibited may have been shared by some Imāmī Shīʿī scholars. Several Shīʿī scholars and poets, such as Bahāʾ al-Dīn al-ʿĀmilī (d. 1621), Ibn Maʿtūq al-Ḥuwayzī (d. 1676), and Ibn Maʿṣūm (d. ca. 1708), composed pederastic love poetry despite the apparent ruling of their school on the matter.[158] Indeed, the above-mentioned jurist Zayn al-Dīn al-ʿĀmilī concluded his discussion of the religious-legal status of love poetry by making the following point:

> It could perhaps be said that . . . saying love poetry of someone unspecified is an art, and that the aim of the poet is to exhibit his skills in that art, not the verisimilitude of what is mentioned, and thus it should not be held to contravene the status of being *ʿadl,* and on the assumption that it is permissible, too much of it is reprehensible.[159]

Ideals and Practices Revisited

The condition that the poet should not specify the identity of the beloved was, as has been shown in the previous chapter, often disregarded. Jurists were aware of this fact. Ibn Ḥajar al-Haytamī, for instance, wrote that "some libertine poets set up hints which lead to identification [of the beloved] and this is undoubtedly like [straightforward] specification of identity."[160] The previous chapter also gave examples of religious scholars who themselves composed such love poetry: ʿAbd al-Ghanī al-Nābulusī composed a poem with his colleague Aḥmad al-Ṣafadī in which they gave away the identity of the beloved Rabāḥ al-Khayyāṭ; the Iraqi scholar ʿAbdallah al-Suwaydī alluded to the name of the youth from Mosul—Ṣāliḥ—to whom his petition in rhymed prose and verse was dedicated. Other examples are not hard to come by. The Egyptian scholar and poet Yūsuf al-Ḥafnī (d. 1764) taught at the Azhar college in Cairo, and was the younger brother of the Rector of the institution, Muḥammad al-Ḥafnī (d. 1767). His *Dīwān* includes several instances of poetry that mention the name of the male beloved. An example is the following couplet:

> O moon, you have let my heart taste the cup of love, so be generous and hold back the swords of harshness.
> I am melting from love—enough harshness! O Aḥmad, has my love not elicited your good will?[161]

Other poems by Ḥafnī seem to provide good examples of what Ibn Ḥajar called "setting up hints that lead to identification," such as the following lines:

> I offer my soul to the one whom I ardently love, but will not name him for fear of the mocker.
> His beginning in code is one-eighth of the following, and the last of his letters is a tenth of the third.[162]

The poet is here using the system of letter-code (*ḥisāb al-jummal*), whereby each letter of the alphabet has a conventional numerical value. The poet is alluding to the name Aḥmad, which in Arabic is written with four letters with the following numerical values: *A* (1)–*Ḥ* (8)–*M* (40)–*D* (4).

Other religious scholars were linked by ties of friendship to offending poets. For instance, Ḥasan al-ʿAṭṭār, who was Rector of the Azhar college in Cairo during Edward Lane's sojourn in the city, was a close friend of the poet Ismāʿīl al-Khashshāb (d. 1815), whose poetry often ignored the restrictions set up by jurists. It was in fact ʿAṭṭār who collected his friend's poetry into a single volume.[163] The following couplet, ʿAṭṭār wrote, was said of a youth called Sharaf whom al-Khashshāb was said to have loved:

> I fell in love with one whose glances are lethal yet languid; a succulent branch; a handsome form; slender.
> When my censurer foolishly blames me for fancying him, I reply: "By God, that's my honor (*sharafī*)."[164]

This was not the only such poem of Khashshāb's that ʿAṭṭār reproduced. A similar couplet was composed of a singer named Wafāʾ:

> By God, a delicate fawn; ravishing; handsome; if he sings for us he cures morbid worries.
> Whenever his luminous guise shines on my companions, I say to them: "There! The beloved appeared (*wafā*)!"[165]

On one occasion when the poem itself does not specify the identity of the beloved, ʿAṭṭār himself informed the reader that the poem was said of a certain young scribe called ʿAlī ibn Muḥammad whom Khashshāb loved passionately.[166]

It may appear that we are once again in the position we were in at the beginning of this study. Having established that the recognized interpreters of Islamic law held that an act was not permissible, we are faced with abundant evidence that it was nevertheless indulged in openly, by belletrists who had close personal ties with religious scholars, and often by religious scholars themselves. However, it is important to resist the temptation to use an anachronistic concept such as "homosexuality" to characterize the transgression committed. That concept is simply not fine-grained enough to capture certain distinctions that are essential to understanding the attitude of urban, literate Arab Muslims in the early Ottoman period. The belletrists and scholars were not openly committing *liwāṭ*. They simply composed love poetry that mainstream jurists held to be inappropriate. This transgression was hardly considered to be a major sin. It is difficult to believe that having intercrural intercourse with a boy was considered to be a minor sin, whereas saying chaste love poetry of a specified boy was considered a major sin. As mentioned previously, committing a minor sin was not held to be incompatible with the status of being an "upright" (*ʿadl*) person whose testimony is acceptable in a court of law, and such a sin was held to be atoned for by overall obedience to the law—unless it was committed repeatedly or habitually to such an extent that it would outweigh a person's pious deeds.

To be sure, Ibn Ḥajar al-Haytamī did mention "saying love poetry of a boy even if his identity is not specified" as a major sin in a work entitled "Warnings against Committing Major Sins" (*al-Zawājir ʿan iqtirāf al-kabāʾir*). However, as the title suggests, the work was avowedly of a homiletic nature, rather than an authoritative work of law. Ibn Ḥajar included all sins that could be said to meet one of the criteria for being a major sin that had at one time or other been suggested by jurists, and this led him to enumerate 467 major sins, whereas the great majority of Islamic scholars who tried to number major sins ended up with a number between seven and thirty.[167] Ibn Ḥajar was clearly not committed to the idea that all 467 listed sins should indeed be considered major sins. For instance, refraining from marriage (*al-tabattul*) is included in Ibn Ḥajar's work as a major sin (number 241) simply because a saying attributed to the Prophet had cursed those who did not marry, and some scholars had suggested that an act qualified as a major sin if it had been cursed in the Qurʾan or in a *ḥadīth*. Ibn Ḥajar himself pointed out to the reader that the position of the Shāfiʿī school to which he belonged was that choosing to remain unmarried was not even a sin, let alone a major one.[168] Ibn Ḥajar listed playing backgammon in *al-Zawājir* as a major sin (number 444), and though his ensuing discussion made it clear that many jurists disputed such a severe assessment of the act, he refrained from explicitly endorsing their view. However, in his major juridical work, *Tuḥfat al-muḥtāj fī sharḥ al-Minhāj,* he simply stated "it is a minor sin" (*wa huwa min al-ṣaghā'ir*).[169] Similarly, looking with lust at a beardless boy, or at a woman other than a wife or concubine, is mentioned in *al-Zawājir* as a major sin (numbers 242 and 245), though Ibn Ḥajar himself pointed out that the considered position of jurists was that "the antecedents of fornication" were minor sins, and added that judging them to be major sins without additional qualification was "very implausible (*ba'īd jiddan*)."[170] Saying love poetry of an unspecified boy was listed in *al-Zawājir* as a major sin because one jurist had held it to disqualify the poet from being a witness in court, and incompatibility with being a witness in court was another proposed criterion for being a major sin. However, Ibn Ḥajar went on to cite a host of other Shāfi'ī jurists who believed that saying love poetry of an unspecified boy was permissible, and hence not even a minor sin.[171]

The fact that an act is listed in Ibn Ḥajar's *al-Zawājir* as a major sin is thus far from sufficient to show that it was actually considered to be a major sin by Islamic jurists, or indeed by Ibn Ḥajar himself. Ibn Ḥajar's assessment of the gravity of the sin of composing love poetry of a specified boy appears in a somewhat different light in a work on love by the Egyptian-born scholar 'Abd al-Mu'īn ibn al-Bakkā' (d. 1630/1). In the summer of 1565, less than a year before he died, Ibn Ḥajar was visited by Ibn al-Bakkā' in his home in Mecca and told him the following story: a man loved a youth named Badr, who fell ill and died on a night in which the moon (*badr*) was full. The lamenting lover addressed the following couplet to the moon:

> Your namesake is in his grave, and you still shine thereafter, O moon?!
> Would that you had been eclipsed, this being your wearing black at his loss!

That night, said Ibn Ḥajar, a lunar eclipse did take place, whereupon the overwhelmed lover died as well.[172] Of course, even the strictest jurists allowed a person to cite the illicit poetry of others. Yet, the tone in which the story is related suggests that the reader is meant to feel sympathy for the unhappy lover, rather than conclude that he has committed a major sin by alluding to the name of his beloved. After relating several such stories of people who died from passionate love, Ibn al-Bakkā' wrote: "It is desirable, indeed it is a duty, to assist the beloved and aid the yearner, and so it has been said: It is the duty of any man of honor to support the passionate lover morally and with money, and if not, with prayer."[173]

Indeed, there is more direct evidence from juridical works themselves which suggest that composing forbidden love poetry was deemed to be at most a minor sin. The Damascene Ḥanafī jurist Ibn ʿĀbidīn seems to have held that love poetry was permissible, unless it was cultivated to an inordinate degree or the poet specified the identity of the beloved woman or boy, in which case it was reprehensible (*makrūh*) if the woman or boy was alive at the time of composition.[174] An act that is deemed "reprehensible" (*makrūh*) is not, strictly speaking, prohibited (*ḥarām*), and committing it thus cannot be called a sin at all, not even a minor one. If one of the four recognized schools of law held the composing of such poetry to be at most reprehensible, then it is very unlikely that the other schools would have held it to be a major rather than minor sin.[175] A handbook of Shāfiʿī law glossed by the Egyptian jurist Aḥmad al-Qalyūbī expounded the principle that witnesses in a court of law should not have committed major sins or persevered in committing minor sins. The handbook gave as examples of major sins manslaughter, fornication, sodomy, drinking alcohol, and stealing, and as examples of minor sins looking at what one is not permitted to look at, telling a harmless lie, and making remarks that were slanderous (*ghībah*) without amounting to false accusation of serious crimes (*qadhf*). The handbook then proceeded to state that playing backgammon (*al-nard*) is prohibited, as is playing chess for money, playing or listening to most musical instruments, and composing poetry which involves the defamation of Muslims or portrays a specified boy or a woman not available for licit intercourse. Qalyūbī commented thus on the statement that playing backgammon is prohibited: "That is, it is one of the minor sins, like what follows from what will be mentioned (*ay wa min al-ṣaghāʾir ka-al-ladhī baʿdahu mimmā yaʾtī*)."[176] Qalyūbī's phrase is crucially ambiguous. He could be referring to all of the sins that follow, or only to the sin that is mentioned immediately after playing backgammon, playing chess for money. However, the latter reading would suggest that Qalyūbī believed that the other sins—playing or listening to musical instruments, and composing poetry that involves defaming Muslims or specifying the beloved woman or boy—were not minor sins. This is very unlikely. Playing or listening to musical instruments, especially wind and string instruments, was prohibited by most jurists. However, other juridical sources reveal that it was held to be a minor sin that did not disqualify the perpetrator from being a witness in a court of law unless he or she did it habitually.[177] Ibn Ḥajar, who belonged to the same school of law as Qalyūbī, wrote a work dealing mainly with the religious status of playing and listening to musical instruments. One chapter of the work is devoted to discussing whether such acts should be considered a major or minor sin. The conclusion of the chapter was unequivocal:

> To sum up, the authoritative verdict of our school is that this is one of the minor sins as long as it is not habitual to such an extent that the perpetrator's transgressions outweigh his compliance with the law, in which case it would be like a major sin in being incompatible with being an upright person and in annulling legal testimony.[178]

Ibn Ḥajar characteristically included the composing of poetry which involves the defamation of Muslims in his *al-Zawājir* as one of the major sins (number 456), but his ensuing discussion makes it clear that the standard position of jurists was that it was a minor sin, and thus only disqualified the person composing such poetry from being a witness in court if done habitually:

> To say without qualification that defamatory poetry annuls legal testimony is implausible, since verse is like prose . . . and thus it should be said that if he [the composer of defamatory poetry] does it excessively, or becomes infamous for such activity, or defames in a manner that is not compatible with being an upright person, by saying things which it is a major sin to say, then his testimony is annulled. However, if he does not defame excessively, and does not become infamous for such activity, and does not say things which it is a major sin to say, then his testimony is not annulled.[179]

The considered opinion of Shāfiʿī jurists thus seems to have been that playing backgammon, playing and listening to musical instruments, and composing defamatory poetry were minor sins. Since an influential handbook of Shāfiʿī law mentions composing love poetry of a specified boy or woman not available for licit sexual intercourse in the same breath as the other three sins, it seems reasonable to conclude that it too was considered to be a minor offense.

The fact that religious jurists disapproved of playing backgammon, listening to musical instruments, or saying love poetry of someone who was not available for licit sexual intercourse of course does not imply that these activities were not an important and visible part of popular culture. Indeed the evidence of travel literature clearly suggests that such activities were as popular in the Arab world in the early Ottoman period as they are now.[180] Then as now, ordinary believers seem to have been able to acknowledge the religious authority of the jurists while at the same time resisting a wholesale adoption of their austere outlook and way of life. In the sixteenth century many jurists expressed their disapproval of the new habit of drinking coffee. In the following century tobacco was introduced into the Middle East and was likewise met with suspicion by many jurists. In both cases, there was obviously little that jurists could do to stop the spread of the habit. An illustration of how ordinary believers could respect the authority of jurists and yet refuse to obey them on such matters is provided by the chronicler ʿAbd al-Raḥmān al-Jabartī (d. 1825/6). According to Jabartī, the prominent Mālikī jurist ʿAlī al-ʿAdawī (d. 1775) was "very unyielding in matters of religion" (*shadīd al-shakīmah fī al-dīn*), and was given to "commanding the good and proscribing the bad." He held smoking tobacco to be prohibited, and when word got around that he was approaching, people would hastily pack away their pipes and hide them from him. Even the de facto ruler of Egypt between 1760 and 1773, ʿAlī Bey, would, according to Jabartī, hide his pipes before ʿAdawī was to enter his presence.[181] Jabartī of course intended the story to illustrate the respect that was accorded the jurist by high and low. However, he inadvertently also illustrated how both high and low had no intention of giving up smoking simply because particularly zealous scholars held it to be forbidden.

It is certainly legitimate to speak of a divergence between the austere ideals expounded by religious jurists and the less austere ways of society at large. However, it is equally certain that it is distortingly simplistic to assimilate the case of "homosexuality" to that of playing backgammon or listening to musical instruments, as one more type of behavior prohibited by Islam but tolerated in Islamic society. Some aspects of what today might be called "homosexuality"—falling in love with a teenage boy and expressing this love in verse—were tolerated or considered to be peccadilloes by most religious scholars. Other aspects, such as repeatedly and flagrantly flouting the religious ban on sodomy, could easily have incurred the censure of ordinary "lay" believers, not to mention severe or capital punishment. The case of two young men convicted of sodomy in Damascus in mid-December 1807 serves as a reminder of the possible consequences. On the order of the governor of the city, they were executed by being thrown off one of the minarets of the Umayyad mosque.[182]

Conclusion

The concept of male homosexuality did not exist in the Arab-Islamic Middle East in the early Ottoman period. There was simply no native concept that was applicable to all and only those men who were sexually attracted to members of their own sex, rather than to women. Distinctions elided by the concept of homosexuality appeared significant to contemporaries: between the active and the passive partner; between passionate but chaste love and carnal lust; between permissible and prohibited sexual acts. Each distinction was central to a particular cultural strand. One influential strand tended to depict sexual intercourse as a polarizing act in which the dominant, "male" penetrator asserts his dominance over the subordinate, "female" penetrated. The active and passive sodomite thus tended to be assimilated to opposing sides of the fundamental dichotomy between genders. From this point of view, the penetrated male was dishonored and stigmatized by being cast in a female role, while the penetrator was not. Another cultural strand tended to idealize a man's love of beautiful women and youths, and implicitly or explicitly dissociated this phenomenon from the fornication and sodomy condemned by religious law. The Platonic love of human beauty was valued either as part of a wider ideal of refined sensibility, or as a way of loving an omnipresent and infinitely beautiful God. The religious-juridical strand focused on acts to the exclusion of desires and inclinations. Sexual acts between men were part of the general category of unlawful intercourse. There was no single juridical concept, and no single punishment, for all kinds of homosexual intercourse. Anal intercourse was a more severe sin than, say, intercrural intercourse, passionate kissing, or caressing. Indeed, the latter acts were considered less grave than certain forms of heterosexual intercourse. Falling in love with a teenage youth and expressing this love in verse were not punishable offenses, and a significant number of Islamic scholars, though not all, asserted that such behavior was not objectionable.

The three strands were relatively self-contained and embodied potentially conflicting ideals: of masculinity, of refined aesthetic sensibility, and of conformity to religious stipulations. Sometimes, the conflict was actualized: what from one perspective appeared as "screwing" was "sodomy" to another; the "inclination to boys" could alternatively be a "sensibility to beauty"; the appreciation of divine beauty could be seen as a willful exposition of the self to temptation. It is possible to speculate as to the relative weight of these ideals among various social groups. It seems clear, for example, that the second ideal was especially influential among belletrists and monist mystics; while the third was more relevant to jurists, ḥadīth-scholars, and ascetic Sufis. One might also suppose that the influence of both mystical aestheticism and austere moralistic asceticism was socially quite limited. The former was self-consciously elitist and was linked to a complex mystical philosophy. The latter, which frowned on such things as music, tobacco, coffee, secular poetry, and looking at youths, probably ran counter to what appears to have been a moderate but persistent hedonistic streak in popular culture.

Other variables than social group also seem relevant to the discussion of the influence of the various cultural perspectives. There is, for example, abundant evidence to suggest that young men in their twenties and early thirties were expected to be more inclined to pursue pleasure than older men, and that their youthful dispositions were condoned to some extent. As has been mentioned previously, graying hair was often depicted as one of the indicators that the time of passionate love and carefree pursuit of fancy was coming to a close. One anonymous couplet portrayed graying hair on the part of the lover as the counterpart of the beard on the cheeks of a beloved:

> I've become gray-haired, and my beloved has become bearded; he has left me and I've left him.
>
> My black [hair] has become white, and his white [cheek] has become black.[1]

The Yemeni scholar Muḥammad ibn Ismāʿīl al-Amīr (d. 1768) expressed a similar sentiment in the following lines of poetry:

> And poetry is only for the young and budding. As for what comes after that: What have older men to do with poetry? . . .
>
> And I do not countenance the disparagement of graying hair, for it indicates sobriety and a forewarning to those who know.
>
> It makes me forget every young woman or man, so I no longer complain of the turning away of a sun [*fem.*] or moon [*masc.*].[2]

The Damascene scholar Ḥasan al-Būrīnī excused himself from an invitation to a banquet with wine, in the following words:

> As for what you have indicated of the words of Abū Nuwās, and of following his way and drinking the cup [of wine], that would have been accepted if the

house of youth was still inhabited . . . but after the coming of gray hair, and the omen from the world to come, there is no possibility of touching the daughter of the vine.[3]

The supposition that young adults were more liable to sin was even enshrined in canonical sayings attributed to the Prophet. According to one such *ḥadīth,* "He [i.e., the Prophet] used to repeat the maxim: Islam and graying hair should be restraint enough for a person."[4] According to another saying: "God is impressed with the youth (*al-shābb*) who is devoid of passion (*ṣabwah*)"; commentators explained that this was because young men were by nature particularly susceptible to concupiscence.[5] Michael Rocke, in his impressive study of homosexual behavior in Renaissance Florence based on particularly rich court records, found that the great majority of cases brought before the authorities involved a teenage boy and a young man in his twenties or early thirties.[6] The same pattern may very well have existed in the urban centers of the Middle East in the period between 1500 and 1800.

The correlation between attitudes and social groups or generations can, however, be pushed too far. A significant number of people, perhaps the majority of urban males, seem to have been receptive to all three ideals and could, depending on context, shift between the various cultural perspectives. Indeed, the perspectives were not necessarily mutually exclusive. It was consistent to conceptualize the active and the passive sodomite in fundamentally different terms and believe that the latter was more contemptible than the former; to tolerate and even value chaste pederastic love; and to condemn transgressions of religious law, particularly those that were flagrant and habitual. The point is not that the various ideals were in principle irreconcilable, though certain individuals might claim that they were. But neither was their coexistence unproblematic, and a particular reconciliation could be questioned or challenged. Issues that were particularly controversial, in light of the delicate balance of ideals, appear to have been the relationship between passionate love and sexual desire; and the extent to which poetry reflected personal experience.

The present study started with what appeared to be a chasm between a "practice" that tolerated homosexuality and a "theory" that condemned it. It ends with an emphasis on the multiplicity of ideals that coexisted in the Arab-Islamic world in the early Ottoman period. A survey of the literature of the period—historical, belletristic, or religious—indicates a complex and variegated reality; a reality that cannot be adequately captured by notions of "tolerance" contra "intolerance," or "ideal" contra "practice." The people of Damascus reacted in two opposing ways to the rape of the womanizing Druze chieftain, and to indications that one of their major religious dignitaries had committed sodomy. The scholar and chronicler Jabartī mentioned with sympathy the refined pederastic love affair of his friends, while condemning the "vulgar" for pursuing handsome youths (presumably for less refined motives) during the saints' fairs of Egypt.[7] Such apparent contradictions were not simply cases of inconsistency or irrationality. Similarly, an adult man who courted handsome youths was not simply failing to conform to ideals in practice, but was living out other, independent ideals. He might even, with some reason, claim that he was not contravening the precepts of religion.

An approach that stresses the various strands or perspectives that are available to members of a culture may also be useful for understanding the development of attitudes in the nineteenth and twentieth centuries. A detailed account of the ways in which attitudes have changed—or remained unchanged—in the modern period remains to be written, and the following remarks are not intended to be more than a tentative sketch that will hopefully be fleshed out by future research.[8]

Between the middle of the nineteenth century and the early decades of the twentieth, the prevalent tolerance of the passionate love of boys was eroded, presumably owing—at least in part—to the adoption of European Victorian attitudes by the new, modern-educated and westernized elite. It has already been mentioned that the Egyptian scholar Rifāʿah al-Ṭahṭāwī (d. 1873), who studied in Paris from 1826 to 1831, noted that the French disapproved of the pederastic themes in Arabic literature, and accordingly changed the gender of the beloved when translating from Arabic into French. Significantly, he endorsed their position, presenting his readers with an argument that he had apparently—witness the analogy with the new European phenomenon of "electricity"—heard in Paris:

> They consider this [the love of boys] to be an example of moral corruption, and they are right. And this is because each gender inclines toward a distinct property possessed by the other gender, just as magnets have distinct properties that attract iron or electricity has distinct properties that attracts things, and so forth. Thus, when the genders are the same the distinct properties are absent, and [the attraction] becomes unnatural (*kharaja ʿan al-ḥālah al-ṭabīʿiyyah*).[9]

Another influential nineteenth-century Arab author who adopted the Victorian European disapproval of pederastic themes in Arabic literature was the Lebanese Protestant Buṭrus al-Bustānī (d. 1883). In his three-volume work *Udabāʾ al-ʿarab*, one of the first modern literary histories of Arabic, he distinguished between two trends in early Arabic love poetry: the chaste love poetry of the bedouins and the "dissolute" love poetry of the townspeople. He wrote that the eighth-century AD saw the strengthening of the latter trend:

> The second became more widespread and gained more adherents, and they invented a new type of it, reflecting the extent of depravity to which they had sunk, and this type is what is called "the love poetry of the male" (*ghazal al-mudhakkar*). The reason for its emergence was the mixing of Arabs with the rich non-Arabs, and the great number of slave boys from Turkish, Daylamite, and Byzantine areas.[10]

Bustānī clearly did not believe that there could be anything other than depravity and moral corruption in this poetic theme. In his chapter on the famous libertine poet Abū Nuwās (d. ca. 815), he repeatedly alluded to the poet's "sick and depraved" character, and to the fact that his "dissolute self turned him away from proper love."[11] Otherwise, Bustānī hardly dealt with the topic at all. One would not suspect from his literary history that there was a millennium-old tradition of chaste Arabic love poetry of boys in the *ʿudhrī* style. As was the case in Victorian Europe, the idealization of passionate love was for Bustānī strictly confined to the love of women.

To be sure, attitudes did not shift overnight. Nineteenth-century Egyptian poets such as Muḥammad Shihāb al-Dīn (d. 1857), Ṣāliḥ Majdī Bey (d. 1881), and ʿAbdallah Fikrī (d. 1889) continued to compose love poetry of boys.[12] Even the famous *fin-de-siècle* poet Ḥāfiẓ Ibrāhīm (d. 1932) composed shorter love poems of handsome young men.[13] In 1908, it was still possible in Cairo to publish a fifteenth-century work devoted entirely to love poetry of boys, entitled *Jannat al-wildān fī al-ḥisān min al-ghilmān,* which roughly translates as "The Paradise of Boys: On Handsome Youths."[14] A fourteenth-century work in rhymed prose describing a man's passionate love for a boy, *Lawʿat al-shākī wa damʿat al-bākī* ("The Plaints of the Lovelorn and Tears of the Disconsolate") was repeatedly printed in Cairo between 1857 and 1929.[15] However, it apparently ceased to be printed after the latter date, and it would seem that tolerance of the theme was quickly being eroded in the first decades of the twentieth century.

A very popular Arabic adaptation of Carl Brockelmann's *Geschichte der arabischen Literatur,* by Jurjī Zaydān (d. 1914), first published in Cairo in 1911–14 and frequently reprinted, condemned the theme of boy love in classical and postclassical Arabic poetry. Zaydān briefly noted the appearance of pederasty as a cultural and literary phenomenon in the early ʿAbbasid period (i.e., the late eighth and ninth centuries), but obviously did not want to dwell on the theme. He wrote:

> As for Abū Nuwās, there is in his Dīwān a special section devoted to descriptions of male youths, called "love poetry of males" (*ghazal al-mudhakkar*), containing around a thousand verses. We merely note its existence, deeming it inappropriate for the reader to look at this poetry. We have also passed over many events relating to the love poetry of boys, revealing the extent of depravity to which people had sunk. Neither education, nor manners, nor prominent position in the state prevented them from indulging in this . . . After this period saying love poetry of male youths became an established genre of poetry.[16]

In 1925, a history of Arabic literature designed for use in secondary and higher education in Egypt stated that love poetry of boys was "a crime against literature and a disgrace to the history of Arabic poetry."[17] Aḥmad Amīn, in a hugely influential multivolume history of the first four centuries of Islamic civilization published between 1928 and 1945 (and frequently reprinted), also touched on the theme of the love of boys with disapproval. Discussing the tenth century AD, he noted:

> The greatest calamity to befall society was the love of boys, which was echoed in literature. Abū Nuwās had hitherto been alone in the field, along with a few others, but in this period most poets would touch on the theme, and indulge in it with reticence or wantonness . . . We even see a strange phenomenon, which is that prominent officials such as viziers and judges did not restrain themselves from an inordinate indulgence of the theme, which shows that the disapproval of public opinion had weakened, and it came to be considered an example of elegant wit and bawdy humor, except in conservative circles.[18]

In 1930, a new edition of *The Arabian Nights* was published in Cairo. In general, it followed the older editions of 1835 and 1890, but made some noteworthy omissions. For example, the few stories that related in a sympathetic tone of pederastic love affairs were quietly left out.[19] Two years later, a heavily expurgated version of the *Dīwān* of Abū Nuwās was published in Cairo. By contrast to the earlier editions of 1898 and 1905, it abandoned the traditional thematic organization of the poems. Thus, whereas the former editions had a section for love poetry of male youths (*ghazal al-mudhakkar*), the 1932 edition did not. Indeed, it would be difficult to gauge from the editor's introduction to the latter edition that Abū Nuwās had said love poetry of youths at all.[20]

It is probably in the 1940s and '50s that the term *shudhūdh jinsī* began to be regularly used by Arab authors to refer generally to phenomena that had traditionally been distinguished, such as active pederasty, effeminate male passivity, the passionate love of boys, and sodomy. Exactly when the term was introduced is a question for further research. However, it does not seem to have been in common use in the early 1930s. The term does not appear, for example, in ʿUmar Farrūkh's study of Abū Nuwās, first published in 1932, even though the author discussed (disapprovingly) the pederastic theme in Abū Nuwās's poetry.[21] By contrast, a series of studies of the same poet published in the late 1940s and early 1950s all used the term.[22]

The term *shudhūdh jinsī* was obviously introduced to express the contemporary European concept of "sexual inversion" or "sexual perversion."[23] The use of the constituent term *jinsī* in the sense of "sexual" was itself a terminological innovation, reflecting the influence of the new European concept of "sexuality."[24] In premodern Arabic, *jins* meant "genus" or "kind," and hence sometimes "biological sex" or "gender," but not "sexuality."[25] It is worth emphasizing that the new concept referred to something distinct from, and more pervasive than, the conscious desire for copulation. When in 1953 the Egyptian critic ʿAbbās Maḥmūd al-ʿAqqād argued that Abū Nuwās was a "narcissist" rather than a "homosexual," he did not want to imply that Abū Nuwās wished to copulate with himself. He defined "narcissism" in much broader terms, as an obsessive infatuation with, and inordinate love of, one's own bodily features, which led the poet to fall in love with, and lust after, individuals with features resembling his own.[26] A man's conscious desire to copulate with other men was analogously not essential to being afflicted with "homosexuality," which ʿAqqād defined as "the inclination toward passionately loving members of one's own sex rather than members of the opposite sex."[27] A defender of the chaste love of boys prior to the twentieth century—such as ʿAbd al-Ghanī al-Nābulusī—could insist on the distinction between lust and passionate love, and argue that to conflate the two would be to "think ill" of others. Such an argument was much more difficult to sustain in a milieu that operated with the modern, nebulous notion of "sexuality."

The introduction of the new concept of *shudhūdh jinsī* thus seems to have cemented the emerging view that all forms of passionate attraction to boys were equally signs of "sickness" and "depravity." Writing in 1946, the Egyptian historian Tawfīq al-Ṭawīl thus denounced what he considered to be widespread *shudhūdh jinsī* in Ottoman Egypt, and expressed his own surprise at Ṭahṭāwī's remarks concerning the unacceptability of pederasty in France, "as if its being widespread was the natural thing." Ṭawīl mentioned examples of scholars being in love with boys as examples of *shudhūdh jinsī:*

> Examples of the third kind [of moral decadence], viz. *shudhūdh jinsī,* are plentiful and almost beyond count. We often read in the works of history and biography that this or that scholar used to love boys, may God forgive him.[28]

The adversity toward all forms of "homosexuality" would seem to be typical of Arab historians writing in the second half of the twentieth century. As has been seen in chapter 2 of this study, many modern Arab literary historians are clearly uncomfortable with the pederastic themes in their literary heritage, and will often write as if it was a marginal phenomenon or did not exist at all. Closely related to this denial is the tendency—mentioned above in connection with *The Arabian Nights* and the *Dīwān* of Abū Nuwās—to publish expurgated versions of pre-nineteenth-century works. For example, the seventeenth-century satirical work *Hazz al-quḥūf,* which is replete with references to pederasty, was still being printed in Cairo in the last decades of the nineteenth century and the first decade of the twentieth.[29] After not being printed for more than half a century, it was published in 1963 in a heavily expurgated form, in which all references to homosexuality (and all explicitly sexual and scatological words and phrases) were removed.[30]

Less reticent historians tended to adopt the dismissive and hostile attitude that came to the forefront in the 1920s and '30s. Thus, Yūsuf Ḥusayn Bakkār, writing in 1971 about currents in Arabic love poetry, distinguishes between "sensual" (*ḥissī*), "perverted" (*shādhdh*), and "chaste" (*'afīf*) love poetry.[31] "Perverted" love poetry is love poetry of boys, and the idea that love poetry of boys could itself be divided into "sensual" or "chaste" is not even considered. al-Khaṭīb al-'Adnānī, in a recent book (published in 1999) on fornication and "homosexuality" in Arabic history, subsumes sodomy, effeminate passivity, the love of boys, and lesbianism under the term *shudhūdh jinsī.*[32] He claims that homosexuals spread AIDS like a plague, upholds the strict Imāmī Shī'ite punishments for sodomy and same-sex intercourse, and deplores what he believes to be the widespread tolerance of homosexuality in the West. He is apparently unaware that the concept of *shudhūdh jinsī* is Western in origin, and that two centuries earlier it was European travelers who complained about the openness with which men in the Ottoman Empire expressed their passion for boys.

In this respect, the cultural change has been quite dramatic. In less than a century, the unsympathetic attitude toward pederastic love that Ṭahṭāwī attributed to the French had been adopted by the articulate classes of Arab societies. Yet, other cultural strands have not disappeared from the scene. Islamic law still considers *liwāṭ,* defined strictly as anal intercourse between men, to be a punishable sin comparable to fornication or the drinking of wine. This traditional position is of course potentially in tension with the view that the desire for same-sex intercourse is pathological. Writers like al-Khaṭīb al-ʿAdnānī who wish to uphold both views accordingly devote some effort to reconciling them.[33] The punishment prescribed for the act in Islamic law has also remained largely unchanged, though—as noted in the previous chapter—the increasing influence of the revivalist and anti-scholastic Salafī movement may have led more Sunnī jurists to favor the death penalty in all cases, regardless of marital status. The rising influence of the Salafī movement has also succeeded in putting Sufism, particularly of the monist, Ibn ʿArabī school, on the defensive.[34] However, the notion of appreciating divine beauty in humans was hardly widespread and uncontroversial before the nineteenth century, and the declining fortunes of monist mysticism hardly amounts to a dramatic shift in cultural attitudes.

The "polarizing" view of phallic penetration still looms large in popular, oral culture. The new literary term *shudhūdh jinsī,* which ignores the question of who does what to whom, has never really been adopted in spoken Arabic, and it is still a common assumption, particularly in the less westernized segments of Arab society, that engaging in homosexual intercourse as an "active" partner does not compromise one's masculinity, nor reveal any constitutional abnormality.[35] From this perspective, the conceptual distinction between the supposed active and the supposed passive partner is maintained, despite the introduction of the new and indiscriminate concept of *shudhūdh jinsī.*

Notes

Introduction

1. Bernard, *L'orient du XVIe siècle,* 200; Rycaut, *The Present State of the Ottoman Empire,* 33–34; Buckingham, *Travels in Assyria, Media, and Persia,* 1:149ff.

2. Pitts, *A Faithful Account of the Religion and Manners of the Mahometans,* 26.

3. Sonnini, *Travels in Upper and Lower Egypt,* 1:251–52.

4. This point is pressed in Matar, *Turks, Moors, and Englishmen in the Age of Discovery,* ch. 4.

5. Miller, *Disorienting Encounters,* 161.

6. Ṭahṭāwī, *Takhlīṣ al-ibrīz,* 78. D. Hopwood cites this passage in *Sexual Encounters in the Middle East,* 247. I have consulted his translation, but deviate from it on some points. Most importantly, he translates the term *ʿarab* as "Arabs," whereas I translate it as "Bedouin." In the history of ʿAbd al-Raḥmān al-Jabartī, written one generation before Ṭahṭāwī's visit to Paris, the term *ʿarab* clearly refers to nomadic Bedouin, not to "Arabs" in the modern sense of the word; see *ʿAjāʾib al-āthār,* 2:89 (line 33), 2:257 (line 13), 3:173 (line 8–9), 3:176 (line 7–8). When Jabartī wishes to designate the Arabic-speaking people of Egypt, in contrast to the Turkish-speaking military elite, he uses the term *awlād al-ʿarab* or *abnāʾ al-ʿarab;* see 2:248 (line 31), 4:265 (line 32). On the supposed absence of pederasty among the Bedouins, as opposed to the settled townspeople, see Burckhardt, *Travels in Arabia,* 1:364.

7. Bullough, *Sexual Variance in Society and History,* ch. 9.

8. Boswell, *Christianity, Social Tolerance, and Homosexuality,* 194–200.

9. Hodgson, *The Venture of Islam,* 2:146.

10. Lewis, *Music from a Distant Drum,* 26.

11. Jabartī, *ʿAjāʾib al-āthār,* 1:209.

12. Shabrāwī, *Dīwān,* 59.

13. Shabrāwī, *Dīwān,* 54.

14. Shabrāwī, *Dīwān,* 69.

15. Shabrāwī, *Dīwān,* 69, 48, 9.

16. Foucault, *The History of Sexuality,* 1:43.

17. This is stated in conscious opposition to constructionist claims, by Johansson and Percy, "Homosexuality," 156, and AbuKhalil, "A Note on the Study of Homosexuality in the Arab/Islamic Civilization," 32a.

18. Nathan, "Medieval Arabic Medical Views on Male Homosexuality."

19. Spencer, *Homosexuality: A History,* 103–4; Greenberg, *The Construction of Homosexuality,* 176–77.

20. The secondary literature may for convenience be divided into four major types:

(i) General overviews of the theme by specialists in Arab-Islamic studies, such as the article "Liwāṭ" (1986) in *Encyclopaedia of Islam;* Bruce Dunne's "Homosexuality in the Middle East: An Agenda for Historical Research" *Arab Studies Quarterly* (1990); Arno Schmitt's "Different Approaches to Male-Male Sexuality-Eroticism from Morocco to Usbekistan," in A. Schmitt and J. Sofer, eds., *Sexuality and Eroticism among Males in Moslem Societies* (1992); As'ad AbuKhalil's article "A Note on the Study of Homosexuality in the Arab/Islamic Civilization," *Arab Studies Journal* (1993); al-Khaṭīb al-'Adnānī's *al-Zinā wa al-shudhūdh fī al-tārīkh al-'arabī* (1999).

(ii) Chapters devoted to Islamic civilization in comparative and historical accounts of homosexuality such as Vern L. Bullough's *Sexual Variance in Society and History* (1976), David Greenberg's *The Construction of Homosexuality* (1988), and Stephen O. Murray's *Homosexualities* (2000). Such chapters are written by nonspecialists who read no (or very little) Arabic, and consequently must rely on secondary studies, travel literature, and the odd translation of an Arabic primary source. The same applies to the contributions to S. O. Murray and W. Roscoe, eds., *Islamic Homosexualities* (1997).

(iii) Remarks on the theme in studies with a more general scope, such as A. Bouhdiba's *La sexualité en Islam* (1975; English translation 1985), Robert Irwin's *The Arabian Nights: A Companion* (1994), and Thomas Bauer's *Liebe und Liebesdichtung in der arabischen Welt des 9. und 10. Jahrhunderts* (1998).

(iv) Discussions of a particular Arabic work or poem, or sometimes even one passage from a work or poem. This includes the discussion of Abū Bakr al-Rāzī's analysis of the disease *ubnah* by Franz Rosenthal (1978), and the discussion of Ibn Sīnā's analysis of the same disease by B. Nathan (1994). Most of the contributions to E. K. Rowson and J. W. Wright Jr., eds., *Homoeroticism in Classical Arabic Literature* (1997), also fall into this category. A few studies have tried to survey a collection of thematically related texts. For instance, Franz Rosenthal has surveyed the theme of "disputation" (*mufākharah*) between lovers of women and lovers of boys in classical Arabic literature (Rosenthal, "Male and Female: Described and Compared"). Arno Schmitt has recently surveyed rulings on sodomy (*liwāṭ*) in Muslim law (Schmitt, "*Liwāṭ* im *Fiqh*").

21. Burton's terminal essay on pederasty was excised from most editions of his translation. It has since been published as a separate monograph under the title *The Sotadic Zone.*

22. Pellat et al., "Liwāṭ." The article has been reprinted in Schmitt and Safer, eds., *Sexuality and Eroticism among Males in Moslem Societies,* 151–64, with critical notes by A. Schmitt. Schmitt trenchantly exposes some of the conceptual confusions that mar the article.

23. Goitein, "The Sexual Mores of the Common People," 47–48.

24. Bouhdiba, *Sexuality in Islam,* 31–33, 200–201.

25. Schmitt, "Different Approaches to Male/Male Sexuality"; Schmitt, "*Liwāṭ* im *Fiqh*"; Rowson, "The Categorization of Gender and Sexual Irregularity"; Rowson, "Two Homoerotic Narratives from Mamluk Literature"; Bauer, *Liebe und Liebesdichtung,* 163–74.

26. For a similar criticism of some of the secondary literature on homosexuality in Arab-Islamic history, see Massad, "Re-Orienting Desire," 362–63.

27. Monroe, "The Striptease That Was Blamed on Abū Bakr's Naughty Son," 116–17.

28. This point is made in a somewhat different context by Gellner, "Doctor and Saint," and by Burke, "Strengths and Weaknesses of the History of Mentalities."

29. In adopting this approach, I have been influenced especially by Frazer and Cameron, "Knowing What to Say: The Construction of Gender in Linguistic Practice"; Loizos and Papataxiarchis, "Gender and Kinship in Marriage and Alternative Contexts"; and Baker, "On the Problem of the Ideological Origins of the French Revolution."

Chapter One

1. Ibn Kannān, *al-Ḥawādith al-yawmiyyah,* 51–52.

2. Nābulusī, *Taʿṭīr al-anām,* 2:210 (*liwāṭ*) and 2:294 (*nikāḥ*); see also Munāwī, *al-Fuyūḍāt al-ilāhiyyah,* fol. 70b–71a.

3. Muḥibbī, *Nafḥat al-rayḥānah,* 1:395–96; Muḥibbī, *Khulāṣat al-athar,* 1:47.

4. Muḥibbī, *Nafḥat al-rayḥānah,* 4:607–8.

5. Vanggaard, *Phallos,* ch. 6.

6. al-Alūsī, Maḥmūd, *Rūḥ al-maʿānī,* 8:152.

7. al-Baḥrānī, *al-Burhān,* 2:348, 4:233.

8. For example, al-Manīnī, *al-Fatḥ al-wahbī,* 1:323, 325; al-Isḥāqī, *Akhbār al-uwal,* 125; the two quotations are from poems cited in al-Manīnī, *al-Fatḥ al-wahbī,* 1:156, and in al-ʿĀmilī, Bahāʾ al-Dīn, *al-Kashkūl,* 1:319.

9. I have adopted the term "polarizing" from Halperin's discussion of the classical Greek attitude toward sexual intercourse (Halperin, *One Hundred Years of Homosexuality,* 30).

10. This seems to me to be the tendency of many of the contributions to Schmitt and Sofer, eds., *Sexuality and Eroticism among Males in Muslim Societies.* For another criticism of the simplistic juxtaposition of "Western" and "Arab" attitudes, see Massad, "Re-Orienting Desire," 363.

11. Ibn Ayyūb, *al-Rawḍ al-ʿāṭir,* 84; Māmāyah al-Rūmī, *Rawḍat al-mushtāq,* fol. 191a. For another example of sexual imagery being used in a case of rivalry for position, see Ṭālawī, *Sāniḥāt dumā al-qaṣr,* 1:217–19.

12. For recent examples, see AbuKhalil, "A Note on the Study of Homosexuality in the Arab/Islamic Civilization"; Hopwood, *Sexual Encounters in the Middle East,* 176.

13. The strict juridical concept of *liwāṭ* will be discussed in chapter 3.

14. Jazāʾirī, *Zahr al-rabīʿ,* 31.

15. al-Ḥurr al-ʿĀmilī, *Wasāʾil al-shīʿah,* 14:248ff. (tradition 12). The term *ityān,* which I have rendered as "carnal penetration of," clearly connotes assuming the active-insertive role in sexual intercourse, and passive forms of the word are regularly used to denote the assumption of the passive-receptive role.

16. See *Dīwān khidmat al-usṭā ʿUthmān.* On *lūṭīs* who are attracted to boys: 12, 26–27; on *bitāʿ al-ṣighār:* 7, 37.

17. Shirbīnī, *Hazz al-quḥūf,* 94; Murādī, *Silk al-durar,* 2:206.

18. Khafājī, *Rayḥānat al-alibbā,* 1:431–32.

19. al-ʿUmarī, ʿUthmān, *al-Rawḍ al-naḍir,* 1:62.

20. al-ʿUmarī, Muḥammad Amīn, *Manhal al-awliyāʾ,* 1:228.

21. The image of the people of Sodom in the Qur'anic commentaries will be discussed in chapter 3.

22. Saffārīnī, *Qar' al-siyāṭ,* fol. 10b. Again, the term *ityān* clearly indicates assuming the insertive role.

23. Bājūrī, *Ḥāshiyah,* 2:240.

24. Jazarī, *Dīwān,* fol. 72a.

25. Irwin, *The Arabian Nights: A Companion,* 169.

26. Compare Tīfāshī, *Nuzhat al-albāb,* 141 (on the helpful tools of the pederast) with 144–45 (on the visible characteristics of boy prostitutes). Incidentally, Irwin's references to hairy ankles, thin legs, and long robes are also inaccurate. Tīfāshī wrote that the boy prostitutes usually remove the hair from their legs and wear short robes that reveal their ankles. It is only those who do not shave their legs, or who have thin legs, who try to conceal this by wearing long robes.

27. E. Rowson makes a similar point in "The Categorization of Gender and Sexual Irregularity in Medieval Arabic Vice Lists," as does T. Bauer, in *Liebe und Liebesdichtung,* 166.

28. For example, *liwāṭ* is called *al-dā' al-ladhī lā dawā' lahu* in a tradition cited i-n Baḥrānī, *al-Burhān,* 2:348; but the very same tradition goes on to state: *fa-ayy dā' adwa'* [variant: *a'dā*] *min al-bukhl?* Muḥammad al-Saffārīnī calls *liwāṭ* a *dā'* in his short tract *Qar' al-siyāṭ* (fol. 10b), which relies heavily on *al-Dā' wa al-dawā'* by Ibn Qayyim al-Jawziyyah (d. 1350). However, the latter work clearly uses the term *dā'* in a broad, nonmedical sense, calling *jahl* the fundamental *dā',* and repentance (*al-tawbah*) the most important antidote.

29. Medieval Latin translations of Avicenna's *Canon* (book 3, chapter 20) refer to *alubuati* (or *aluminati* or *alguagi*). Joan Cadden takes these to be Latinizations of the Arabic *al-liwāṭ* ("Western Medicine and Natural Philosophy," 64). They are in fact Latinizations of the Arabic *al-ubnah.* See Ibn Sīnā, *al-Qānūn fī al-ṭibb,* 3:228–29. See also the discussion of this passage in Nathan, "Medieval Arabic Medical Views on Male Homosexuality." Nathan, however, insists on using the unhelpful term "homosexual" to translate the Arabic term *ma'būn,* even though, as he himself admits, the latter term only applied to the passive partner.

30. Ibn Ayyūb, *al-Rawḍ al-'āṭir,* 23; Ibn Kannān, *al-Ḥawādith al-yawmiyyah,* 38; al-Makkī al-Mūsawī, *Nuzhat al-jalīs,* 1:242; Tietze, *Mustafa 'Ali's Description of Egypt,* 60.

31. *Nuzhat al-udabā',* MS I, 95a; MS II, 208a. This work is sometimes attributed to a certain 'Umar al-Halabī, who seems to have flourished in the seventeenth century. See Brockelmann, *Geschichte der arabischen Literatur,* Supplement, 2:414; and Arberry, *A Second Supplementary Hand-List,* no. 128.

32. *Dīwān khidmat al-usṭā 'Uthmān,* 13, 31.

33. Māmāyah al-Rūmī, *Rawḍat al-mushtāq,* fol. 192b–193a.

34. On Rāzī's diagnosis of *ubnah,* see Rosenthal, "Ar-Razi on the Hidden Illness." The Arabic text is reproduced in al-Tīfāshī, *Nuzhat al-albāb,* 302–8.

35. Anṭākī, *al-Nuzhah al-mubhijah,* 2:216; Sha'rānī, *Mukhtaṣar,* 55; Qalyūbī, *al-Tadhkirah,* 58. See also Jazā'irī, *Zahr al-rabī',* 511; Isḥāqī, *Akhbār al-uwal,* 48; Sha'rānī, *Laṭā'if al-minan,* 2:211.

36. This last remedy is also mentioned in the discussions of Sha'rānī, Qalyūbī, and Jazā'irī. The idea goes back at least to Pliny the Elder (d. 79), see Williams, *Roman Homosexuality,* 180–81. A variant also appears in the medieval Western medical tradition. Albertus

Magnus (d. 1280) suggested burnt and ground fur from the neck of *alzabo* (Arabic *al-ḍabʿ*) as an effective cure for "sodomy." As pointed out by J. Boswell, Albertus's source was probably a Latin translation or adaptation of an earlier Arabic medical or zoological work (*Christianity, Social Tolerance, and Homosexuality,* 316–17). Apparently, the Arabic *ubnah,* which refers to a condition of the passive partner, became role-unspecified *sodomia* in Latin.

37. Isḥāqī, *Akhbār al-uwal,* 47; Ibn Nujaym, *al-Baḥr al-rāʾiq,* 5:50; Ibn ʿĀbidīn, *Radd al-muḥtār,* 3:201–2.

38. Buhūtī, *Sharḥ muntahā al-irādāt,* 3:358; a similar ruling is given in Ibn Ḥajar, *al-Fatāwā al-kubrā al-fiqhiyyah,* 4:201.

39. Ibn Ayyūb, *al-Rawḍ al-ʿāṭir,* 101; al-Isḥāqī, *Akhbār al-uwal,* 47.

40. *Nuzhat al-udabāʾ,* MS I, fol. 93b–97a; MS II, fol. 208a–209a (ch. 11: *fī al-mustaṭrab min aḥādīth al-maʾābīn wa al-mukhannathīn*); Tīfāshī, *Nuzhat al-albāb,* 249–308 (ch. 12: *fī al-khināth wa al-mukhannathīn*); Isḥāqī, *Akhbār al-uwal,* 44–48.

41. al-Khāl, *Dīwān,* fol. 35b. The term *ʿilq* is a colloquial term with the same meaning as *mukhannath* or *maʾbūn*. This is explicitly stated in Barbīr, *al-Sharḥ al-jalī,* 230. See also M. Hinds and E. Badawi, *A Dictionary of Egyptian Arabic,* 593, and *Dīwān khidmat al-usṭā ʿUthmān,* 37: "No one washes his arse except the *ʿilq* boy so that he will be loved by *bitāʿ al-ṣighār.*"

42. Ibn Ayyūb, *al-Rawḍ al-ʿāṭir,* 79–80; Khafājī, *Rayḥānat al-alibbā,* 2:125; Muḥibbī, *Khulāṣat al-athar,* 1:47; al-ʿUmarī, ʿUthmān, *al-Rawḍ al-naḍir,* 68. The same insult (*euruprôktos*) was used in classical Greece, see Dover, *Greek Homosexuality,* 140; Thornton, *Eros,* 110.

43. Winter, *Egyptian Society under Ottoman Rule,* 9–10 (citing the chronicle of Ibn Iyyās), 230 (citing the chronicle of Aḥmad Çelebī).

44. Būrīnī, *Tarājim al-aʿyān,* 2:280; Jabartī, *ʿAjāʾib al-āthār,* 1:413.

45. Tietze, *Mustafa ʿAlī's Description of Egypt,* 51–54.

46. Ibn Ayyūb, *al-Rawḍ al-ʿāṭir,* 87–88; Māmāyah al-Rūmī, *Rawḍat al-mushtāq,* fol. 219b. Majnūn and Laylah and Kuthayyir and ʿAzzah are legendary (male/female) love couples from the early Islamic period.

47. Dardīr, *al-Sharḥ al-kabīr,* 4:339.

48. Ḥaṣkafī, *al-Durr al-muntaqā,* 1:609–10.

49. See the anecdotes in Isḥāqī, *Akhbār al-uwal,* 113–16; and Tīfāshī, *Nuzhat al-albāb,* 99–126.

50. Bullough, *Sexual Variance in Society and History,* 232; Irwin, *The Arabian Nights,* 175. Both works cite *The Arabian Nights.*

51. Shaykhzāde, *Majmaʿ al-anhur,* 1:595–96; Ibn Nujaym, *al-Baḥr al-rāʾiq,* 5:17–18.

52. Gilmore, "Introduction: The Shame of Dishonour," 9.

53. ʿĀmilī, Bahāʾ al-Dīn, *al-Kashkūl,* 1:361; Jazāʾirī, *Zahr al-rabīʿ,* 45.

54. For example, Buhūtī, *Sharḥ muntahā al-irādāt,* 3:345: "*wa lūṭī fāʿil wa mafʿūl bihi . . .*"

55. Būrīnī, *Tarājim al-aʿyān,* 1:252.

56. Būrīnī, *Tarājim al-aʿyān,* 2:73–74. For another independent allusion to this incident, see Ibn Ayyūb, *al-Rawḍ al-ʿāṭir,* 30.

57. Nābulusī, *Taʿṭīr al-anām,* 2:210 (*liwāṭ*), 236–38 (*mujāmaʿah*), 294 (*nikāḥ*). Compare the strikingly similar interpretations of Artemidorus (2nd century AD), analyzed in

Foucault, *The History of Sexuality,* 3:4–36, and Winkler, *The Constraints of Desire,* 17–44. On this theme, see also Oberhelman, "Hierarchies of Gender, Ideology, and Power in Medieval Greek and Arabic Dream Literature."

58. *Nuzhat al-udabā',* MS I, fol. 95a; MS II, fol. 208a–b.

59. This is one of the main points in Bourdieu, *The Logic of Practice;* see especially "The Social Uses of Kinship," 162–99.

60. Pitt-Rivers, *The Fate of Shechem,* 16.

61. Gilmore, "Introduction: The Shame of Dishonour," 10–11 (speaking of contemporary Mediterranean culture in general).

62. Nābulusī, *Ta'ṭīr al-anām,* 1:223–27 (*dhakar insān*), 19 (*unthayān*), 192 (*khaṣī*). See also Munāwī, *al-Fuyūḍāt al-ilāhiyyah,* fol. 68b–69a. For a similar observation concerning the contemporary Mediterranean area, see Pitt-Rivers, *The Fate of Shechem,* 22.

63. For example, Jabartī, *'Ajā'ib al-āthār,* 1:100, 111; see also Lane, *An Account of the Manners and Customs of the Modern Egyptians,* 37, 561 (n. 4); and Volney, *Travels through Syria and Egypt,* 1:118.

64. Nābulusī, *Ta'ṭīr al-anām,* 2:206–8 (*liḥya*), 1:223–27 (*dhakar insān*). See also Munāwī, *al-Fuyūḍāt al-ilāhiyyah,* fol. 66b (*al-ṭūl fī al-liḥyah*) and fol. 68 (*kibr al-dhakar wa ṭūluhu*). On the symbolic importance of the beard or moustache in the Mediterranean area, see Gilmore, *Manhood in the Making,* 31, 47 (Italy and Greece); and Bourdieu, *The Logic of Practice,* 211 (the Kabyle of Algeria).

65. Ibn al-Ḥanbalī, *Durr al-ḥabab,* 2:145; Ghazzī, *al-Kawākib al-sā'irah,* 3:23.

66. Jabartī, *'Ajā'ib al-āthār,* 2:217. For al-Khashshāb's love of the scribe, see ibid, 4:238–41.

67. Muḥibbī, *Khulāṣat al-athar,* 4:35–36; Muḥibbī, *Nafḥat al-rayḥānah,* 1:380.

68. The theme will be dealt with at greater length in the following chapter.

69. Shawkānī, *al-Badr al-ṭāli',* 1:281–82 (the editor's footnote, quoting an unpublished biographical dictionary of eighteenth-century Yemeni poets).

70. Barbīr, *al-Sharḥ al-jalī,* 220.

71. Ibn Ḥajar al-Haytamī, *al-Fatāwā al-kubrā al-fiqhiyyah,* 4:359.

72. Ibn al-Wakīl al-Mallawī, *Bughyat al-musāmir,* fol. 131b–133a.

73. Ibn al-Ḥanbalī, *Durr al-ḥabab,* 1:688–89, 2:159.

74. Ibn Ayyūb al-Anṣārī, *al-Rawḍ al-'āṭir,* 23.

75. Būrīnī, *Tarājim al-a'yān,* 1:108. For another example, see Ghazzī, *Luṭf al-samar,* 2:581–82.

76. Māmāyah al-Rūmī, *Rawḍat al-mushtāq,* fol. 331b–334a.

77. 'Urḍī, *Ma'ādin al-dhahab,* 244–45; Ibn al-Ḥanbalī, *Durr al-ḥabab,* 1:687–93; al-Budayri al-Ḥallāq, *Ḥawādith Dimashq al-yawmiyyah,* 185.

78. Lane, *An Account of the Manners and Customs of the Modern Egyptians,* 159–60; Russell, *The Natural History of Aleppo,* 1:281–82; Volney, *Travels through Syria and Egypt,* 2:485–86; Marcus, *The Middle East on the Eve of Modernity,* 196.

79. Jabartī, *'Ajā'ib al-āthār,* 1:67, 361.

80. Pitts, *A Faithful Account,* 98–100; Burckhardt, *Travels in Arabia,* 1:364; Jabartī, *'Ajā'ib al-āthār,* 1:144, 3:219; al-Budayrī al-Ḥallāq, *Ḥawādith Dimashq al-yawmiyyah,* 39, 57, 92, 112, 134; al-Suwaydī 'Abdallah, *al-Nafḥah al-miskiyyah,* fol. 95a.

81. For related remarks on courtship of boys in ancient Greece, see Cohen, *Law, Sexuality, and Society,* 185–87.

82. Volney, *Travels through Syria and Egypt,* 1:185.

83. Zabīdī, *Tāj al-ʿarūs,* 9:166 (m-r-d).

84. Shirbīnī, *Hazz al-quḥūf,* 94. This is strikingly similar to the pre-Meiji Japanese views analyzed in Pflugfelder, *Cartographies of Desire,* 31.

85. Ibn Kannān, *al-Ḥawādith al-yawmiyyah,* 417.

86. Būrīnī, *Tarājim al-aʿyān,* 2:241; Muḥibbī, *Nafḥat al-rayḥānah,* 1:412; Khafājī, *Rayḥānat al-alibbā,* 1:247. An eighteenth-century Turkish work of bawdy comedy also states that for pederasts the ideal age of boys is fourteen (see Schmidt, "Sünbülzāde," 24).

87. Blount, *A Voyage into the Levant,* 14.

88. Murādī, *Silk al-durar,* 1:247; Ghazzī, *al-Wird al-unsī,* fol. 110b–111a; al-Alūsī, Maḥmūd Shukri, *al-Misk al-adhfar,* 98–99. In these cases, the last hemistich of the poems contains the date of composition in letter-code. Together with the date of birth, they allow the calculation of the age of the youth at the time.

89. Ibn al-Ḥanbalī, *Durr al-ḥabab,* 1:1109. Ibn al-Ḥanbalī knew the son in question personally.

90. Ibn Ayyūb, *Nuzhat al-khāṭir,* 2:204.

91. al-ʿUmarī, ʿUthmān, *al-Rawḍ al-naḍir,* 2:270–73.

92. Shirbīnī, *Hazz al-quḥūf,* 233.

93. Tīfāshī, *Nuzhat al-albāb,* 198; for a concrete example, see Ibn Kannān, *al-Ḥawādith al-yawmiyyah,* 180.

94. Anṭākī, *Tazyīn al-aswāq,* 2:84; the above-mentioned poem of Qāṣim al-Rāmī also stated that the handsome boy himself fell in love, when he was fourteen.

95. Muḥibbī, *Nafḥat al-rayḥānah,* 1:301.

96. al-ʿĀmilī, Bahāʾ al-Dīn, *al-Kashkūl,* 1:361; Jazāʾirī, *Zahr al-rabīʿ,* 287.

97. Shirbīnī, *Hazz al-quḥūf,* 94.

98. This is a recurrent theme in Schmitt and Sofer, eds., *Sexuality and Eroticism among Males in Muslim Societies.* For a criticism of the "blind phallus" stereotype that infects some of the contributions to that work, see Murray, *Homosexualities,* 266–72.

99. al-ʿUmarī, Muḥammad Amīn, *Manhal al-awliyāʾ,* 1:228.

100. Būrīnī, *Tarājim al-aʿyān,* 1:87; Khafājī, *Rayḥānat al-alibbā,* 1:62. For another example, see Ibn Kannān, *al-Ḥawādith al-yawmiyyah,* 38.

101. Tietze, *Mustafa ʿAli's Description of Egypt,* 54.

102. Chamberlain, *Knowledge and Social Practice in Medieval Damascus,* ch. 2; Berkey, *The Transmission of Knowledge in Medieval Cairo,* ch. 2. By the eighteenth century, the Azhar college in Cairo does seem to have gained a reputation as an institution, but certificates were still conferred by individual teachers.

103. Shīrāzī, *al-Ḥikmah al-mutaʿāliyah,* 7:171–72; Mullā Ṣadra's discussion is quoted in the miscellany of Rāghib Pāshā (d. 1763), *Safīnat al-rāghib,* 317–18.

104. Ikhwān al-Ṣafā, *Rasāʾil,* 3:277; Plato, *Symposium,* 208e–209e.

105. Ibn Ḥajar, *Taḥrīr al-maqāl,* 65.

106. Muḥibbī, *Khulāṣat al-athar,* 2:407, 3:223–24; Murādī, *Silk al-durar,* 4:222.

107. Būrīnī, *Tarājim al-aʿyān,* 1:124–25; Ghazzī, *Lutf al-samar,* 2:539–40; Muḥibbī, *Khulāṣat al-athar,* 2:337; al-ʿUmarī, Muḥammad Amīn, *Manhal al-awliyāʾ,* 1:257.

108. Shabrāwī, *Dīwān,* 69–70.

109. Murādī, *Silk al-durar,* 4:130.

110. Jabartī, *ʿAjāʾib al-āthār,* 1:79–80. The recent English translation of Jabartī's history renders the Arabic term *bidāyātihim* as "their nurses," taking *bi* as a preposition prefixed to the term *dāyātihim* (Phillip and Perlmann, *ʿAbd al-Rahman al-Jabarti's History of Egypt,* 1:131). However, a seventeenth-century tract reveals that at least one disreputable order called their young novices *bidāyāt;* see Dajjānī, *al-ʿIqd al-mufrad,* fol. 6a–8a.

111. Dajjānī, *al-ʿIqd al-mufrad,* fol. 6a–8a; Tawil, *al-Taṣawwuf fī Miṣr,* 112, 176–77 (citing a *fatwā* by al-ʿAdawī). A similarly motivated condemnation of the Muṭāwiʿah order was composed by Muḥammad al-Ghamrī (d. 1445); see Shaʿrānī, *al-Anwār al-qudsiyyah,* 1:47.

112. Ritter, *Das Meer der Seele,* ch. 26.

113. Bakrī, *al-Suyūf al-ḥidād,* fol. 24b–25a.

114. Ghazzī, *Lutf al-samar,* 1:269–70; Ibn al-Ḥanbalī, *Durr al-ḥabab,* 1:525–27; Būrīnī, *Tarājim al-aʿyān,* 1:256; Ghulāmī, *Shammāmat al-ʿanbar,* 193–94.

115. Ibn Maʿṣūm, *Sulāfat al-ʿaṣr,* 98; Muḥibbī, *Nafḥat al-rayḥānah,* 4:79; Muḥibbī, *Khulāṣat al-athar,* 1:271.

116. Shirbīnī, *Hazz al-quḥūf,* 90–93.

117. Jazāʾirī, *Zahr al-rabīʿ,* 304.

118. Westermarck, *Ritual and Belief in Morocco,* 1:108.

119. Lane, *An Account of the Manners and Customs of the Modern Egyptians,* 229.

120. Shaʿrānī, *al-Ṭabāqat al-kubrā,* 2:122.

121. Ramlī, Khayr al-Dīn, *al-Fatāwā al-khayriyyah,* 2:179.

122. Shaʿrānī, *al-Anwār al-qudsiyyah,* 1:46, 2:96.

123. Winter, *Society and Religion in Early Ottoman Egypt,* 116.

124. Ibn Ḥajar, *al-Zawājir,* 2:143.

125. Russell, *The Natural History of Aleppo* (1756 ed.), 113.

126. Nābulusī, *al-Qawl al-muʿtabar,* fol. 186a–b.

127. Shaʿrānī, *Laṭāʾif al-minan,* 2:135.

128. Shaʿrānī, *Laṭāʾif al-minan,* 2:105.

129. Būrīnī, *Tarājim al-aʿyān,* 1:327, 2:133–37; Muḥibbī, *Khulāṣat al-athar,* 2:219–20, 3:412; Ibn Ayyūb, *al-Rawḍ al-ʿāṭir,* 81; Khafājī, *Rayḥānat al-alibbā,* 1:100; Muḥibbī, *Nafḥat al-rayḥānah,* 2:237.

130. ʿUrḍī, *Maʿādin al-dhahab,* 82.

131. Ibn Ayyūb, *al-Rawḍ al-ʿāṭir,* 5.

132. ʿAlwān al-Ḥamawī, *ʿArāʾis al-ghurar,* 68.

133. Blount, *A Voyage into the Levant,* 14.

134. Saffārīnī, *Qarʿ al-siyāṭ,* fol. 10b. Nevertheless, the remark is an interesting example of apparent ethnic resentment predating the spread of nationalism proper in the second half of the nineteenth century.

135. Jazarī, *Dīwān,* fol. 73b. See also the defamatory poems on fol. 73b–74a and fol. 116a–117a. For the idea that black African men were popular with *mukhannaths* because of their reputed virility and endowment, see Tīfāshī, *Nuzhat al-albāb,* 270–71.

136. Ghazzī, *al-Kawākib al-sāʾirah,* 2:111–12.

137. Hattox, *Coffee and Coffeehouses,* 109.

138. Marcus, *The Middle East on the Eve of Modernity,* 232; Rafeq, "Public Morality in Eighteenth-Century Damascus," 183. For an interesting parallel, see the image of the boy waiters of the *sake* shops in pre-Meiji Japan described in Pflugfelder, *Cartographies of Desire,* 79.

139. Būrīnī, *Tarājim al-aʿyān,* 1:93.

140. ʿInāyātī, *Dīwān,* MS(1), fol. 100a; MS(2), fol. 71a.

141. Lane, *An Account of the Manners and Customs of the Modern Egyptians,* 339.

142. Shirbīnī, *Hazz al-quḥūf,* 219.

143. Munāwī, *al-Nuzhah al-zahiyyah,* 36.

144. Kawkabānī, *Ḥadāʾiq al-nammām,* 93.

145. Kawkabānī, *Ḥadāʾiq al-nammām,* 99–100.

146. Kawkabānī, *Ḥadāʾiq al-nammām,* 179–201.

147. al-Makkī al-Mūsawī, *Nuzhat al-jalīs,* 2:318–19. The word "shave" probably refers to shaving the head, not the beard.

148. McIntosh, "The Homosexual Role," 36.

149. Bray, *Homosexuality in Renaissance England,* 31.

150. Bray, *Homosexuality in Renaissance England,* 103.

151. Huussen, "Sodomy in the Dutch Republic during the Eighteenth Century"; Rey, "Parisian Homosexuals Create a Lifestyle, 1700–1750"; Greenberg, *The Construction of Homosexuality,* 310–46.

152. Foucault, *The History of Sexuality,* 1:43.

153. For example, Boswell, "Revolutions, Universals, and Sexual Categories"; Murray, "Homosexual Acts and Selves in Early Modern Europe"; Saslow, "Homosexuality in the Renaissance"; Cady, "Masculine Love, Renaissance Writing, and the New Invention of Homosexuality." For a recent study that challenges the findings of Bray on Renaissance England, see Young, *James VI and I and the History of Homosexuality,* esp. 3–4, 141–55.

154. For similar remarks on the Greek stereotype of the passive *kinaidos,* see Winkler, *The Constraints of Desire,* 45–46.

155. Isḥāqī, *Akhbār al-uwal,* 48.

156. Tīfāshī, *Nuzhat al-albāb,* 251–308.

157. In fact, Foucault elsewhere explicitly allows that in classical Greece a man's preference for boys rather than women could be seen as a "character-trait" (*The History of Sexuality,* 2:190). D. Halperin has recently addressed simplistic distortions of Foucault's position in "Forgetting Foucault" and *How to Do the History of Homosexuality,* ch. 1.

158. Sibṭ al-Marṣafī, *al-Bahjah al-unsiyyah,* MS. fol. 12a.

159. Sibṭ al-Marṣafī, *al-Bahjah al-unsiyyah,* MS. fol. 17a.

160. Sibṭ al-Marṣafī, *al-Bahjah al-unsiyyah,* MS. fol. 15b, 16b.

161. Ibn al-Ḥanbalī, *Durr al-ḥabab,* 1:1034–35, 2:414–18, 435–36; Ibn Ayyūb, *al-Rawḍ al-ʿāṭir,* 49, 68–69.

162. Ghazzī, *al-Kawākib al-sāʾirah,* 3:172–73; Ibn Ayyūb, *al-Rawḍ al-ʿāṭir,* 49; Ibn Ṭūlūn, *al-Thaghr al-bassām,* 318–19.

163. Murādī, *Silk al-durar,* 4:222; Muḥibbī, *Khulāṣat al-athar,* 3:244–45.

164. Ramlī, Khayr al-Dīn, *al-Fatāwā al-khayriyyah,* 1:65.

165. Ibn Ḥajar, *al-Zawājir,* 2:141; ʿAlwān al-Ḥamawī, *ʿArāʾis al-ghurar,* 176.

166. See for example, Ibn al-Ḥanbalī, *Durr al-ḥabab,* 2:201 (drug addicts), 1:175, 2:269 (Ibn ʿArabī), 1:216 (music); Būrīnī, *Tarājim al-aʿyān,* 2:241–42 (alcohol), 2:331 (solitude); Murādī, *Silk al-durar,* 3:67 (luxury), 3:246 (pure-blood horses), 4:3 (anecdotes and jokes); Ibn Ayyūb, *al-Rawḍ al-ʿāṭir,* 16 (Ethiopian slave girls); Jabartī, *ʿAjāʾib al-āthār,* 1:165 (poetry), 1:339 (the sciences of language).

167. Muḥibbī, *Khulāṣat al-athar,* 2:16, 3:37; Ghazzī, *Lutf al-samar,* 1:326, 2:716–17; Ibn Ayyūb, *al-Rawḍ al-ʿāṭir,* 84; Ibn al-Ḥanbalī, *Durr al-ḥabab,* 1:142, 169, 835, 2:219.

168. Ibn Ayyūb, *al-Rawḍ al-ʿāṭir,* 68–69; Ghazzī, *al-Kawākib al-sāʾirah,* 1:153–54; Ibn al-Ḥanbalī, *Durr al-ḥabab,* 2:278–79.

169. Muḥibbī, *Khulāṣat al-athar,* 2:219–20.

170. ʿUrḍī, *Maʿādin al-dhahab,* 37.

171. Shawkānī, *al-Badr al-ṭāliʿ,* 2:162. See also Muḥibbī's comments on the works of Ghazzī and Ibn Maʿṣūm in *Khulāṣat al-athar,* 4:197, 1:476; and Būrīnī's introduction to his *Tarājim al-aʿyān,* 1:5–6.

172. Ibn Ayyūb, *al-Rawḍ al-ʿāṭir,* 49.

Chapter Two

1. Muḥibbī, *Khulāṣat al-athar,* 1:99–100.

2. Muḥibbī, *Khulāṣat al-athar,* 3:225–26; Muḥibbī, *Nafḥat al-rayḥānah,* 1:405–8.

3. Muḥibbī, *Khulāṣat al-athar,* 1:42, 4:16.

4. For example, Ibn al-Ḥanbalī, *Durr al-ḥabab,* 1:1033, 2:68; Murādī, *Silk al-durar,* 4:228–29, 2:142; Jabartī, *ʿAjāʾib al-āthār,* 2:169–70, 259–60; Kanjī, *Bulūgh al-munā,* 69, 75; Shawkānī, *al-Badr al-ṭāliʿ,* 2:161.

5. Zabīdī, *Itḥāf al-sādah al-muttaqīn,* 9:555 (margin); Kāshānī, *al-Ḥaqāʾiq,* 178–79. Emphasis added.

6. Shabrāwī, *Dīwān,* 60.

7. Būrīnī, *Tarājim al-aʿyān,* 2:71.

8. *Kaḥal* refers to a natural blackness and should therefore be distinguished from the kohl (black dye) applied to the eye by women; see Būrīnī, *Sharḥ Dīwān Ibn al-Fāriḍ,* 2:112; Barbīr, *al-Sharḥ al-jalī,* 206. For the term *kaḥīl* applied to males, see Shirbīnī, *Hazz al-quḥūf,* 157; Nābulusī, *Ghāyat al-maṭlūb,* 53; Ghazzī, *al-Kawākib al-sāʾirah,* 3:125.

9. Būrīnī, *Tarājim al-aʿyān,* 2:254, 2:127–28.

10. Būrīnī, *Tarājim al-aʿyān,* 1:125, 2:241, 1:30.

11. Quoted in Muḥibbī, *Khulāṣat al-athar,* 1:280.

12. Ṭālawī, *Sāniḥāt dumā al-qaṣr,* 1:165.

13. al-Suwaydī, ʿAbdallah, *al-Nafḥah al-miskiyyah,* fol. 143a.

14. al-Suwaydī, ʿAbd al-Raḥmān, [*Risālah fī al-maḥabbah*], fol. 113a. This short tract is included in a manuscript including several other works in the Cambridge University Library. The relevant catalogue by E. G. Browne mistakenly states that the manuscript dates from 1603 (*A Supplementary Hand-List,* 112–13). This cannot be true, since it mentions ʿAbd al-Ghanī al-Nābulusī (d. 1731) on fol. 101a, and Maḥmūd al-Alūsī (d. 1854) on fol. 129b. The author of the tract is stated at the outset to be Abū al-Khayr ʿAbd al-Raḥmān, the son of Abū al-Barakāt ʿAbdallah al-Suwaydī. This is certainly the Iraqi scholar ʿAbd al-Raḥmān al-Suwaydī (d. 1786), who was known as Abū al-Khayr, and whose father ʿAbdallah (d. 1761)

was known as Abū al-Barākāt (see al-Alūsī, Maḥmūd Shukrī, *al-Misk al-adhfar,* 125ff. and 131ff.). Browne also mistakenly states that the tract in question was written *for* ʿAbd al-Raḥmān al-Suwaydī by "his brother." The tract was written by al-Suwaydī at the request of "one of his brothers among his contemporaries" (fol. 101b–102a).

15. ʿUrḍī, *Maʿādin al-dhahab,* 120–21, 233.

16. For the general theme of old age or gray hair signaling the end of the love of the beautiful, see Muḥibbī, *Khulāṣat al-athar,* 2:53, 387–88; Muḥibbī, *Nafḥat al-rayḥānah,* 4:200; Ibn Maʿṣūm, *Sulāfat al-ʿaṣr,* 554; Khafājī, *Rayḥānat al-alibbā,* 1:175; Murādī, *Silk al-durar,* 1:237–38 (stated to be an exception to the norm). For a similar *topos* in Medieval and Renaissance Europe, see Singer, *The Nature of Love,* 2:55, 130.

17. For example, Murādī, *Silk al-durar,* 1:15, 4:242; Ibn al-Ḥanbalī, *Durr al-ḥabab,* 1:832, 2:256; Jabartī, *ʿAjāʾib al-āthār,* 4:238–41; Khafājī, *Rayḥānat al-alibbā,* 1:53, 2:78; ʿĀmilī, Bahāʾ al-Dīn, *al-Kashkūl,* 1:78; Ibn Maʿṣūm, *Sulāfat al-ʿaṣr,* 310; Kanjī, *Bulūgh al-munā,* 20, 109; Anṭākī, *Tazyīn al-aswāq,* 1:209, 2:21.

18. For discussions of this cultural ideal in earlier periods, see Enderwitz, *Liebe als Beruf,* 53ff.; Bauer, "Raffinement und Frömmigkeit."

19. For renunciations of secular poetry, see Muḥibbī, *Khulāṣat al-athar,* 2:276, 4:266; Muḥibbī, *Nafḥat al-rayḥānah,* 1:448–49, 4:574; Ibn al-Ḥanbalī, *Durr al-ḥabab,* 1:1005–6.

20. Ibn ʿĀbidīn, *Radd al-muḥtār,* 1:32.

21. Muḥibbī, *Nafḥat al-rayḥānah,* 4:585.

22. Shīrāzī, *al-Ḥikmah al-mutaʿāliyah,* 7:171–72; quoted in Rāghib Pāshā, *Safīnat al-rāghib,* 317–18.

23. Nābulusī, *Dīwān al-ḥaqāʾiq,* 1:129.

24. Muḥibbī, *Khulāṣat al-athar,* 1:167–68.

25. Muḥibbī, *Khulāṣat al-athar,* 2:288–89; Muḥibbī, *Nafḥat al-rayḥānah,* 1:38; Murādī, *Silk al-durar,* 1:142.

26. ʿUṭayfī, *Riḥlah,* 16.

27. The three traditions were included in *al-Jāmiʿ al-ṣaghīr,* the renowned compilation of the Prophet's sayings by Jalāl al-Dīn al-Suyūṭī (d. 1505); see Munāwī, *al-Fayḍ al-qadīr,* 1:74, 540, 2:224, 3:313 (*ḥadīths* 44, 1107, 1720, 3486). For citations of such sayings in belles-lettres, see Ṭālawī, *Sāniḥāt dumā al-qaṣr,* 2:178; Khafājī, *Rayḥānat al-alibbā,* 1:417; Murādī, *Silk al-durar,* 3:100–101, 4:73; Nābulusī, *Khamrat bābil,* 177–78.

28. Nābulusī, *Dīwān al-ḥaqāʾiq,* 1:36.

29. al-ʿUmarī, ʿUthmān, *al-Rawḍ al-naḍir,* 2:180–81; Ghulāmī, *Shammāmat al-ʿanbar,* 277.

30. Marcus, *The Middle East on the Eve of Modernity,* 35–36. For the association of *riqqah* and *ḥaḍārah,* see ʿĀmilī, Bahāʾ al-Dīn, *al-Kashkūl,* 2:148; Ibn Maʿṣūm, *Sulāfat al-ʿaṣr,* 369; Muḥibbī, *Khulāṣat al-athar,* 3:311.

31. Shaʿrānī, *Laṭāʾif al-minan,* 1:33.

32. Baer, "Shirbīnī's *Hazz al-quḥūf* and its significance."

33. In this and the following section I draw on material from my article "The Love of Boys in Arabic Love-Poetry of the Early Ottoman Period, 1500–1800," *Middle Eastern Literatures* 8 (2005): 3–22.

34. Muḥibbī, *Khulāṣat al-athar,* 1:151; Muḥibbī, *Nafḥat al-rayḥānah,* 3:447, 4:207, 3:88; Kaywānī, *Dīwān,* 133. On *maṭbūʿ* poetry see Manīnī, *al-Fatḥ al-wahbī,* 1:115.

35. Ṭālawī, *Sāniḥāt dumā al-qaṣr,* 2 : 287.

36. The major poetic anthologies from the period are *Rayḥānat al-alibbā,* by Aḥmad al-Khafājī (d. 1659); *Sulāfat al-ʿaṣr,* by Ibn Maʿṣūm (d. ca. 1708); *Nafḥat al-rayḥānah,* by Muḥammad Amīn al-Muḥibbī (d. 1699); *al-Rawḍ al-naḍir,* by ʿUthmān al-ʿUmarī (d. 1770/1); and *Shammāmat al-ʿanbar,* by Muḥammad al-Ghulāmī (d. 1772/3).

37. Muḥibbī, *Khulāṣat al-athar,* 1 : 406.

38. For examples of love poetry using the feminine, see Muḥibbī, *Nafḥat al-rayḥānah,* 1 : 198–200, 2 : 273, 2 : 392, 2 : 425–27, 3 : 65, 3 : 499–500, 4 : 48; Kanjī, *Bulūgh al-munā,* 15–16, 68.

39. Lane, *An Account of the Manners and Customs of the Modern Egyptians,* 257.

40. Ṭahṭāwī, *Takhlīṣ al-ibrīz,* 78.

41. Amīn, *Muṭālaʿāt fī al-shiʿr al-mamlūkī wa al-ʿUthmānī,* 117–27. The author, however, admits at the very end of his discussion that love poetry of boys was not uncommon.

42. Bāshā, *Tārīkh al-adab al-ʿarabī: al-adab al-ʿuthmānī,* 593; Jundi, *Dīwān,* 123–43.

43. Anouti, *al-Ḥarakah al-adabiyyah,* 59 (footnote 1). Anouti wrote that these four examples are all he could find.

44. al-ʿUmarī, ʿUthmān, *al-Rawḍ al-naḍir,* 1 : 458; Kaywānī, *Dīwān,* 108; Muḥibbī, *Nafḥat al-rayḥānah,* 1 : 126.

45. Murādī, *Silk al-durar,* 1 : 16, 129, 167, 196, 247; 2 : 251, 262, 263; 3 : 199; 4 : 181, 204, 208, 262.

46. Bauer, *Liebe und Liebesdichtung,* 255–80.

47. Muḥibbī, *Khulāṣat al-athar,* 3 : 409, 1 : 331; Murādī, *Silk al-durar,* 1 : 196; Kanjī, *Bulūgh al-munā,* 26; Muḥibbī, *Nafḥat al-rayḥānah,* 1 : 218; al-ʿUmarī, ʿUthmān, *al-Rawḍ al-naḍir,* 1 : 457; Shabrāwī, *Dīwān,* 69; Nābulusī, *Khamrat bābil,* 272.

48. Ibn al-Ḥanbalī, *Durr al-ḥabab,* 1 : 250.

49. For manuscripts of these works, see the index to Brockelman, *Geschichte der arabischen Literatur.*

50. There are, however, examples of a poet describing the beard-down of his beloved, only to go on to describe his earrings (*qurṭ*) and pigtail (*ghadāʾir*) or his veil (Murādī, *Silk al-durar,* 2 : 263; al-ʿUmarī, ʿUthmān, *al-Rawḍ al-naḍir,* 1 : 252–53). For a male youth with earrings, see ʿĀmilī, Bahāʾ al-Dīn, *al-Kashkūl,* 2 : 286; for a veiled youth, see Ibn al-Ḥanbalī, *Durr al-ḥabab,* 1 : 1109.

51. For beard-down as an indication of the gender of the beloved in Persian love poetry, see Bürgel, "Love, Lust, and Longing," 95.

52. Ibn al-Ḥanbalī, *Durr al-ḥabab,* 1 : 689.

53. Ibn Ḥajar, *Tuḥfat al-muḥtāj,* 7 : 190; Ramlī, Sham al-Dīn, *Nihāyat al-muḥtāj,* 6 : 193; Bājūrī, *Ḥāshiyah,* 2 : 101–2.

54. Būrīnī, *Tarājim al-aʿyān,* 1 : 124; Nābulusī, *Khamrat bābil,* 120, 159; Williams, *Roman Homosexuality,* 242 (citing Lucretius).

55. Quoted in Muḥibbī, *Khulāṣat al-athar,* 3 : 316.

56. Ibn Maʿṣūm, *Sulāfat al-ʿaṣr,* 528; Muḥibbī, *Khulāṣat al-athar,* 2 : 384; Murādī, *Silk al-durar,* 3 : 254–55; Muḥibbī, *Khulāṣat al-athar,* 2 : 405.

57. Freud, *Three Essays on the Theory of Sexuality,* 144.

58. Ibn al-Wakīl al-Mallawī, *Bughyat al-musāmir,* fol. 67a–72a.

59. ʿAlwān al-Ḥamawī, *ʿArāʾis al-ghurar,* 68. Beardless youths were also depicted as

being attractive to both women and men in classical Roman literature (Williams, *Roman Homosexuality,* 59).

60. al-ʿUmarī, ʿUthmān, *al-Rawḍ al-naḍir,* 1:353; Ghulāmī, *Shammāmat al-ʿanbar,* 127.

61. Munāwī, *al-Fayḍ al-qadīr,* 2:2 (*ḥadīth* 1178). There was some disagreement among scholars about whether this equation included the Prophet Muḥammad.

62. Jāḥiẓ, *Mufākharat al-jawārī wa al-ghilmān,* in *Rasāʾil,* 2:87–137. See Rosenthal's survey of this theme in classical Arabic literature in "Male and Female: Described and Compared." The theme also features in late-classical Greek literature (see Foucault, *The History of Sexuality,* 3:193ff.; Goldhill, *Foucault's Virginity,* 82ff.); and in the literature of premodern Japan (see Pflugfelder, *Cartographies of Desire,* 59–63).

63. *Alf laylah wa laylah,* 1:598–602 (Nights 419–23).

64. Ibn al-Ḥanbalī, *Durr al-ḥabab,* 1:983–84; Ghazzī, *al-Kawākib al-sāʾirah,* 1:266.

65. Muḥibbī, *Khulāsāt al-athar,* 3:257. The quotation is a saying attributed to the Prophet.

66. Barbīr, *al-Sharḥ al-jalī,* 219.

67. Quoted in Murādī, *Silk al-durar,* 3:244.

68. Khafājī, *Rayḥānat al-alibbā,* 1:350.

69. Muḥibbī, *Khulāṣat al-athar,* 4:84.

70. Ghulāmī, *Shammāmat al-ʿanbar,* 276–77.

71. I use the adjective "heterosexual" in such contexts merely to avoid more cumbersome locutions, and not because the couples involved can appropriately be described as "heterosexual."

72. Ibn al-Wakīl al-Mallawī, *Bughyat al-musāmir,* fol. 140b.

73. On dark-skinned Ethiopians versus the fair-skinned, see Anṭākī, *Tazyīn al-aswāq,* 2:137–38; Ghazzī, *al-Kawākib al-sāʾirah,* 3:106–7; Ibn Maʿṣūm, *Sulāfat al-ʿaṣr,* 80.

74. Nābulusī, *Ghāyat al-maṭlūb,* 163.

75. For similar remarks on "disputations" in classical antiquity, see Halperin, "Historicizing the Subject of Desires" (revised and reprinted as ch. 3 of *How to Do the History of Sexuality*), and Williams, *Roman Homosexuality,* 171–72.

76. Khafājī, *Rayḥānat al-alibbā,* 1:100–102.

77. Murādī, *Silk al-durar,* 4:182.

78. Usāmah ibn Munqidh composed a much-cited couplet endorsing the creed of the Mosulites. See al-ʿUmarī, Muḥammad Amīn, *Manhal al-awliyāʾ,* 1:228; al-ʿUmarī, ʿUthmān, *al-Rawḍ al-naḍir,* 1:456.

79. Muḥibbī, *Khulāṣat al-athar,* 3:114; Murādī, *Silk al-durar,* 2:206.

80. Ibn al-Sammān, [*Tārīkh*], fol. 145b–149a.

81. Ibn al-Sammān, [*Tārīkh*], fol. 151a.

82. Ibn al-Sammān, [*Tārīkh*], fol. 159b–160a.

83. Murādī, *Silk al-durar,* 3:234–45. Anouti mentions this tract in passing, describing its subject matter as "strange"; see *al-Ḥarakah al-adabiyyah,* 93.

84. Murādī, *Silk al-durar,* 4:208.

85. Muḥibbī, *Nafḥat al-rayḥānah,* 2:447.

86. For example, Muḥibbī, *Nafḥat al-rayḥānah,* 2:148; Ibn Maʿtūq al-Ḥuwayzī, *Dīwān,* 225.

87. ʿUṭayfī, *Riḥlah,* 18–19.

88. al-ʿUmarī, ʿUthmān, *al-Rawḍ al-naḍir,* 1:549–58.

89. T. Bauer has convincingly argued that already by the ninth and tenth centuries, love poetry of boys was at least as common as love poetry of women in Arabic literature (*Liebe und Liebesdichtung,* 150–63).

90. This seems to be true of elite poetry produced in the major cities of the Arabic-speaking parts of the Ottoman Empire, as evinced by the literary anthologies and the poetic excerpts in the biographical dictionaries of the period. It may not be true of folk poetry or the poetry of, say, Oman.

91. This is close to the position of T. Bauer in "Raffinement und Frömmigkeit." Bauer, however, seems not to take seriously the dimension of chastity in such poetry, and thus makes the contrast between the secular-hedonist ideal expressed in amatory belles-lettres more at odds with the religious condemnation of fornication and sodomy than I think it was.

92. Bray, *Homosexuality in Renaissance England,* 60–61. For a critical discussion of similar claims about Judeo-Arabic poetry in medieval Spain, see Schirmann, "The Ephebe in Medieval Hebrew Poetry," 67.

93. Bürgel, "Literatur und Wirklichkeit," 254.

94. Rosenthal, "Male and Female: Described and Compared," p. 43.

95. Enderwitz, *Liebe als Beruf,* 7 and 224.

96. Ibn Ḥajar, *Kaff al-raʿāʿ,* 274. The same point is made by Ghazālī in his *Iḥyāʾ ʿulūm al-dīn;* see Zabīdī, *Itḥāf al-sādah al-muttaqīn,* 1:249 (margin), 6:496 (margin).

97. Shawkānī, *al-Badr al-ṭāliʿ,* 1:281.

98. Barbīr, *al-Sharḥ al-jalī,* 219. It is generally agreed that pederastic themes first appear in Arabic literature in the second half of the eighth century.

99. Karmī, *Munyat al-muḥibbīn,* fol. 34b.

100. Karmī, *Munyat al-muḥibbīn,* fol. 41a.

101. See Barbīr, *al-Sharḥ al-jalī,* 219; Karmī, *Munyat al-muḥibbīn,* fol. 41b.

102. Muḥibbī, *Khulāṣat al-athar,* 1:333–34.

103. Murādī, *Silk al-durar,* 4:208.

104. Ibn Maʿtūq al-Ḥuwayzī, *Dīwān,* 225.

105. Muḥibbī, *Khulāṣat al-athar,* 1:10; Muḥibbī, *Nafḥat al-rayḥānah,* 2:653–54.

106. Jabartī, *ʿAjāʾib al-āthar,* 4:239–40.

107. Muḥibbī, *Khulāṣat al-athar,* 4:98–99; Muḥibbī, *Nafḥat al-rayḥānah,* 2:393–94.

108. Bürgel, "Love, Lust, and Longing," 83, and Bürgel, "Literatur und Wirklichkeit," 248.

109. This is clearly the underlying motivation behind Bürgel's attempt to stress the possible fictionality of love poetry; see "Literatur und Wirklichkeit," 254, and "Die beste Dichtung ist die lügenreichste," 35. Modern scholars who regard medieval courtly love in the West as a literary *topos* with no social basis have supported their position by pointing to the severity with which adultery was regarded at the time (see Benton, "Clio and Venus," and the critical discussion of Benton's position in Boas, *The Origin and Meaning of Courtly Love,* 111–14). For recent attempts to vindicate the social reality of medieval courtly love, see Keen, "Chivalry and Courtly Love," and Jaeger, *Ennobling Love.*

110. Karmī, *Munyat al-muḥibbīn,* fol. 39a–b.

111. Khafājī, *Rayḥānat al-alibbā,* 1:335, 338.

112. Muḥibbī, *Nafḥat al-rayḥānah,* 1:31, 1:127.

113. Muḥibbī, *Nafḥat al-rayḥānah,* 1:411–13. The poet is making a pun based on the similarity of the name of the youth to the term for "dividends" or "profits" (*arbāḥ,* plural of *ribḥ*). The friendship between Muḥibbī and Ṣafadī is also apparent from the entry on the latter in Muḥibbī, *Khulāṣat al-athar,* 1:356–59.

114. Nābulusī, *Khamrat bābil,* 223. The term Çelebī in this context probably denotes a "gentlemanly" status in general, not any specific rank. Nābulusī cites another poem composed by Ṣafadī which features the name Rabāḥ in the final line in *Khamrat bābil,* 142.

115. Ghulāmī, *Shammāmat al-ʿanbar,* 381–82. Suwaydī confirmed that Muḥammad al-Ghulāmī was a close friend of his, in *al-Nafḥah al-miskiyyah* (see fol. 3a–b).

116. al-Suwaydī, ʿAbdallah, *al-Nafḥah al-miskiyyah,* MS fol. 142b–147b.

117. Murādī, *Silk al-durar,* 2:275. Murādī quotes the second passage from an anthology of poets by Muḥammad Saʿīd ibn al-Sammān (d. 1759); see Ibn al-Sammān, [*Tārīkh*], fol. 217a.

118. Muḥibbī, *Khulāṣat al-athar,* 2:175. The dates of death may suggest otherwise, but Zakariyyā al-Būsnawī was eighteen years younger than Manjak.

119. Ṭālawī, *Sāniḥāt dumā al-qaṣr,* 1:177; Ibn al-Ḥanbalī, *Durr al-ḥabab,* 2:145; Ghazzī, *al-Kawākib al-sāʾirah,* 3:23.

120. Dover, *Greek Homosexuality,* 66.

121. Kanjī, *Bulūgh al-munā,* 73, 90. The editor of this work assumes that it was written in the nineteenth century. Internal evidence (in particular the formulaic expressions after mentioning a person which reveal whether he was dead or alive at the time of writing) shows that the work was written between 1107/1695–96 and 1117/1705–6. The author is almost certainly the Muḥammad ibn Aḥmad al-Kanjī who is mentioned by Muḥibbī (d. 1699) in *Dhayl Nafḥat al-rayḥānah,* 55–74. The same person is mentioned in the entry on his father Aḥmad (d. 1695/6) in Murādī, *Silk al-durar,* 1:196–99. His date of death is given in Ibn Kannān al-Ṣāliḥī, *al-Ḥawādith al-yawmiyyah,* 518.

122. Jabartī, *ʿAjāʾib al-āthār,* 2:248. A mosque-preacher (*khaṭīb*) aged seventeen is mentioned in Murādī, *Silk al-durar,* 2:2–3.

123. Murādī, *Silk al-durar,* 4:138.

124. Muḥibbī, *Khulāṣat al-athar,* 1:105.

125. Muḥibbī, *Khulāṣat al-athar,* 3:430.

126. Anṭākī, *Tazyīn al-aswāq,* 1:46. For a similar belief in ancient Greece, see Plato, *Symposium,* 196e.

127. Muḥibbī, *Nafḥat al-rayḥānah,* 1:60–61, 2:145; Muḥibbī, *Khulāṣat al-athar,* 4:249, 3:151; Murādī, *Silk al-durar,* 2:142.

128. Ghazzī, *al-Kawākib al-sāʾirah,* 3:22.

129. Ibn al-Sammān, [*Tārīkh*], fol. 160a.

130. Ibn ʿAbd al-Bāqī, *Dīwān,* 54.

131. Khafājī, *Rayḥānat al-alibbā,* 2:55; Muḥibbī, *Nafḥat al-rayḥānah,* 1:599–600; Murādī, *Silk al-durar,* 1:261.

132. Lane, *The Manners and Customs of the Modern Egyptians,* 196.

133. The works composed by these scholars were almost exclusively in the fields of belles-lettres, history, and the sciences of language.

134. al-ʿĀmilī, Bahāʾ al-Dīn, *al-Kashkūl,* 1:76.

135. Zabīdī, *Tāj al-ʿarūs,* 26:158–59.

136. al-ʿĀmilī, Bahāʾ al-Dīn, *al-Kashkūl,* 2:300; Jazāʾirī, *al-Anwār al-nuʿmāniyyah,* 3:161.

137. Ṣaltī, *Ṣabābat al-muʿānī,* fol. 14b.

138. Anṭākī, *Tadhkirat ulī al-albāb,* 3:176–77.

139. Anṭākī, *Tazyīn al-aswāq,* 1:46; see also Plato, *Symposium,* 195b–196b.

140. Anṭākī, *Tazyīn al-aswāq,* 1:29; Nābulusī, *Ghāyat al-maṭlūb,* 149.

141. Ibn al-Bakkāʾ, *Ghawānī al-ashwāq,* fol. 19b–20a.

142. Muḥibbī, *Nafḥat al-rayḥānah,* 1:283; Kanjī, *Bulūgh al-munā,* 55–56.

143. Compare Anṭākī, *Tazyīn al-aswāq,* 1:43–44 and 1:50–59.

144. Singer, *The Nature of Love;* see especially 1:122–23, 2:3–4.

145. Giffen, *Theory of Profane Love among the Arabs,* 117.

146. Shirbīnī, *Hazz al-quḥūf,* 90–93. For other examples: ʿUrḍī, *Maʿādin al-dhahab,* 332 (*maʿshūq*); Muḥibbī, *Khulāṣat al-athar,* 4:35 (*ʿāshiq*); Anṭākī, *Tazyīn al-aswāq,* 2:54 (*ʿishq*).

147. Anṭākī, *Tazyīn al-aswāq,* 2:171.

148. Muḥibbī, *Nafḥat al-rayḥānah,* 4:454.

149. The point is made by Meisami, "Arabic *Mujūn* Poetry," 24.

150. This tradition and the controversy surrounding it is discussed in Giffen, *Theory of Profane Love among the Arabs,* 99–115.

151. In Islamic law, a martyr (*shahīd*) in the strict sense, who is to be buried without being washed, shrouded, and (according to some) prayed for, is the Muslim who dies fighting for his faith. However, jurists allowed martyr status in an extended sense to Muslims who, for example, died of plague, in childbirth, were murdered, and so on. Such martyrs were to be buried in the normal way, but were thought to gain immediate access to heaven. See Kohlberg, "Shahīd."

152. Giffen, *Theory of Profane Love among the Arabs,* 127–29. Such an argument is cited in Karmī, *Munyat al-muḥibbīn,* fol. 24a–b.

153. Saffārīnī, *Ghidhāʾ al-albāb,* 1:72.

154. Ṣaltī, *Ṣabābat al-muʿānī,* fol. 11b–12a; compare Karmī, *Munyat al-muḥibbīn,* fol. 32a–b.

155. Nābulusī, *Ghāyat al-maṭlūb,* 18.

156. Muḥibbī, *Khulāṣat al-athar,* 2:329.

157. Murādī, *Silk al-durar,* 3:45.

158. Ibn al-Ḥanbalī, *Durr al-ḥabab,* 1:148–49.

159. Murādī, *Silk al-durar,* 4:243.

160. Karmī, *Munyat al-muḥibbīn,* fol. 28a; al-ʿUmarī, ʿUthmān, *al-Rawḍ al-naḍir,* 1:39–40.

161. Kaywānī, *Dīwān,* 100.

162. Shabrāwī, *Dīwān,* 69–70.

163. ʿUshārī, *Dīwān,* 218.

164. Hamori, "Love Poetry (*ghazal*)," 205. The tradition of pederastic but *ʿudhrī* love poetry goes back at least to Khālid ibn Yazīd al-Kātib (d. 876); see Arazi, *Amour divin et amour profane.*

165. Quoted in Muḥibbī, *Khulāṣat al-athar,* 2:452.

166. For such military imagery in love poetry, see Ibn al-Ḥanbalī, *Durr al-ḥabab,* 2:145–46; Ibn Maʿṣūm, *Sulāfat al-ʿaṣr,* 227; Muḥibbī, *Khulāṣat al-athar,* 2:330, 3:452.

167. Būrīnī, *Sharḥ Dīwān Ibn al-Fāriḍ,* 1:33.

168. Ibn al-Ḥanbalī, *Durr al-ḥabab,* 1:1034–35.

169. Quoted in Muḥibbī, *Khulāṣat al-athar,* 1:105.

170. Muḥibbī, *Khulāṣat al-athar,* 1:118.

171. Būrīnī, *Sharḥ Dīwān Ibn al-Fāriḍ,* 2:55.

172. Muḥibbī, *Khulāṣat al-athar,* 2:275.

173. The point is made by al-Suwaydī, ʿAbd al-Raḥmān, [*Risālah fī al-maḥabbah*], fol. 104b.

174. This argument is used in Rāghib Pāshā, *Safīnat al-rāghib,* 322; Munāwī, *al-Fayḍ al-qadīr,* 6:179–80.

175. Ghazzī, Kamāl al-Dīn, *al-Wird al-unsī,* fol. 140b; a similar theory is to be found in Ibn Ḥazm (d. 1037), *Ṭawq al-ḥamāmah;* see Giffen, *Theory of Profane Love among the Arabs,* 80.

176. Ṣaltī, *Ṣabābat al-muʿānī,* fol. 11a–b.

177. Buckingham, *Travels in Assyria, Media, and Persia,* 1:149. This source was brought to my attention by S. O. Murray's article "Some Nineteenth-Century Reports of Islamic Homosexualities." I am not as convinced as Murray seems to be that the discussion tells us more about Buckingham's culture than about Ismael's.

178. Buckingham, *Travels in Assyria, Media, and Persia,* 1:160.

179. Buckingham, *Travels in Assyria, Media, and Persia,* 1:163.

180. In the legends surrounding the *ʿudhrī* lovers, the couples sometimes marry, and this is said not to have affected their love. Yet the marriage invariably features as a lull in the narrative, which picks up when the lovers are separated again, by travel, parental intervention, or death (see, for example, Anṭākī, *Tazyīn al-aswāq,* 1:131, 205, 286). Hamori succinctly describes marriage as a "much too prosaic relief" for *ʿudhrī* idealization of passionate, unconsummated love ("Love Poetry (*ghazal*)," 205).

181. Anṭākī, *Tazyīn al-aswāq,* 2:53–54.

182. Ibn al-Wakīl al-Mallawī, *Bughyat al-musāmir,* fol. 140b.

183. Saffārīnī, *Qarʿ al-siyāṭ,* fol. 24b–25a. Saffārīnī is quoting Ibn Qayyim al-Jawziyyah, *al-Dāʾ wa al-dawāʾ,* 371–72.

184. Manīnī, *al-Fatḥ al-wahbī,* 2:56–57.

185. al-Suwaydī, ʿAbd al-Raḥmān, [*Risālah fī al-maḥabbah*], fol. 106b–107a.

186. Zabīdī, *Itḥāf al-sādah al-muttaqīn,* 6:184 (margin); Kāshānī, *al-Ḥaqāʾiq,* 321.

187. For instance, Nābulusī invoked Ghazālī's claim in his defense of the chaste love of boys; see *Ghāyat al-maṭlūb,* 77.

188. Ramlī, *Nihāyat al-muḥtāj,* 2:497.

189. For the metaphysics of Ibn ʿArabī, I have relied most heavily on Izutsu, *Sufism and Taoism,* part I. Helpful shorter surveys include Affifi, "Ibn ʿArabī"; Schimmel, *Mystical Dimensions of Islam,* ch. 6; Chittick, *The Sufi Path of Knowledge,* ch. 1.

190. The analogy with Platonism is made in Izutsu, *Sufism and Taoism,* 163–64.

191. Lines 242–43 and 261–62 of Ibn al-Fāriḍ's *al-Tāʾiyyah al-kubrā* entitled *Naẓm al-sulūk.* The translation is my own. For annotated translations of the poem, see Nicholson, *Studies in Islamic Mysticism,* 199ff.; and Homerin, *ʿUmar ibn al-Fāriḍ,* 73ff.

192. Nābulusī, *Kashf al-sirr al-ghāmiḍ,* fol. 3a–b.

193. Nābulusī, *Kashf al-sirr al-ghāmiḍ,* fol. 4a–b.

194. Nābulusī, *Sharḥ Dīwān Ibn al-Fāriḍ,* 1:61.

195. Nābulusī, *Sharḥ Dīwān Ibn al-Fāriḍ,* 2:234.

196. Nābulusī, *Sharḥ Dīwān Ibn al-Fāriḍ,* 1:201.

197. Nābulusī, *Sharḥ Dīwān Ibn al-Fāriḍ,* 1:34, 1:61.

198. Nicholson, *The Tarjuman al-ashwaq,* 1–9.

199. See the discussions in Munāwī, *al-Fayḍ al-qadīr,* 3:445 (tradition 3928); al-ʿAzīzī al-Būlāqī, *al-Sirāj al-munīr,* 2:251; ʿAjlūnī, *Kashf al-khafāʾ,* 1:379.

200. Nicholson, *Studies in Islamic Mysticism,* 121 (quoting *al-Insān al-kāmil* by ʿAbd al-Karīm al-Jīlī [d. 1428]). See also, Izutsu, *Sufism and Taoism,* 218ff.

201. Burton, *The Sotadic Zone,* pp. 18–19.

202. Ritter, *Das Meer der Seele,* ch. 26.

203. Discussions of the theme available in English also focus almost exclusively on the Persian mystical tradition; see Schimmel *Mystical Dimensions of Islam,* 287ff.; Schimmel, "Eros—Heavenly and Not So Heavenly—in Sufi Literature and Life"; Wafer, "Vision and Passion"; Wilson, *Scandal,* 93ff.

204. Unless otherwise indicated, information on Ayyūb is taken from Muḥibbī, *Khulāṣat al-athar,* 1:428–33.

205. al-Ḥanbalī, Abū al-Mawāhib, *Mashyakhah,* 89.

206. Baytimānī, *al-Jawāb al-maṭlūb,* fol. 174b. Ḥusayn al-Baytimānī (d. 1762), who was an acquaintance of Bakrī, composed a commentary on this poem, entitled *al-Jawāb al-maṭlūb ʿan sharḥ mawwāl al-shaykh Ayyūb.* It is very unlikely that Bakrī did not know who composed the poem.

207. See Murādī, *Silk al-durar,* 3:30–38.

208. The idea, recurrent in for example Schimmel's *Mystical Dimensions of Islam,* that the Naqshbandī mystics were opposed to the idea of the unity of existence is untenable. Several prominent mystics of the order subscribed to the idea; see Algar, "A Brief History of the Naqshbandī Order," 21.

209. See his *Īḍāḥ al-dalālāt fī samāʿ al-ālāt* and *Ghāyat al-maṭlūb fī maḥabbat al-maḥbūb.*

210. Nābulusī, *Dīwān al-ḥaqāʾiq,* 2:134.

211. Nābulusī, *Dīwān al-ḥaqāʾiq,* 1:202.

212. Nābulusī, *Dīwān al-ḥaqāʾiq,* 1:87. The "spirit of essences" (*Rūḥ al-dhawāt*) is presumably the Perfect Man, who—as mentioned earlier—is "the spirit of the universe" (*Rūḥ al-ʿālam*). The "most comprehensive attribute" (*atamm al-ṣifāt*) is presumably existence, which in one sense is an all-embracing attribute and in another sense is identical to God; see Izutsu, *Sufism and Taoism,* 116.

213. Nābulusī, *Sharḥ Dīwān Ibn al-Fāriḍ,* 1:70.

214. Nābulusī, *Dīwān al-ḥaqāʾiq,* 1:148. The tradition is rejected by Shawkānī, *al-Fawāʾid al-majmūʿah,* 275 (tradition 275), and more mildly assessed by al-Qāriʾ al-Harawī (*al-Asrār al-marfūʿah,* 416–17) as a variant of the acceptable saying: "Seek the good from handsome countenances."

215. Trimingham, *The Sufi Orders in Islam,* 212 (note 1).

216. Schimmel, *Mystical Dimensions of Islam,* 286; Schimmel, *As Through a Veil,* 46.

217. Nābulusī, *Ghāyat al-maṭlūb,* 1.

218. Nābulusī, *Ghāyat al-maṭlūb,* 52.

219. Nābulusī, *Ghāyat al-maṭlūb,* 93–117. For some of the traditions on which Nābulusī relies, see Munāwī, *al-Fayḍ al-qadīr,* 1:483 (tradition 964), 5:325 (tradition 7469), 6:420 (tradition 9864).

220. Munāwī, *al-Fayḍ al-qadīr,* 6:212 (tradition 8985).

221. Nābulusī, *Ghāyat al-maṭlūb,* 92.

222. Nābulusī, *Ghāyat al-maṭlūb,* 40.

223. Nābulusī, *Ghāyat al-maṭlūb,* 80, 82.

224. Nābulusī, *Ghāyat al-maṭlūb,* 73–76. For similar ideas among earlier mystics, see Ritter, *Das Meer des Seele,* 452, 477.

225. Nābulusī, *Dīwān al-ḥaqā'iq,* 1:270. The first quotation is from the above-mentioned Qur'anic passages.

226. Nābulusī, *Ghāyat al-maṭlūb,* 80–82; Nābulusī, *Dīwān al-ḥaqā'iq,* 2:132. For the traditions, see Munāwī, *al-Fayḍ al-qadīr,* 1:514 (tradition 1041), 3:517 (tradition 4172).

227. On Rūmī and Ḥusām al-Dīn, see Nābulusī, *Ghāyat al-maṭlūb,* 149; Schimmel, *As Through a Veil,* 92–94.

228. Murādī, *Silk al-durar,* 4:25.

229. Nābulusī, *Khamrat bābil,* 53–54. In the last line, Nābulusī is alluding to the dogma that someone who loves Muḥammad—the Prophet—does not deserve to be confined to hell-fire. Note, however, that the line loses much of its force unless we suppose that the portrayed beloved is also called Muḥammad.

230. al-Ghazzī, Kamāl al-Dīn, *al-Wird al-unsī,* fol. 58a–b.

231. Unless otherwise indicated, information on ʿAydarūsī is taken from Jabartī, *ʿAjā'ib al-āthār,* 2:27–34.

232. See ʿAydarūsī, *Tanmīq al-asfār,* 161–62.

233. ʿAydarūsī, *Tarwīḥ al-bāl,* 118.

234. ʿAydarūsī, *Tarwīḥ al-bāl,* 50.

235. According to Ibn ʿArabī, man is called *insān* (which in Arabic also means pupil of the eye) "because God sees His creatures through man." See Izutsu, *Sufism and Taoism,* 227; and Nicholson, *Studies in Islamic Mysticism,* 155–56.

236. ʿAydarūsī, *Tanmīq al-asfār,* 205–6.

237. The practice of indicating the name of the beloved by acrostics was common at the time. See, for instance, Nābulusī, *Khamrat bābil,* 223; al-Ḥafnī, Yūsuf, *Dīwān,* fol. 34b and fol. 36b; ʿUshārī, *Dīwān,* 520 and 534.

238. The Light of Muḥammad was considered to be the first "determination" (*taʿayyun*) of God, and the principle from which the universe was formed. See Nicholson, *Studies in Islamic Mysticism,* 103–21; Izutsu, *Sufism and Taoism,* 236–38.

239. ʿAydarūsī, *Tanmīq al-asfār,* 23.

240. ʿAydarūsī, *Tanmīq al-asfār,* 102.

241. Knysh, *Ibn ʿArabi in the Later Islamic Tradition,* 87ff., 209ff., 263ff.

242. al-Ghazzī, Najm al-Dīn, *al-Kawākib al-sā'irah,* 1:203–4 (on Zakariyyā al-Anṣārī); Ibn ʿĀbidīn, *Radd al-muḥtār,* 3:294 (who cites the opinion of Suyūṭī and Pāshāzāde); Winter, *Society and Religion in Early Ottoman Egypt,* 163–64.

243. The completion of the mosque and the first Friday prayer there, attended by Sultan Salīm himself, are described by the contemporary chronicler Ibn Ṭūlūn, *Mufākahat al-khillān,* 2:79–80.

244. On the Wahhābi condemnation of Ibn al-Fāriḍ and Ibn ʿArabī, see *Majmūʿat al-rasāʾil,* 1:47. On Ibn al-Amīr's condemnation, see Ibn al-Amīr, *Dīwān,* 168–69.

245. The few scholars who continued to criticize Ibn ʿArabī were by the eighteenth century clearly treated as mavericks. See Jabartī, *ʿAjāʾib al-āthār,* 1:313; al-ʿUmarī, Yāsīn, *Ghāyat al-marām,* 384.

246. Nābulusī, *Sharḥ Dīwān Ibn al-Fāriḍ,* 1:29.

247. Shaʿrānī, *al-Anwār al-qudsiyyah,* 1:46.

248. Shaʿrānī, *al-Anwār al-qudsiyyah,* 2:137.

249. See Shaʿrānī's comments on what he called *al-waḥdah al-muṭlaqah* in his *Laṭāʾif al-minan,* 1:23, and *al-Ṭabaqāt al-kubrā,* 2:42. On the later "interpolations" in Ibn ʿArabī's works, see *Laṭāʾif al-minan,* 1:42, 2:29.

250. Shaʿrānī, *Laṭāʾif al-minan,* 2:29.

251. Shaʿrānī, *Laṭāʾif al-minan,* 2:103.

252. Nābulusī, *Ghāyat al-maṭlūb,* 22.

253. Nābulusī, *Ghāyat al-maṭlūb,* 79.

254. Ghazzī, *al-Wird al-unsī,* fol. 136a.

Chapter Three

1. Ibn Ḥajar, *al-Zawājir,* 2:211.

2. Bürgel, "Die beste Dichtung ist die lügenreichste," 35.

3. See the representative discussion in ʿAlwān al-Ḥamawī, *ʿArāʾis al-ghurar,* 75ff.

4. See, for example, the Shāfiʿī jurists Ibn Ḥajar, *Tuḥfat al-muḥtāj,* 7:193; al-Ramlī, Shams al-Dīn, *Fatāwā,* 3:169–70; Qalyūbī, *Ḥāshiyah,* 1:177; the Ḥanafī jurists Ḥaṣkafī, *al-Durr al-mukhtār,* 1:298 (with the glosses of Ibn ʿĀbidīn); the Ḥanbalī jurist Buhūtī, *Kashshāf al-qināʿ,* 1:266; the Mālikī jurists Dardīr, *al-Sharḥ al-ṣaghīr,* 1:289; Nafarāwī, *al-Fawākih al-dawānī,* 2:367. Apparently, only a few Mālikī scholars still left it open whether women had to veil their faces (see the glosses of Ṣāwī in Dardīr, *al-Sharḥ al-ṣaghīr,* 1:289).

5. Ibn Ḥajar, *al-Zawājir,* 2:6; Ibn Ḥajar, *Taḥrīr al-maqāl,* 63.

6. Ibn Ḥajar, *al-Zawājir,* 2:5.

7. Ibn Ḥajar, *Tuḥfat al-muḥtāj,* 7:199.

8. Ibn Ḥajar, *al-Zawājir,* 2:141.

9. ʿAlwān al-Ḥamawī, *ʿArāʾis al-ghurar,* 99.

10. Ibn Ḥajar, *Taḥrīr al-maqāl,* 64; Ibn Ḥajar, *al-Zawājir,* 2:6; ʿAlwān al-Ḥamawī, *ʿArāʾis al-ghurar,* 175.

11. Ibn Ḥajar, *Taḥrīr al-maqāl,* 63–64; Ibn Ḥajar, *al-Zawājir,* 2:6; Ramlī, Khayr al-Dīn, *Fatāwā,* 1:65; Ibn ʿĀbidīn, *Radd al-muḥtār,* 5:233.

12. ʿAlwān al-Ḥamawī, *ʿArāʾis al-ghurar,* 106.

13. Ibn Ḥajar, *al-Zawājir,* 2:141; Ibn Ḥajar, *Taḥrīr al-maqāl,* 63.

14. This was the position of ʿAbd al-Ghanī al-Nābulusī on music; see his *Īḍāḥ al-dalālāt,* 72–73; see also al-Ghazzī, Kamāl al-Dīn, *al-Wird al-unsī,* fol. 167b–168a.

15. Ibn ʿAllān, *Dalīl al-fāliḥīn,* 8:137.

16. *al-Qawl al-muʿtabar fī bayān al-naẓar;* Nābulusī also polemicized against the position of Nawawī in *Ghāyat al-maṭlūb,* 23–41 (*al-faṣl al-thānī: fī bayān ḥukm al-naẓar ilā al-wujūh al-ḥisān*).

17. Nābulusī, *Ghāyat al-maṭlūb,* 38–39.

18. al-Ghazzī, Kamāl al-Dīn, *al-Wird al-unsī,* fol. 167a–b. Nābulusī's attitude here is consistent with his stand on the traditional duty of "commanding the right and forbidding the wrong," which he in effect neutralizes by stressing the need to avoid a self-righteous preoccupation with the faults of others; see Cook, *Commanding the Right,* 325–28.

19. This applies to jurists of the Ḥanafī and Mālikī schools of law. The Ḥanbalī and Shāfiʿī jurists held that the face was not taboo during prayer, but was taboo to unrelated men. See the discussions cited in note 4 to chapter 3, above.

20. Shaykhzāde, *Majmaʿ al-anhur,* 1:81; Ḥaṣkafī, *Durr al-muntaqā,* 1:81; Ibn Nujaym, *al-Baḥr al-rāʾiq,* 1:284; Ibn ʿĀbidīn, *Radd al-muḥtār,* 1:298.

21. Nābulusī, *al-Qawl al-muʿtabar,* fol. 187a.

22. Ibn Ḥajar, *al-Zawājir,* 2:143; in fact, premodern Arabic zoology knew of animals who practiced *liwāṭ* or were afflicted with *ubnah;* see Pellat, "Liwāṭ," 777a (citing *al-Ḥayawān* of Jāḥiẓ).

23. Zurqānī, *Sharḥ al-mukhtaṣar,* 1:88 (with the glosses of Bannānī); Kharāshī, *Sharḥ al-mukhtaṣar,* 1:155 (with the glosses of ʿAdawī); Dardīr, *al-Sharḥ al-ṣaghīr,* 1:144–45 (with the glosses of Ṣāwī); Dardīr, *al-Sharḥ al-kabīr,* 1:106 (with the glosses of Dasūqī).

24. Ibn Ḥajar, *Tuḥfat al-muḥtāj,* 7:198–99; Ramlī, Shams al-Dīn, *Nihāyat al-muḥtāj,* 6:192 (who cites the argument of the followers of Nawawī but ends by adopting the position of Rāfiʿī).

25. Buhūtī, *Kashshāf al-qināʿ,* 5:16; Ḥaṣkafī, *al-Durr al-mukhtār,* 5:254–55.

26. Ramlī, Shihab al-Dīn, *Fatāwā,* 3:172; Ramlī, Shams al-Dīn, *Nihāyat al-muḥtāj,* 6:192–93; al-Khaṭīb al-Shirbīnī, *Mughnī al-muḥtāj,* 3:130–31; Qalyūbī, *Ḥāshiyah,* 3:210; Bujayrimī, *Tuḥfat al-ḥabīb,* 3:341–42; Bājūrī, *Ḥāshiyah,* 2:99.

27. Ibn ʿĀbidīn, *Radd al-muḥtār,* 5:233.

28. Buhūtī, *Sharḥ al-muntahā,* 3:4–6.

29. Karmī, *Ghāyat,* 3:7.

30. Ramlī, Shams al-Dīn, *Nihāyat al-muḥtāj,* 6:192; Bājūrī, *Ḥāshiyah,* 2:99.

31. Zurqānī, *Sharḥ al-mukhtaṣar,* 1:176.

32. al-Ramlī, Khayr al-Dīn, *Fatāwā,* 1:64–65. The verdict was reiterated by later jurists; see Ibn ʿĀbidīn, *al-ʿUqūd al-durriyyah,* 1:75.

33. Ibn ʿĀbidīn, *Radd al-muḥtār,* 1:378.

34. Cited by Shabrāmallisī, *Ḥāshiyah,* 6:193.

35. Karmī, *Ghāyat al-muntahā,* 3:7.

36. Murādī, *Silk al-durar,* 3:242–43.

37. Ibn al-Ḥanbalī, *Durr al-ḥabab,* 2:278.

38. Schacht, *An Introduction to Islamic Law,* 175–79.

39. See Shaykhzāde, *Majmaʿ al-anhur,* 1:595ff.; Ḥaṣkafī, *al-Durr al-muntaqā,* 1:595ff.; Ibn Nujaym, *al-Baḥr al-rāʾiq,* 5:17ff.; Ibn ʿĀbidīn, *Radd al-muḥtār,* 3:169ff.; Ḥaṣkafī, *al-Durr al-mukhtār,* 3:169ff.; al-Ṭahṭāwī, Aḥmad, *Ḥāshiyah,* 2:397ff.; Kawākibī, *al-Fawāʾid*

al-samiyyah, 2 : 355. On the authoritativeness of the works cited for each school, see Schacht, *An Introduction to Islamic Law,* 261–63, and the articles devoted to each school in the *Encyclopaedia of Islam.*

40. Heyd, *Studies in Old Ottoman Criminal Law,* 102–3.

41. See Ramlī, Shams al-Dīn, *Nihāyat al-muḥtāj,* 7 : 422ff.; Ibn Ḥajar, *Tuḥfat al-muḥtāj,* 9 : 101ff.; Bujayrimī, *Tuḥfat al-ḥabīb,* 4 : 153ff.; Bājūrī, *Ḥāshiyah,* 2 : 235ff.; Qalyūbī, *Ḥāshiyah,* 4 : 178ff.

42. Bujayrimī, *Tuḥfat al-ḥabīb,* 4 : 153.

43. See the discussions of the relevant *ḥadīth* in Suyūṭī, *al-Ḥāwī,* 2 : 110ff.; Ibn Ḥajar, *al-Fatāwā,* 4 : 242; al-Qāriʾ al-Harawī, *Mirqāt al-mafātīḥ,* 7 : 162–63.

44. The first is included in *al-Sunan al-kubrā,* by al-Bayhaqī (d. 1066), and the second in *al-Muʿjam al-kabīr,* by al-Ṭabarānī (d. 971).

45. Qannawjī, *al-Rawḍah al-nadiyyah,* 2 : 273–75; Ibn al-Amīr, *Subul al-salām,* 3 : 17–19; Saffārīnī, *Qarʿ al-siyāṭ,* fol. 15a–16b (quoting Ibn Qayyim al-Jawziyyah, *al-Dāʾ wa al-dawāʾ,* 260–63).

46. See Buhūtī, *Kashshāf al-qināʿ,* 6 : 89ff.; Buhūtī, *Sharḥ al-muntahā,* 3 : 342ff.; Karmī, *Ghāyat al-muntahā,* 3 : 317ff.; Taghlibī, *Nayl al-maʾārib,* 2 : 355ff.; Najdī, *Hidāyat al-rāghib,* 2 : 762ff.; Ḥajjāwī, *al-Iqnāʿ,* 4 : 220.

47. See the editor's footnote in Buhūtī, *Kashshāf al-qināʿ,* 6 : 94.

48. See Zurqānī, *Sharḥ al-mukhtaṣar,* 8 : 74ff. (with glosses of Bannānī); Kharāshī, *Sharḥ al-mukhtaṣar,* 8 : 74ff. (with glosses of ʿAdawī); Dardīr, *al-Sharḥ al-ṣaghīr,* 4 : 447ff. (with glosses of Ṣāwī); Dardīr, *al-Sharḥ al-kabīr,* 4 : 321ff. (with glosses of Dasūqī); Nafarāwī, *al-Fawākih al-dawānī,* 2 : 286.

49. Pellat, "Liwāṭ," 777b.

50. al-ʿĀmilī, Zayn al-Dīn, *al-Rawḍah al-bahiyyah,* 9 : 141ff.; al-ʿĀmilī, Zayn al-Dīn, *Masālik al-afhām,* 14 : 401ff.; al-Najafī, *Jawāhir al-kalām,* 41 : 374ff.; al-Ḥurr al-ʿĀmilī, *Wasāʾil al-shīʿah,* 18 : 416ff.

51. Bullough, *Sexual Variance in Society and History,* 221–22.

52. Abū al-Suʿūd, *Irshād al-ʿaql al-salīm,* 1 : 324–25; Alūsī, *Rūḥ al-maʿānī,* 5 : 211–13.

53. Jamal, *Ḥāshiyah ʿalā tafsīr al-Jalālayn,* 1 : 365–66.

54. al-Qāriʾ al-Harawī, *Fatḥ bāb al-ʿināyah,* 3 : 195.

55. Shaʿrānī, *Laṭāʾif al-minan,* 1 : 207.

56. Ibn Nujaym, *al-Baḥr al-rāʾiq,* 5 : 5; Ibn ʿĀbidīn, *Radd al-muḥtār,* 3 : 156; Zurqānī, *Sharḥ al-mukhtaṣar,* 7 : 176–77; Ramlī, *Nihāyat al-muḥtāj,* 8 : 307; Ibn ʿAllān, *Dalīl al-fāliḥīn,* 3 : 20.

57. Dardīr, *al-Sharḥ al-ṣaghīr,* 4 : 455 (the glosses of Ṣāwī); Ibn ʿĀbidīn, *Radd al-muḥtār,* 3 : 140; Ibn Ḥajar, *Fatāwā,* 4 : 33.

58. Shaykhzāde, *Majmaʿ al-anhur,* 1 : 586; Buhūtī, *Kashshāf al-qinaʾ,* 6 : 78; Ramlī, *Nihāyat al-muḥtāj,* 7 : 425; Munāwī, *al-Fayḍ al-qadīr,* 1 : 226–29.

59. Imber, "*Zina* in Ottoman Law," 63. The position was endorsed by some Ḥanafī jurists (e.g., Ibn Nujaym, *al-Baḥr al-rāʾiq,* 5 : 19–20; Shaykhzāde, *Majmaʿ al-anhur,* 1 : 595), but denied by others within the same school (e.g., Ḥaṣkafī, *al-Durr al-mukhtār,* 1 : 595; Ibn ʿĀbidīn, *Munḥat al-khāliq,* 5 : 20).

60. Shaykhzāde, *Majmaʿ al-anhur,* 1 : 595; Ibn Nujaym, *al-Baḥr al-rāʾiq,* 5 : 18; Ibn ʿĀbidīn, *Radd al-muḥtār,* 3 : 156; Ḥaṣkafī, *Durr al-mukhtār,* 3 : 155.

61. Kawākibī, *al-Fawā'id al-samiyyah,* 2:355.

62. This is clearly stated in, for example, Ibn Ḥajar al-Haytamī, *Tuḥfat al-muḥtāj,* 9:103; Ramlī, Shams al-Dīn, *Nihāyat al-muḥtāj,* 7:424; Dardīr, *al-Sharḥ al-ṣaghīr,* 4:447; Kharāshī, *Sharḥ,* 5:316; Buhūtī, *Kashshāf al-qinā',* 6:94; Najdī, *Hidāyat al-rāghib,* 2:764. The Ḥanafī assumption about the position of other schools may reflect an uncertainty among Shāfiʿī and Mālikī jurists of earlier centuries on whether to apply *ḥadd* in cases of anal intercourse with male slaves; see on this point Schmitt, "*Liwāṭ* im *Fiqh,*" 80–86. Schmitt, focusing mainly on earlier juridical texts, suggests that only the Ḥanbalī school was unequivocal in applying *ḥadd* in this case. This is not true of the early Ottoman period.

63. Ḥaṣkafī, *Durr al-muntaqā,* 1:595; Dardīr, *al-Sharḥ al-ṣaghīr,* 4:448 (the glosses of Ṣāwī).

64. Ibn ʿĀbidīn, *Radd al-muḥtār,* 3:156.

65. Ṭahṭāwī, *Ḥāshiyah,* 2:397.

66. For discussions of the Qur'anic passages dealing with the people of Lot, see Jamal, "The Story of Lot and the Qur'an's Perception of the Morality of Same-Sex Sexuality," and Rowson, "Homosexuality."

67. These are cited in Ibn Ḥajar, *al-Zawājir,* 2:139–40.

68. Ibn Ḥajar, *al-Zawājir,* 2:140–41.

69. Jamal, *Ḥāshiyah ʿalā tafsīr al-Jalālayn,* 3:374.

70. Abū al-Suʿūd, *Irshād al-ʿaql al-salīm,* 2:178–79; Būrsawī, *Rūḥ al-bayan,* 3:197.

71. Alūsī, *Rūḥ al-maʿānī,* 12:94; Jamal, *Ḥāshiyah ʿalā tafsīr al-Jalālayn,* 2:412; Būrsawī, *Rūḥ al-bayan,* 4:166; Shawkānī, *Fatḥ al-qadīr,* 2:489; Baḥrānī, *al-Burhān,* 2:227; Kāshānī, *Tafsīr al-ṣāfi,* 2:461.

72. Abū al-Suʿūd, *Irshād al-ʿaql al-salīm,* 4:136.

73. Abū al-Suʿūd, *Irshād al-ʿaql al-salīm,* 2:178–79; Būrsawī, *Rūḥ al-bayān,* 3:197; Alūsī, *Rūḥ al-maʿānī,* 8:147–48; al-Khaṭīb al-Shirbīnī, *al-Sirāj al-munīr,* 1:471.

74. Shaʿrānī, *al-Mīzān al-kubrā,* 2:135–36; al-ʿAzīzī al-Būlāqī, *al-Sirāj al-munīr,* 1:486–87.

75. Karmī, *Ghāyat al-muntahā,* 3:317.

76. al-Ḥurr al-ʿĀmilī, *Wasā'il al-shīʿah,* 14:248ff. (tradition 2).

77. Ibn Nujaym, *al-Baḥr al-rā'iq,* 5:17–18; Ḥaṣkafī, *al-Durr al-mukhtār,* 3:156; Munāwī, *al-Fayḍ al-qadīr,* 2:420.

78. Abū al-Suʿūd, *Irshād al-ʿaql al-salīm,* 4:169; see also Jamal, *Ḥāshiyah ʿalā tafsīr al-Jalālayn,* 3:374 (citing Bayḍāwī).

79. Munāwī, *al-Fayḍ al-qadīr,* 2:420.

80. Abū al-Suʿūd, *Irshād al-ʿaql al-salīm,* 2:178–79; Jamal, *Ḥāshiyah ʿalā tafsīr al-Jalālayn,* 3:320; Alūsī, *Rūḥ al-maʿānī,* 8:149; al-Shawkānī, *Fatḥ al-qadīr,* 2:212; al-Khaṭīb al-Shirbīnī, *al-Sirāj al-munīr,* 1:471. The commentators are quoting or paraphrasing a remark that appears in the influential thirteenth-century commentary of Bayḍāwī, see Kāzarūnī, *Ḥāshiyah,* 3:17.

81. Shabrāmallisī, *Ḥāshiyah,* 6:192.

82. Saffārīnī, *Qarʿ al-siyāṭ,* fol. 15a.

83. Shaʿrānī, *al-Mīzān al-kubrā,* 2:136.

84. Ibn Nujaym, *al-Baḥr al-rā'iq,* 5:4; Ibn ʿĀbidīn, *Radd al-muḥtār,* 3:153–54; Ramlī, Shams al-Dīn, *Nihāyat al-muḥtāj,* 7:423; Ibn Ḥajar, *Tuḥfat al-muḥtāj,* 9:101.

85. Munāwī, *al-Fayḍ al-qadīr,* 2:420.

86. Jamal, *Ḥāshiyah ʿalā tafsīr al-Jalālayn,* 2:161–62.

87. Zabīdī, *Itḥāf al-sādah al-muttaqīn,* 7:430.

88. al-Ḥurr al-ʿĀmilī, *Wasāʾil al-shīʿah,* 14:248ff. (tradition 12).

89. Ibn Ḥajar, *al-Zawājir,* 2:255–64; see also Gardet, "Djanna," who also notes the increasing reticence of modern Muslim scholars concerning these matters.

90. Ḥamawī, *Ghamz ʿuyūn al-baṣāʾir,* 1:287. The passage is a quotation from a work entitled *Manāqib Abī Ḥanīfah* by Muḥammad al-Kardarī (d. 1424).

91. Ḥamawī, *Ghamz ʿuyūn al-baṣāʾir,* 1:287; Ibn ʿĀbidīn, *Radd al-muḥtār,* 3:156.

92. Ibn Nujaym, *al-Baḥr al-rāʾiq,* 5:18. The Qurʾan (21:74) mentions that "foul deeds" (*khabāʾith*) were committed by the people of Lot.

93. Ḥamawī, *Ghamz ʿuyūn al-baṣāʾir,* 1:287; Shaykhzāde, *Majmaʿ al-anhur,* 1:596 (citing Tumurtāshī's *Tanwīr al-abṣār*).

94. Ibn ʿĀbidīn, *Radd al-muḥtār,* 3:156.

95. Ibn Nujaym, *al-Baḥr al-rāʾiq,* 5:17.

96. Ibn ʿĀbidīn, *Radd al-muḥtār,* 3:156.

97. Ṭaḥṭāwī, *Ḥāshiyah,* 2:398.

98. Greenberg, *The Construction of Homosexuality,* 274–77; Brundage, "Sex and Canon Law," 43.

99. Ibn ʿĀbidīn, *Radd al-muḥtār,* 3:156; Ibn ʿĀbidīn, *Munḥat al-khāliq,* 5:18–19; Ramlī, Khayr al-Dīn, *Nuzhat al-nawāẓir,* 22; Munāwī, *al-Fayḍ al-qadīr,* 6:226. Ibn ʿĀbidīn quotes Khayr al-Dīn al-Ramlī, who in turn quotes *Dhayl al-Wishāḥ fī ʿilm al-nikāḥ,* by Jalāl al-Dīn al-Suyūṭī (d. 1505). Munāwī quotes *al-Tadhkirah,* by Ṣāliḥ al-Bulqīnī (d. 1464). Suyūṭī and Bulqīnī both quote from an unnamed work by Ibn ʿAqīl al-Ḥanbalī (d. 1119), who was a student of Abū ʿAlī ibn al-Walīd al-Muʿtazilī; see Makdisi, *Ibn ʿAqil,* 18–20.

100. Alūsī, *Rūḥ al-maʿānī,* 8:152.

101. Ḥaskafī, *al-Durr al-mukhtār,* 3:169; Nābulusī, *Risālat al-ajwibah,* fol. 81b; Ṭaḥṭāwī, *Ḥāshiyah,* 2:397–98.

102. Ḥafnī, *Ḥāshiyah,* 3:389.

103. Zīrekzāde, *Ḥāshiyah,* fol. 51a.

104. Būrsawī, *Rūḥ al-bayān,* 3:198–99.

105. Jamal, *Ḥāshiyah ʿalā tafsīr al-Jalālayn,* 4:272–73.

106. Abū al-Suʿūd, *Irshād al-ʿaql al-salīm,* 5:217.

107. Abū al-Suʿūd, *Irshād al-ʿaql al-salīm,* 5:130; Alūsī, *Rūḥ al-maʿānī,* 27:117; Shawkānī, *Fayḍ al-qadīr,* 5:146.

108. al-Khaṭīb al-Shirbīnī, *al-Sirāj al-munīr,* 4:438.

109. Jazāʾirī, *Zahr al-rabīʿ,* 183.

110. Būrīnī, *Tarājim al-aʿyān,* 2:199.

111. Murādī, *Silk al-durar,* 3:19.

112. Murādī, *Silk al-durar,* 2:308.

113. Buhūtī, *Sharḥ al-muntahā,* 3:348.

114. Ibn Ḥajar, *al-Zawājir,* 2:143–44; Shabrāmallisī, *Ḥāshiyah,* 7:425.

115. Ibn ʿĀbidīn, *Radd al-muḥtār,* 3:174.

116. Zurqānī, *Sharḥ al-mukhtaṣar,* 8:88 (the glosses of Bannānī).

117. The sources are intriguingly silent concerning oral intercourse, especially *fellatio.* I

have not come across a single clear-cut reference to this act in the juridical sources, or indeed in any other source, from the period. There are references to *fellatio* in the erotic work *Rujūʿ al-shaykh ilā ṣibāh,* attributed to Aḥmad al-Tīfāshī (d. 1253), and this work was known to at least one author in the early Ottoman period (Isḥāqī, *Akhbār al-uwal,* 115). For references to *cunnilingus,* see Buhūtī, *Sharḥ muntahā al-irādāt,* 3:8; Kharāshī, *Sharḥ al-mukhtaṣar,* 3:165–66 (the glosses of ʿAdawī).

118. Ramlī, Shams al-Dīn, *Nihāyat al-muḥtāj,* 7:424.

119. Buhūtī, *Kashshāf al-qināʿ,* 6:89 and 6:95.

120. Dardīr, *al-Sharḥ al-kabīr,* 4:321–24.

121. The Imāmī Shīʿī jurists disagreed on this point, as pointed out above.

122. Bujayrimī, *Tuḥfat al-ḥabīb,* 4:153.

123. al-Khaṭīb al-Shirbīnī, *Mughnī al-muḥtājj,* 4:144.

124. Ibn Ḥajar, *al-Zawājir,* 1:7.

125. Ibn Ḥajar, *al-Zawājir,* 2:4–5.

126. Dasūqī, *Ḥāshiyah,* 4:170.

127. Zurqānī, *Sharḥ al-mukhtaṣar,* 1:176.

128. Ibn ʿAllān, *Dalīl al-fāliḥīn,* 2:141. Repentance from all sins was, of course, still a duty.

129. Ibn ʿAllān, *Dalīl al-fāliḥīn,* 4:73–74.

130. Shawkānī, *Fatḥ al-qadīr,* 5:110.

131. Ramlī, Shihāb al-Dīn, *Fatāwā,* 4:73–74; Jamal, *Ḥāshiyah ʿalā Sharḥ al-Manhaj,* 2:193–94.

132. al-Muttaqī al-Hindī, *Kanz al-ʿummāl,* 3:372 (traditions 6999 and 7000).

133. Ibn Qayyim al-Jawziyyah, *al-Dāʾ wa al-dawāʾ,* 372–75.

134. al-Qāriʾ al-Harawī, *al-Asrār al-marfūʿah,* 238–39; Zurqānī, *Mukhtaṣar,* 196; ʿAjlūnī, *Kashf al-khafāʾ,* 2:263–64; Zabīdī, *Itḥāf al-sādah al-muttaqīn,* 7:439–40. A weak tradition is distinct from a fabrication; it may be used in moralistic and exhortatory literature, but not to establish a point of law; see Robson, "Ḥadīth," 25a–b.

135. Saffārīnī, *Nafathāt ṣadr al-mukmad,* 2:702–3; Shawkānī, *al-Fawāʾid al-majmūʿah,* 320.

136. Anṭākī, *Tazyīn al-aswāq,* 1:29–30; Ṣaltī, *Ṣabābat al-muʿānī,* fol. 18b–19a; Karmī, *Munyat al-muḥibbīn,* fol. 29a; Karmī, *al-Fawāʾid al-mawḍūʿah,* 109.

137. Munāwī, *al-Fayḍ al-qadīr,* 6:179; Zabīdī, *Itḥāf al-sādah al-muttaqīn,* 7:439.

138. Ḥafnī, *Ḥāshiyah,* 3:373.

139. Ibn Ḥajar, *Fatāwā,* 2:15.

140. Ramlī, Shams al-Dīn, *Nihāyat al-muḥtāj,* 2:497.

141. Cited in Shabrāmallisī, *Ḥāshiyah,* 2:497.

142. Qalyūbī, *Ḥāshiyah,* 1:339; Bājūrī, *Ḥāshiyah,* 1:254; Bujayrimī, *Tuḥfat al-ḥabīb,* 2:261; Bujayrimī, *Ḥāshiyah,* 1:539; al-Khaṭīb al-Shirbīnī, *Mughnī al-muḥtāj,* 1:350; Ibn Ḥajar, *Tuḥfat al-muḥtāj,* 3:166 (with glosses of Shirwānī); Jamal, *Ḥāshiyah ʿalā Sharḥ al-Manhaj,* 2:193.

143. Sharqāwī, *Ḥāshiyah,* 1:337.

144. Rāghib Pāshā, *Safīnat al-rāghib,* 322–26; Būrīnī, *Sharḥ Dīwān Ibn al-Fāriḍ,* 2:65; Nābulusī, *Ghāyat al-maṭlūb,* 19.

145. Ibn Ḥajar, *al-Zawājir,* 2:211; Ibn ʿĀbidīn, *Radd al-muḥtār,* 1:35; Zabīdī, *Itḥāf*

al-sādah al-muttaqīn, 6:508–9; Ramlī, Shams al-Dīn, *Nihāyat al-muḥtāj,* 8:299; Qalyūbī, *Ḥāshiyah,* 4:320–21; Alūsī, *Rūḥ al-maʿānī,* 19:137.

146. Qalyūbī, *Ḥāshiyah,* 4:320–21.

147. Zabīdī, *Itḥāf al-sādah al-muttaqīn,* 6:509.

148. Buhūtī, *Sharḥ muntahā al-irādāt,* 3:592; Taghlibī, *Nayl al-maʾārib,* 2:477; Najafī, *Jawāhir al-kalām,* 41:49.

149. al-ʿĀmilī, Zayn al-Dīn, *Masālik al-afhām,* 14:182.

150. Saffārīnī, *Ghidhā' al-albāb,* 1:170.

151. Saffārīnī, *Ghidā' al-albāb,* 1:151.

152. Nābulusī, *Ghāyat al-maṭlūb,* 153. See in general chapter 5 of the work (140–65).

153. Muḥibbī, *Khulāṣat al-athar,* 4:360–61; Muḥibbī, *Nafḥat al-rayḥānah,* 2:260–61.

154. Karmī, *Ghāyat al-muntahā,* 3:500.

155. Ibn ʿĀbidīn, *Radd al-muḥtār,* 1:35.

156. Karmī, *Munyat al-Muḥibbīn,* fol. 41b.

157. Karmī, *Munyat al-Muḥibbīn,* fol. 47b–53b.

158. Examples of the pederastic love poetry of al-Ḥuwayzī and Ibn Maʿṣūm have been cited in the previous chapter. On this aspect of ʿĀmilī's poetry, see Tūnjī, *Bahā' al-Dīn al-ʿĀmilī,* 88–90.

159. al-ʿĀmilī, Zayn al-Dīn, *Masālik al-afhām,* 14:182.

160. Ibn Ḥajar, *Tuḥfat al-muḥtāj,* 10:224; Ramlī, Shams al-Dīn, *Nihāyat al-muḥtāj,* 8:299.

161. Ḥafnī, Yūsuf, *Dīwān,* fol. 46a.

162. Ḥafnī, Yūsuf, *Dīwān,* fol. 37a–b.

163. Jabartī, *ʿAjā'ib al-āthār,* 4:239.

164. Khashshāb, *Dīwān,* 375.

165. Khashshāb, *Dīwān,* 376. On the same page, there is a somewhat longer poem of a handsome youth known as Abyaḍ.

166. Khashshāb, *Dīwān,* 374.

167. See the lists cited in the article "Khaṭī'a" in the *Encyclopaedia of Islam,* or by Ibn Ḥajar himself in the introduction to *al-Zawājir,* 1:9–12. The work on which Ibn Ḥajar's *al-Zawājir* was modeled, *Kitāb al-kabā'ir,* by Muḥammad al-Dhahabī (d. 1348), enumerated seventy major sins.

168. Ibn Ḥajar, *al-Zawājir,* 2:3.

169. Ibn Ḥajar, *Tuḥfat al-muḥtāj,* 10:216; Ibn Ḥajar, *al-Zawājir,* 2:198–99.

170. Ibn Ḥajar, *al-Zawājir,* 2:4.

171. Ibn Ḥajar, *al-Zawājir,* 2:211–12.

172. Ibn al-Bakkā', *Ghawānī al-ashwāq,* fol. 53a–53b. Ibn al-Bakkā' was told the story by Ibn Ḥajar in the month of Muḥarram in the year 973 of the Hijra (i.e., roughly August 1565), seven months before Ibn Ḥajar died.

173. Ibn al-Bakkā', *Ghawānī al-ashwāq,* fol. 59b.

174. Ibn ʿĀbidīn, *Radd al-muḥtār,* 1:35. This seems to be the position suggested by the quotations adduced by Ibn ʿĀbidīn, though he does not spell out the conclusion in his own words.

175. For the tendency of the four schools not to stray too far from each other in their evaluative scaling of acts, see Schacht, *An Introduction to Islamic Law,* 67–68.

176. Qalyūbī, *Ḥāshiyah,* 4:319.

177. Dardīr, *al-Sharḥ al-ṣaghīr,* 2:503 (the glosses of Ṣāwī); Dasūqī, *Ḥāshiyah,* 4:171; Kharāshī, *Sharḥ,* 5:178 (the glosses of al-ʿAdawī).

178. Ibn Ḥajar, *Kaff al-raʿāʿ,* 314.

179. Ibn Ḥajar, *al-Zawājir,* 2:213. Ibn Ḥajar is quoting the jurist Shihāb al-Dīn al-Adhraʿī (d. 1381), but this is the last quotation adduced on this particular issue, and seems to reflect Ibn Ḥajar's own opinion.

180. Lane, *An Account of the Manners and Customs,* chs. 17–18; Russell, *The Natural History of Aleppo* [1794], 1:142, 150–56.

181. Jabartī, *ʿAjāʾib al-āthār,* 1:415–16.

182. al-ʿAbd, *Hawādith bilād al-shām,* 140. I am grateful to Malek Shareef for drawing my attention to this passage.

Conclusion

1. Jazāʾirī, *Zahr al-rabīʿ,* 274.

2. Ibn al-Amīr, *Dīwān,* 227.

3. Quoted in Muḥibbī, *Khulāṣat al-athar,* 2:53.

4. Munāwī, *al-Fayḍ al-qadīr,* 5:203 (tradition 6977).

5. Munāwī, *al-Fayḍ al-qadīr,* 2:263 (tradition 1799).

6. Rocke, *Forbidden Friendships,* 113–19, 228–29.

7. Compare Jabartī, *ʿAjāʾib al-āthār,* 1:124–25, 202–3, with 2:260–61, 4:238–41.

8. Joseph Massad is currently preparing a study on attitudes toward sex in Arabic literature in the late nineteenth and twentieth centuries. I have benefited from discussions with him about the development of attitudes during the period.

9. Ṭahṭāwī, *Takhlīṣ al-ibrīz,* 78.

10. Bustānī, *Udabāʾ al-ʿarab,* 2:27.

11. Bustānī, *Udabāʾ al-ʿarab,* 2:75–80.

12. See Shihāb al-Dīn, *Dīwān,* pt. 4 (*fī al-ikhwān wa al-nudmān wa al-ḥisān min al-jawārī wa al-ghilmān*); Majdī Bey, *Dīwān,* pp. 88, 118, 123, 241, 242, 247–48, 284, 306, 313–14, 317–18, 319–20, 335, 354, 377; Fikrī, *al-Āthār al-fikriyyah,* pp. 17, 34, 35, 47, 47–48.

13. Ḥāfiẓ Ibrāhīm, *Dīwān,* 1:246–49.

14. Naṣīr, *al-Kutub al-ʿarabiyyah al-latī nushirat fī miṣr bayna ʿāmay 1900–1925* (no. 8/235). On this work see Rosenthal, "Male and Female: Described and Compared," 33.

15. Naṣīr, *al-Kutub al-ʿarabiyyah al-latī nushirat fī miṣr fī al-qarn al-tāsiʿ ʿashar,* nos. 8/1051–55; Naṣīr, *al-Kutub al-ʿarabiyyah al-latī nushirat fī miṣr bayna ʿāmay 1900–1925,* no. 8/1362; Naṣīr, *al-Kutub al-ʿarabiyyah al-latī nushirat bayna ʿāmay 1926–1940,* no. 8/50; Manṣūr, *Dalīl al-maṭbūʿāt al-miṣriyyah: 1940–1956.* For other printed editions between 1857 and 1929, not cited by Naṣīr, see Brockelmann, *Geschichte der arabischen Literatur,* 2:32 (and Supplement). For a discussion of the contents of *Lawʿat al-shākī,* see Rowson, "Two Homoerotic Narratives from Mamluk Literature." I give the translation of the title suggested by Rowson.

16. Zaydān, *Tārīkh ādāb al-lughah al-ʿarabiyyah,* 2:47.

17. Zayyāt, *Tārīkh al-adab al-ʿarabī,* 268.

18. Amīn, *Ẓuhr al-Islām,* 138–39.

19. Thus, the story of Abū Nuwās and the three boys, and the story of a teacher's love for the brother of Badr al-Dīn, the Vizier of the Yemen, were omitted in the 1930 edition. Compare *Alf laylah wa laylah* [1835], 1:562ff., and *Alf laylah wa laylah* [1890], 2:190ff., with *Alf laylah wa laylah* [1930], 2:317ff.

20. *Dīwān Abī Nuwās* [1932]. Compare with *Dīwān Abī Nuwās* [1898], 402–36, and *Dīwān Abī Nuwās* [1905], 398–439.

21. Farrūkh, *Abū Nuwās,* 83–86.

22. Ṣidqī, *Alḥān al-ḥān,* 270–92; Nuwayhī, *Nafsiyyat Abī Nuwās,* 54–99; ʿAqqād, *Abū Nuwās,* 39 and 51.

23. Like its European counterparts, the term *shudhūdhdh jinsī* is used primarily of homosexuality. To say of someone that he is *shādhdh jinsiyyan* will be understood to mean that he is a homosexual, and not, say, a sadist or exhibitionist.

24. On the formation of the concept of "sexuality" in late nineteenth-century European psychiatry, see Davidson, *The Emergence of Sexuality,* esp. chapters 1 and 2. Classical Arabic has terms for the desire for intercourse (*shahwat al-wiqāʿ*) and for sexual prowess (*bāh*), but not for "sexuality."

25. The point is also made in Massad, "Re-Orienting Desire," 265.

26. ʿAqqād, *Abū Nuwās,* 36. I would like to thank Joseph Massad for drawing my attention to this work.

27. ʿAqqād, *Abū Nuwās,* 39.

28. Ṭawīl, *al-Taṣawwuf fī Miṣr,* 157.

29. Naṣīr, *al-Kutub al-ʿarabiyyah al-latī nushirat fī Miṣr fī al-qarn al-tāsiʿ ʿashar,* nos. 8/95–98; Naṣīr, *al-Kutub al-ʿarabiyyah al-latī nushirat fī Miṣr bayna ʿāmay 1900–1925,* no. 8/1638; Naṣīr, *al-Kutub al-ʿarabiyyah al-latī nushirat bayna ʿāmay 1926–1940;* Manṣūr, *Dalīl al-maṭbūʿāt al-miṣriyyah: 1940–1956.*

30. Baer, "Shirbīnī's *Hazz al-quḥūf,*" 26 and 31. In the same year, a heavily expurgated version of *Thamarāt al-awrāq,* by Ibn Ḥijjah al-Ḥamawī (d. 1434), was published; see ʿAbd al-Nabī, *al-Mukhtār min kitāb Thamarāt al-awrāq.*

31. Bakkār, *Ittijāhāt al-ghazal.*

32. ʿAdnānī, *al-Zinā wa al-shudhūdh.*

33. ʿAdnānī, *al-Zinā wa al-shudhūdh,* 126–29.

34. Trimingham, *The Sufi Orders in Islam,* 246ff.

35. This is a recurrent theme in Schmitt and Sofer, eds., *Sexuality and Eroticism among Males in Muslim Societies.*

Bibliography

Arabic Primary Sources

al-ʿAbd, Ḥasan Āghā. *Ḥawādith bilād al-shām*. Edited by Y. J. al-Naʿīsah. Damascus, 1986.

Abū al-Suʿūd Efendī, Muḥammad (d. 1574). *Irshād al-ʿaql al-salīm ilā mazāyā al-Qurʾān al-karīm*. Cairo, 1952.

al-ʿAjlūnī, Ismāʿīl (d. 1749). *Kashf al-khafāʾ wa muzīl al-ilbās ʿammā ishtahara min al-aḥādīth ʿalā alsunat al-nās*. Cairo, 1351H.

Alf laylah wa laylah. Edited by M. Q. al-ʿAdawi. Cairo, 1835.

Alf laylah wa laylah. Cairo, 1890.

Alf laylah wa laylah. Cairo, 1930.

al-Alūsī, Shihāb al-Dīn Maḥmūd (d. 1854). *Rūḥ al-maʿānī fī tafsīr al-Qurʾān*. Cairo, 1345H.

al-Alūsī, Maḥmūd Shukrī (d. 1924). *al-Misk al-adhfar fī nashr mazāyā al-qarn al-thānī ʿashar wa al-thālith ʿashar*. Edited by ʿA. al-Jabbūrī. Riyad, 1982.

ʿAlwān al-Ḥamawī, ʿAlī ibn ʿAtiyyah (d. 1530). *ʿArāʾis al-ghurar wa gharāʾis al-fikar fī aḥkām al-naẓar*. Edited by M. al-Murād. Beirut and Damascus, 1990.

al-ʿĀmilī, Bahāʾ al-Dīn (d. 1621). *al-Kashkūl*. Edited by Ṭ. al-Zāwī. Cairo, 1961.

al-ʿĀmilī, Zayn al-Dīn (d. 1558). *Masālik al-afhām ilā tanqīḥ Sharāʾiʿ al-islām*. Qum, 1413–19H.

——. *al-Rawḍah al-bahiyyah fī sharḥ al-Lumʿah al-dimashqiyyah*. Najaf, 1386H.

al-Anṭākī, Dāwūd (d. 1599). *al-Nuzhah al-mubhijah fī tashḥīdh al-adhhān wa taʿdīl al-amzijah*. [Printed on the margins of Anṭākī's *Tadhkirat ulī al-albāb*.]

——. *Tadhkirat ulī al-albāb wa al-jāmiʿ li-al-ʿajab al-ʿujjāb*. Cairo, 1294H.

——. *Tazyīn al-aswāq bi tafṣīl ashwāq al-ʿushshāq*. Edited by M. al-Tūnjī. Beirut, 1993.

al-ʿAydarūsī, ʿAbd al-Raḥmān (d. 1778). *Tanmīq al-asfār fīmā jarā lahu maʿ al-ikhwān fī baʿḍ al-asfār*. Cairo, 1304H.

——. *Tarwīḥ al-bāl wa tahyīj al-bilbāl*. Cairo, 1283H.

al-ʿAzīzī al-Būlāqī, ʿAlī (d. 1659). *al-Sirāj al-munīr sharḥ al-Jāmiʿ al-ṣaghīr*. Bulaq, 1304H.

al-Baḥrānī, Ḥāshim (d. ca. 1696). *al-Burhān fī tafsīr al-Qurʾan*. Tehran, 1375H.

al-Bakrī, Muṣṭafā (d. 1749). *al-Suyūf al-ḥidād fī aʿnāq ahl al-zandaqah wa al-ilḥād*. MS, Princeton University Library, New Series, 1109.

al-Bājūrī, Ibrāhīm (d. 1860). *Ḥāshiyah ʿalā al-Fatḥ al-qarīb*. Cairo, 1354H.

al-Barbīr, Aḥmad (d. 1817). *al-Sharḥ al-jalī ʿalā baytay al-Mawṣilī*. Beirut, 1303H.

al-Baytimānī, Ḥusayn (d. 1762). *al-Jawāb al-maṭlūb ʿan sharḥ mawwāl al-shaykh Ayyūb*. MS, Princeton University Library, Yahuda 509.

al-Budayrī al-Ḥallāq (d. ca. 1762). *Ḥawādith dimashq al-yawmiyyah.* Edited by A. ʿAbd al-Karīm. Cairo, 1959.

al-Buhūtī, Manṣūr (d. 1641). *Kashshāf al-qināʿ ʿan matn al-Iqnāʿ.* Edited by Ḥ. Hilāl. Riyad, n.d.

——. *Sharḥ Muntahā al-irādāt.* Beirut, 1993.

al-Bujayrimī, Sulaymān (d. 1806). *Ḥāshiyah ʿalā sharḥ Manhaj al-ṭullāb.* Cairo, 1286H.

——. *Tuḥfat al-ḥabīb ʿalā sharḥ al-Khaṭīb.* Cairo, 1284H.

al-Būrīnī, Ḥasan (d. 1615). *Sharḥ dīwān Ibn al-Fāriḍ.* Edited by R. al-Daḥdāḥ. Cairo, 1289H.

——. *Tarājim al-aʿyān min abnāʾ al-zamān.* Edited by Ṣ. al-Munajjid. Damascus, 1959–63.

al-Būrsawī, Ismāʿīl Ḥaqqī (d. 1724). *Tafsīr Rūḥ al-bayān.* Istanbul, 1928.

al-Bustānī, Buṭrus (d. 1883). *Udabāʾ al-ʿarab.* Beirut, n.d. [Dār Ṣādir].

al-Dajjānī, Muḥammad ibn Ṣāliḥ (d. 1660). *al-ʿIqd al-mufrad fī ḥukm al-amrad.* MS, Princeton University Library, New Series, 1952.

al-Dardīr, Aḥmad (d. 1786). *al-Sharḥ al-kabīr ʿalā Mukhtaṣar Khalīl.* [Printed on the margins of Dasūqī's *Ḥāshiyah.*]

——. *al-Sharḥ al-ṣaghīr ʿalā Aqrab al-masālik ilā madhhab al-imām Mālik* [with the glosses of Aḥmad al-Ṣāwī (d. 1825/6)]. Edited by M. Waṣfī. Cairo, 1972–74.

al-Dasūqī, Muḥammad ibn ʿArafah (d. 1815). *Ḥāshiyah ʿalā al-Sharḥ al-kabīr ʿalā Mukhtaṣar Khalīl.* Cairo, 1911.

Dīwān Abī Nuwās. Edited by Maḥmūd Efendī Wāṣif. Cairo, 1898.

Dīwān Abī Nuwās. Cairo, 1905.

Dīwān Abī Nuwās. Edited by Maḥmūd Kamāl Farīd. Cairo, 1932.

Dīwān khidmat al-usṭā ʿUthmān ʿind al-amīr Baybars [lith.]. Cairo, 1289H.

al-Fayḍ al-Kāshānī, Muḥammad Muḥsin (d. 1680). *al-Ḥaqāʾiq fī maḥāsin al-akhlāq.* Beirut, 1989.

——. *al-Tafsīr al-ṣāfī.* Beirut, 1979.

Fikrī, ʿAbdallah (d. 1889). *al-Āthār al-Fikriyyah.* Cairo, 1897.

al-Ghazzī, Kamāl al-Dīn Muḥammad (d. 1799). *al-Wird al-unsī wa al-wārid al-qudsī fī tarjamat al-ʿārif bi-allah ʿAbd al-Ghanī al-Nābulusī.* MS, American University of Beirut, Mic-MS 243.

al-Ghazzī, Najm al-Dīn Muḥammad (d. 1651). *al-Kawākib al-sāʾirah bi aʿyān al-miʾah al-ʿāshirah.* Edited by J. Jabbur. Beirut, 1979.

——. *Luṭf al-samar wa qaṭf al-thamar min tarājim aʿyān al-ṭabaqah al-ūlā min al-qarn al-ḥādī ʿashar.* Edited by M. al-Shaykh. Damascus, 1981–82.

al-Ghulāmī, Muḥammad (d. 1772/3). *Shammāmat al-ʿanbar wa al-zahr al-muʿanbar.* Edited by S. al-Nuʿaymī. Baghdad, 1977.

Ḥafiẓ Ibrāhīm (d. 1932). *Dīwān.* Beirut, n.d. [Dār al-ʿAwdah reprint].

al-Ḥafnī, Muḥammad (d. 1767). *Ḥāshiyah ʿalā sharḥ al-Jāmiʿ al-ṣaghīr.* [Printed on the margins of al-ʿAzīzī al-Būlāqī's *al-Sirāj al-munīr.*]

al-Ḥafnī, Yūsuf (d. 1764). *Dīwān.* MS, Cambridge University Library, Qq. 49.

al-Hajjāwī, Mūsā (d. 1560). *al-Iqnāʿ li-ṭālib al-intifāʿ.* Edited by ʿA. al-Turkī. Riyad, 1999.

al-Ḥamawī, Aḥmad (d. 1687). *Ghamz ʿuyūn al-baṣāʾir sharḥ al-Ashbāh wa al-naẓāʾir.* Cairo, 1290H.

al-Ḥanbalī, Abū al-Mawāhib (d. 1714). *Mashyakhah.* Edited by M. M. al-Ḥāfiẓ. Damascus, 1990.

al-Ḥaṣkafī, ʿAlāʾ al-Dīn Muḥammad (d. 1677). *Durr al-mukhtār sharḥ Tanwīr al-abṣār.* [Printed on the margins of Ibn ʿĀbidin, *Radd.*]

——. *al-Durr al-muntaqā fī sharḥ al-Multaqā.* [Printed on the margins of Shaykhzāde, *Majmaʿ.*]

al-Ḥurr al-ʿĀmilī, Muḥammad (d. 1693). *Wasāʾil al-shīʿah ilā taḥṣīl masāʾil al-sharīʿah.* Edited by ʿA. al-Shīrāzī. Beirut [reprint of Tehran, 1391H].

Ibn ʿAbd al-Bāqī, Ḥasan (d. 1744/5). *Dīwān.* Edited by M. S. al-Jalīlī. Mosul, 1966.

Ibn ʿĀbidīn, Muḥammad Amīn (d. 1836). *Munḥat al-khāliq ʿalā al-Baḥr al-rāʾiq.* [Printed on the margins of Ibn Nujaym, *Baḥr.*]

——. *Radd al-muḥtār ʿalā al-Durr al-mukhtār.* Bulaq, 1272H.

——. *al-ʿUqūd al-durriyyah fī tanqīḥ al-fatāwā al-Ḥāmidiyyah.* Cairo, 1278H.

Ibn ʿAllān, Muḥammad ʿAlī (d. 1648). *Dalīl al-fāliḥīn li-ṭuruq Riyāḍ al-ṣāliḥīn,* Cairo, 1938.

Ibn al-Amīr al-Ṣanʿānī, Muḥammad ibn Ismāʿīl (d. 1768). *Dīwān.* Medina, 1986.

——. *Subul al-salām sharḥ Bulūgh al-marām.* Cairo, 1369H.

Ibn Ayyūb al-Anṣārī, Mūsā (d. ca. 1592). *Nuzhat al-khāṭir wa bahjat al-nāẓir.* Edited by ʿA. M. Ibrāhīm. Damascus, 1991.

——. *al-Rawḍ al-ʿāṭir fīmā tayassara min akhbār ahl al-qarn al-sābiʿ ilā khitām al-qarn al-ʿāshir.* Partial ed., A. Gunes. Berlin, 1981.

Ibn al-Bakkāʾ, ʿAbd al-Muʿīn (d. 1630/1). *Ghawānī al-ashwāq fī maʿānī al-ʿushshāq.* MS, Cambridge University Library, Or. 1415(9).

Ibn Ḥajar al-Haytamī, ʿAlī (d. 1566). *al-Fatāwā al-kubrā al-fiqhiyyah.* Cairo, 1308H.

——. *Kaff al-raʿāʿ ʿan muḥarramāt al-lahū wa al-samāʿ.* [Printed as appendix to Ibn Ḥajar, *Zawājir.*]

——. *Taḥrīr al-maqāl fī ādāb wa aḥkām wa fawāʾid yaḥtāj ilayhā muʾaddib al-aṭfāl.* Edited by M. al-Dibs. Beirut and Damascus, 1987.

——. *Tuḥfat al-muḥtāj bi sharḥ al-Minhāj.* Cairo, 1315H.

——. *al-Zawājir ʿan iqtirāf al-kabāʾir.* Beirut, n.d. [Dār al-Maʿrifah].

Ibn al-Ḥanbalī, Raḍī al-Dīn (d. 1563). *Durr al-ḥabab fī tārīkh aʿyān Ḥalab.* Edited by M. al-Fākhūrī and Y. ʿAbbārah. Damascus, 1972–74.

Ibn Kannān al-Ṣāliḥī, Muḥammad (d. 1740). *al-Ḥawādith al-yawmiyyah min tārīkh iḥdā ʿashar wa alf wa miʾah.* Partial ed., A. ʿUlabī [with the title *Yawmiyyāt shāmiyyah*]. Damascus, 1994.

Ibn Maʿṣūm, ʿAlī (d. ca. 1708). *Sulāfat al-ʿaṣr fī maḥāsin al-shuʿarāʾ bi kulli miṣr.* Cairo, 1324H.

Ibn Maʿtūq al-Ḥuwayzī, Shihāb al-Dīn al-Mūsawī (d. 1676). *Dīwān.* Edited by S. al-Shartūnī. Beirut, 1885.

Ibn Nujaym, Zayn al-ʿĀbidīn (d. 1563). *al-Baḥr al-rāʾiq sharḥ Kanz al-daqāʾiq.* Cairo, 1311H.

Ibn Qayyim al-Jawziyyah, Shams al-Dīn Muḥammad (d. 1350). *al-Dāʾ wa al-dawāʾ.* Edited by ʿA. al-Atharī. Dammām, 1999.

Ibn al-Sammān, Muḥammad Saʿīd (d. 1759). [*Tārīkh*]. MS, Berlin Staatsbibliothek, Wetzstein II, 140.

Ibn Sīnā, Abū ʿAlī al-Ḥusayn (d. 1037). *al-Qānūn fī al-ṭibb.* Edited by S. al-Laḥḥām. Beirut and Damascus, 1994.

Ibn Ṭūlūn, Shams al-Dīn Muḥammad (d. 1546). *Mufākahat al-khillān fī ḥawādith al-zamān.* Edited by M. Muṣṭafā. Cairo, 1962–64.

——. *al-Thagr al-bassām fī man waliya qaḍā' dimashq al-shām.* Edited by Ṣ. al-Munajjid. Damascus, 1956.

Ibn al-Wakīl al-Mallawī, Yūsuf (d. ca. 1719). *Bughyat al-musāmir wa ghinyat al-musāfir.* MS, Cambridge University Library, Qq. 194.

Ikhwān al-Ṣafā. *Rasā'il Ikhwān al-Ṣafā wa khillān al-wafā.* Beirut, n.d. [Dār Ṣādir].

al-ʿInāyātī, Aḥmad (d. 1606). *Dīwān.* MS, British Library, [i] Add. 19486; [ii] Add. 19541.

al-Isḥāqī, Muḥammad (d. ca. 1650). *Akhbār al-uwal fī-man taṣarrafa fī Miṣr min arbāb al-duwal.* Cairo, 1310H.

al-Jabartī, ʿAbd al-Raḥmān (d. 1825/6). *ʿAjā'ib al-āthār fī al-tarājim wa al-akhbār.* Cairo, 1297H.

al-Jāḥiẓ, ʿAmr (d. 869). *Rasā'il.* Edited by ʿA. Hārūn. Cairo, 1964–65.

al-Jamal, Sulaymān (d. 1790). *Ḥāshiyah ʿalā sharḥ Manhaj al-ṭullāb.* Cairo, 1305H.

——. *Ḥāshiyah ʿalā Tafsīr al-Jalālayn.* Cairo, 1933.

al-Jazā'irī, Niʿmatallah (d. 1702). *al-Anwār al-nuʿmāniyyah fī bayān maʿrifat al-nash'ah al-insāniyyah.* Beirut, 1984.

——. *Zahr al-rabīʿ fī al-ṭarā'if wa al-mulaḥ wa al-maqāl al-badīʿ.* Beirut, 1990. [al-Irshād li-al-ṭibāʿah wa al-nashr]

al-Jazarī, Ḥusayn (d. ca. 1624). *Dīwān.* MS, Cambridge University Library, Or. 1464(8).

al-Jundī, Amīn (d. 1841). *Dīwān.* Damascus, 1903.

al-Kanjī, Muḥammad (d. 1740). *Bulūgh al-munā fī tarājim ahl al-ghinā.* Edited by R. Murād. Damascus, 1988.

al-Karmī, Marʿī ibn Yūsuf (d. 1624). *al-Fawā'id al-mawdūʿah fī al-aḥādīth al-mawḍūʿah.* Edited by M. Ṣabbāgh. Beirut, 1977.

——. *Ghāyat al-muntahā fī al-jamʿ bayna al-Iqnāʿ wa al-Muntahā.* Edited by M. al-Shaṭṭī and M. al-Shāwīsh. Damascus, 1959.

——. *Munyat al-muḥibbīn wa bughyat al-ʿāshiqīn.* MS, Dār al-Kutub al-Miṣriyyah, Ṭalʿat, Adab 4648.

al-Kawākibī, Muḥammad ibn Ḥasan (d. 1685). *al-Fawā'id al-samiyyah fī sharḥ al-Farā'id al-saniyyah.* Cairo, 1322–28H.

al-Kawkabānī, Aḥmad (d. 1738/9). *Ḥadā'iq al-nammām fī al-kalām ʿalā mā yataʿallaq bi al-ḥammām.* Edited by ʿA. al-Ḥibshī. Beirut, 1986.

al-Kaywānī, Aḥmad (d. 1760). *Dīwān.* Damascus, 1301H.

al-Kāzarūnī, Abū al-Faḍl (d. 1539). *Ḥāshiyah ʿalā Tafsīr al-Bayḍāwī.* Cairo, 1912.

al-Khafājī, Aḥmad (d. 1659). *Rayḥānat al-alibbā wa zahrat al-ḥayāt al-dunyā.* Edited by ʿA. al-Ḥilū. Cairo, 1967.

al-Khāl, ʿAbd al-Ḥayy ibn al-Ṭawīl (d. 1706). *Dīwān.* MS, Berlin Staatsbibliothek, Wetzstein II, 179.

al-Kharāshī, Muḥammad (d. 1689). *Sharḥ ʿalā Mukhtaṣar Khalīl* [with the glosses of ʿAlī al-ʿAdawī (d. 1775)]. Cairo, 1316H.

al-Khashshāb, Ismāʿīl (d. 1815). *Dīwān.* Istanbul, 1300H.

al-Khaṭīb al-Shirbīnī, Muḥammad (d. 1570). *Mughnī al-muḥtāj ilā maʿrifat maʿānī alfāẓ al-Minhāj.* Cairo, 1933.

——. *al-Sirāj al-munīr fī al-iʿānah ʿalā maʿrifat baʿḍ maʿānī kalām Rabbinā al-ḥakīm al-khabīr.* Cairo, 1299H.

Majdī Bey, Ṣāliḥ (d. 1881). *Dīwān.* Cairo, 1893.

Majmū'at al-masā'il wa al-rasā'il al-najdiyyah. Cairo, 1928.

al-Makkī al-Mūsawī, 'Abbās (fl. 1736). *Nuzhat al-jalīs wa munyat al-adīb al-anīs*. Najaf, 1967.

Māmāyah al-Rūmī, Muḥammad (d. 1579). *Rawḍat al-mushtāq wa bahjat al-'ushshāq*. MS, British Library, Add. 7581.

al-Manīnī, Aḥmad (d. 1759). *al-Fatḥ al-wahbī 'alā tārīkh Abī Naṣr al-'Utbī*. Cairo, 1286H.

al-Muḥibbī, Muḥammad Amīn (d. 1699). *Dhayl Nafḥat al-rayḥānah*. Edited by 'A. al-Ḥilū. Cairo, 1971.

———. *Khulāṣat al-athar fī tarājim ahl al-qarn al-ḥādī 'ashar*. Cairo, 1284H.

———. *Nafḥat al-rayḥānah wa rashḥat ṭilā' al-ḥānah*. Edited by 'A. al-Ḥilū. Cairo, 1967–69.

al-Munāwī, 'Abd al-Ra'ūf (d. 1622). *al-Fayḍ al-qadīr sharḥ al-Jāmi' al-ṣaghīr*. Cairo, 1938.

———. *al-Fuyuḍāt al-ilāhiyyah fī sharḥ al-Alfiyyah al-Wardiyyah*. MS, Princeton, Yahuda 3280.

———. *al-Nuzhah al-zahiyyah fī aḥkām al-ḥammām al-shar'iyyah wa al-ṭibbiyyah*. Edited by 'A. Ḥamdān. Cairo and Beirut, 1987.

al-Murādī, Muḥammad Khalīl (d. 1791). *Silk al-durar fī a'yān al-qarn al-thānī 'ashar*. Cairo and Istanbul, 1291–1301.

al-Muttaqī al-Hindī, 'Alī (d. 1567/8). *Kanz al-'ummāl fī sunan al-aqwāl wa al-af'āl*. Hyderabad, 1951.

al-Nābulusī, 'Abd al-Ghanī (d. 1731). *Dīwān al-ḥaqā'iq wa majmā' al-raqā'iq*. Cairo, 1270H.

———. *Ghāyat al-maṭlūb fī maḥabbat al-maḥbūb*. Edited by S. Pagani. *Rivista Degli Studi Orientali: Supplemento No. 1* 68 (1995).

———. *Īḍāḥ al-dalālāt fī samā' al-ālāt*. Edited by A. Ḥammūsh. Damascus, 1981.

———. *Kashf al-sirr al-ghāmiḍ fī sharḥ Dīwān Ibn al-Fāriḍ*. MS, British Library, Add. 7564.

———. *Khamrat bābil wa ghinā' balābil*. Edited [with the title *Burj bābil wa shadū al-balābil*] by A. al-Jundī. Damascus, 1988.

———. *al-Qawl al-mu'tabar fī bayān al-naẓar*. MS, Berlin Staatsbibliothek, Wetzstein II, 1631.

———. *Risālat al-ajwibah 'an al-mi'ah wa-wāḥid wa-sittūna su'āl*. MS, British Library, Or. 9768.

———. *Sharḥ Dīwān Ibn al-Fāriḍ*. [Excerpts printed with Būrīnī's *Sharḥ*.]

———. *Ta'ṭīr al-anām fī ta'bīr al-manām*. Cairo, 1935.

al-Nafarāwī, Aḥmad (d. 1713/4). *al-Fawākih al-dawānī 'alā Risālat Ibn Abī Zayd al-Qayrawānī*. Beirut, n.d.

al-Najafī, Muḥammad Ḥasan (d. 1850). *Jawāhir al-kalām fī sharḥ Sharā'i' al-islām*. Najaf, 1378H.

al-Najdī, 'Uthmān (d. 1686). *Hidāyat al-rāghib li-sharḥ 'Umdat al-ṭālib*. Edited by H. Makhlūf. Ṭā'if, 1996.

Nuzhat al-udabā' wa salwat al-qurabā'. (i) MS, Cambridge University Library, Or. 1256(8); (ii) MS, British Library, Or. 1357.

al-Qalyūbī, Aḥmad (d. 1659). *Ḥāshiyah 'alā sharḥ al-Minhāj*. Cairo, 1949.

———. *al-Tadhkirah fī al-ṭibb*. [Printed on the margins of Sha'rānī's *Mukhtaṣar*.]

al-Qannawjī, Muḥammad Ṣiddīq ibn Ḥasan Khān (d. 1889). *al-Rawḍah al-nadiyyah sharḥ al-Durar al-bahiyyah*. Cairo, n.d.

al-Qāri' al-Harawī, 'Alī ibn Sulṭān (d. 1614). *al-Asrār al-marfū'ah fī al-akhbār al-mawḍū'ah*. Edited by M. al-Ṣabbāgh. Beirut and Damascus, 1986.

——. *Fatḥ bāb al-ʿināyah bi-sharḥ al-Niqāyah*. Edited by M. N. Tamīm and H. N. Tamīm. Beirut, 1997.

——. *Mirqāt al-mafātīḥ sharḥ Mishkāt al-maṣābīḥ*. Edited by S. al-ʿAṭṭār. Beirut, 1992.

Rāghib Pāshā, Muḥammad (d. 1763). *Safīnat al-rāghib wa dafīnat al-maṭālib*. Cairo, 1282H.

al-Ramlī, Khayr al-Dīn (d. 1671). *al-Fatāwā al-khayriyyah li-nafʿ al-barriyyah*. Cairo, 1300H.

——. *Nuzhat al-nawāẓir ʿalā al-Ashbāh wa al-naẓāʾir*. [Printed as an appendix (with independent pagination) to Ḥamawī's *Ghamz*.]

al-Ramlī, Shams al-Dīn Muḥammad (d. 1596). *Nihāyat al-muḥtāj bi-sharḥ al-Minhāj*. Cairo, 1969.

al-Ramlī, Shihāb al-Dīn Aḥmad (d. 1550). *al-Fatāwā*. [Printed on the margins of Ibn Ḥajar al-Haytamī's *Fatāwā*.]

al-Saffārīnī, Muḥammad (d. 1774). *Ghidhāʾ al-albāb li-sharḥ Manẓūmat al-ādāb*. Cairo, 1324–25H.

——. *Nafathāt ṣadr al-mukmad wa qurrat ʿayn al-musʿad li-sharḥ thulāthiyyāt musnad al-imām Aḥmad*. Damascus, 1380H.

——. *Qarʿ al-siyāṭ fī qamʿ ahl al-liwāṭ*. MS, Chester Beatty, Ar. 4907.

al-Ṣaltī, Muḥyī al-Dīn (d. 1702). *Ṣabābat al-muʿānī wa ṣabbābat al-maʿānī*. MS, Berlin Staatsbibliothek, Wetzstein II 219.

al-Shabrāmallisī, ʿAlī (d. 1676). *Ḥāshiyah ʿalā Nihāyat al-muḥtāj*. [Printed with Shams al-Dīn al-Ramlī's *Nihāyat*.]

al-Shabrāwī, ʿAbdallah (d. 1758). *Dīwān*. Cairo, 1282H.

al-Shaʿrānī, ʿAbd al-Wahhāb (d. 1565). *al-Anwār al-qudsiyyah fī maʿrifat qawāʿid al-ṣūfiyyah*. Edited by Ṭ. Surūr and M. al-Shāfiʿī. Cairo, n.d.

——. *Laṭāʾif al-minan wa al-akhlāq*. Cairo, 1321H.

——. *al-Mīzān al-kubrā*. Cairo, 1306H.

——. *Mukhtaṣar tadhkirat al-Suwaydī fī al-ṭibb*. Cairo, 1304H.

al-Sharqāwī, ʿAbdallah (d. 1811). *Ḥāshiyah ʿalā sharḥ al-Taḥrīr*. Cairo, n.d.

al-Shawkānī, Muḥammad (d. 1834). *al-Badr al-ṭāliʿ bi-maḥāsin man baʿd al-qarn al-sābiʿ*. Cairo, 1348H.

——. *Fatḥ al-qadīr al-jāmiʿ bayn fannay al-riwāyah wa al-dirāyah min ʿilm al-tafsīr*. Cairo, 1349H.

——. *al-Fawāʾid al-majmūʿah fī al-aḥādīth al-ḍaʿīfah wa al-mawḍūʿah*. Mecca, 1415H.

Shaykhzāde, Damad Efendī (d. 1667). *Majmaʿ al-anhur fī sharḥ Multaqā al-abḥur*. Cairo, 1276H.

al-Shīrāzī, Mullā Ṣadr al-Dīn (d. 1640/1). *al-Ḥikmah al-mutaʿāliyah fī al-asfār al-ʿaqliyyah al-arbaʿah*. Najaf, 1387H.

al-Shirbīnī, Yūsuf (fl. 1686). *Hazz al-quḥūf fī sharḥ qaṣīdat Abī Shādūf*. Cairo, 1322H.

Sibṭ al-Marṣafī, Muḥammad al-Ghamrī (fl. 1555). *al-Bahjah al-unsiyyah fī al-firāsah al-insāniyyah*. MS, British Library, Or. 8878.

al-Suwaydī, ʿAbdallah (d. 1761). *al-Nafḥah al-miskiyyah fī al-riḥlah al-makkiyyah*. MS, British Library, Add. 18518.

al-Suwaydī, ʿAbd al-Raḥmān ibn ʿAbdallah (d. 1786). [*Risālah fī al-maḥabbah*]. MS, Cambridge University Library, Or. 51(8).

al-Suyūṭī, Jalāl al-Dīn ʿAbd al-Raḥmān (d. 1505). *al-Ḥāwī li-al-fatāwā*. Cairo, 1352H.

al-Taghlibī, ʿAbd al-Qādir (d. 1723). *Nayl al-ma'ārib bi-sharḥ Dalīl al-ṭālib*. Edited by M. al-Ashqar. Kuwait, 1983.

al-Ṭahṭāwī, Aḥmad (d. 1816). *Ḥāshiyah ʿalā al-Durr al-mukhtār*. Cairo, 1254H.

al-Ṭahṭāwī, Rifāʿah Rāfiʿ (d. 1873). *Takhlīṣ al-ibrīz fī talkhīṣ Bārīz*. In M. ʿAmmārah, ed., *al-Aʿmāl al-kāmilah li Rifāʿah Rāfiʿ al-Ṭahṭāwī*, vol. 2. Beirut, 1973–81.

al-Ṭālawī, Darwīsh (d. 1606). *Sāniḥāt dumā al-qaṣr fī muṭāraḥāt banī al-ʿaṣr*. Edited by M. al-Khawlī. Beirut, 1983.

al-Tīfāshī, Aḥmad (d. 1253). *Nuzhat al-albāb fī-mā lā yūjad fī kitāb*. Edited by J. Jumʿa. London, 1992.

al-ʿUmarī, Muḥammad Amīn (d. 1788). *Manhal al-awliyā' wa mashrab al-aṣfiyā' min sādāt al-Mawṣil al-ḥadbā'*. Edited by S. al-Dīwahji. Mosul, 1967–68.

al-ʿUmarī, ʿUthmān (d. 1770/1). *al-Rawḍ al-naḍir fī tarjamat udabā' al-ʿaṣr*. Edited by S. al-Nuʿaymī. Baghdad, 1974–75.

al-ʿUmarī, Yāsīn (d. 1816/7). *Ghāyat al-marām fī tārīkh maḥāsin Baghdād dār al-salām*. Baghdad, 1968.

al-ʿUrḍī, Abū al-Wafā' (d. 1660). *Maʿādin al-dhahab fī al-aʿyān al-musharrafah bi-him Ḥalab*. Edited by M. al-Tūnjī. Aleppo, 1986.

al-ʿUshārī, Ḥusayn (d. ca. 1781). *Dīwān*. Edited by ʿI. Ra'ūf and W. al-Aʿẓamī. Baghdad, 1977.

al-ʿUṭayfī, Ramaḍān (d. 1684). *Riḥlah min dimashq al-shām ilā ṭarābulus al-shām*. Edited by S. Wild. Beirut and Wiesbaden, 1979.

al-Zabīdī, Muḥammad Murtaḍā (d. 1791). *Itḥāf al-sādah al-muttaqīn bi sharḥ Iḥyā' ʿulūm al-dīn*. Cairo, 1311H.

———. *Tāj al-ʿarūs bi sharḥ jawāhir al-Qāmūs*. Kuwait, 1965–2001.

Zaydān, Jurjī (d. 1914). *Tārīkh ādāb al-lughah al-ʿarabiyyah*. Cairo, 1914–31.

Zīrekzāde, Muḥammad (d. 1601). *Ḥāshiyah ʿalā al-Ashbāh wa al-naẓā'ir*. MS, Princeton University Library, Yahuda 5470.

al-Zurqānī, ʿAbd al-Bāqī (d. 1688). *Sharḥ mukhtaṣar Khalīl*. Cairo, 1307H.

al-Zurqānī, Muḥammad ibn ʿAbd al-Bāqī (d. 1720). *Mukhtaṣar al-Maqāṣid al-ḥasanah fī bayān kathīr min al-aḥādīth al-mushtaharah ʿalā al-alsinah*. Edited by M. al-Ṣabbāgh. Riyad, 1995.

Western Travel Literature

Blount, H. *A Voyage into the Levant*. London, 1636.

Buckingham, J. S. *Travels in Assyria, Media, and Persia*. London, 1830.

Burckhardt, J. L. *Travels in Arabia*. London, 1829.

Lane, E. W. *An Account of the Manners and Customs of the Modern Egyptians*. London, 1842.

Niebuhr, C. *Travels through Arabia and Other Countries in the East*. Translated by R. Heron. Edinburgh, 1792.

Pitts, J. *A Faithful Account of the Religion and Manners of the Mahometans*. London, 1731.

Russell, A. *The Natural History of Aleppo*. 1st ed., London, 1756. 2nd ed., London, 1794.

Rycaut, P. *The Present State of the Ottoman Empire*. London, 1668.

Sonnini, C. S. *Travels in Upper and Lower Egypt*. Translated by H. Hunter. London, 1799.

Volney, C. F. *Travels through Syria and Egypt in the Years 1783, 1784, and 1785*. London, 1787.

Secondary Sources

ʿAbd al-Nabī, Y. *al-Mukhtār min kitāb Thamarāt al-awrāq*. Cairo, 1963.

AbuKhalil, A. "A Note on the Study of Homosexuality in the Arab/Islamic Civilization." *Arab Studies Journal* 1 (1993): 32–34, 48.

al-ʿAdnānī, al-Khaṭīb. *al-Zinā wa al-shudhūdh fī al-tārīkh al-ʿarabī*. London and Beirut, 1999.

Affifi, A. E. "Ibn ʿArabī." In M. M. Sharif, ed., *A History of Muslim Philosophy,* vol. 1: 398–420. Wiesbaden, 1963.

Ahlwardt, W. *Verzeichniss der Arabischen Handschriften der Königlichen Bibliothek zu Berlin*. Berlin, 1887–99.

Algar, H. "A Brief History of the Naqshbandī Order." In M. Gaborieau et al., eds., *Naqshbandis: Cheminements et situation actuelle d'un ordre mystique musulman*. Istanbul, 1990.

Amīn, Aḥmad. *Ẓuhr al-Islām*. Cairo, 1945.

Amīn, Bakrī Shaykh. *Muṭālaʿāt fī al-shiʿr al-mamlūkī wa al-ʿuthmānī*. Beirut and Cairo, 1972.

Anouti, O. *al-Ḥarakah al-adabiyyah fī bilād al-shām khilāl al-qarn al-thāmin ʿashar*. Beirut, 1971.

al-ʿAqqād, ʿAbbās Maḥmūd. *Abū Nuwās*. In *Mawsūʿat aʿmāl ʿAbbās Maḥmūd al-ʿAqqād*, vol. 16. Cairo and Beirut, 1994.

Arazi, A. *Amour divin et amour profane dans l'Islam médiéval à travers le diwan de Khālid al-Kātib*. Paris, 1990.

Arberry, A. J. *A Handlist of the Arabic Manuscripts in the Chester Beatty Library*. Dublin, 1955–66.

———. *A Second Supplementary Hand-List of the Muhammadan Manuscripts in the University and Colleges of Cambridge*. Cambridge, 1952.

Baer, G. "Shirbīnī's *Hazz al-quḥūf* and its significance." In G. Baer, *Fellah and Townsmen in the Middle East: A Study in Social History*. London, 1982.

Baker, K. M. "On the Problem of the Ideological Origins of the French Revolution." In K. M. Baker, *Inventing the French Revolution*. Cambridge, 1990.

Bakkār, Yūsuf Ḥusayn. *Ittijāhāt al-ghazal fī al-qarn al-thānī al-hijrī*. Cairo, 1971.

Bāshā, ʿUmar Mūsā. *Tārīkh al-adab al-ʿarabī: al-ʿaṣr al-ʿuthmānī*. Damascus, 1989.

Bauer, T. *Liebe und Liebesdichtung in der arabischen Welt des 9. und 10. Jahrhunderts*. Wiesbaden, 1998.

———. "Raffinement und Frömmigkeit." *Asiatische Studien* 50 (1996): 275–95.

Bellamy, J. A. "Sex and Society in Islamic Popular Literature." In A. L. al-Sayyid-Marsot, ed., *Society and the Sexes in Medieval Islam*. Malibu, 1979.

Benton, J. F. "Clio and Venus: An Historical View of Medieval Love." In F. X. Newman ed., *The Meaning of Courtly Love*. Albany, 1968.

Berger, P. L. *Invitation to Sociology: A Humanist Perspective*. Harmondsworth, 1963.

Berkey, J. *The Transmission of Knowledge: A Social History of Islamic Education*. Princeton, 1992.

Bernard, Y. *L'Orient du XVIe siècle: à travers les récits des voyageurs français*. Paris, 1988.

Boase, R. *The Origin and Meaning of Courtly Love: A Critical Study of European Scholarship*. Manchester, 1977.

Boswell, J. *Christianity, Social Tolerance, and Homosexuality: Gay People in Western Europe from the Beginning of the Christian Era to the Fourteenth Century.* Chicago, 1980.

———. "Revolutions, Universals, and Sexual Categories." In M. Duberman et al. eds., *Hidden from History: Reclaiming the Gay and Lesbian Past.* Harmondsworth, 1991.

Bouhdiba, A. *Sexuality in Islam.* London, 1985.

Bourdieu, P. *The Logic of Practice.* Cambridge, 1990.

Bousquet, G. H. *L'éthique sexuelle de l'Islam.* Paris, 1966.

Bray, A. *Homosexuality in Renaissance England.* London, 1982.

Brockelmann, C. *Geschichte der arabischen Literatur.* Leiden, 1937–49.

Browne, E. G. *A Hand-List of the Muhammadan Manuscripts in the Library of the University of Cambridge.* Cambridge, 1900.

———. *A Supplementary Hand-List of the Muhammadan Manuscripts Preserved in the Libraries of the University and Colleges of Cambridge.* Cambridge, 1922.

Brundage, J. A. "Sex and Canon Law." In V. L. Bullough and J. A. Brundage, eds., *Handbook of Medieval Sexuality.* New York and London, 1996.

Bullough, V. *Sexual Variance in Society and History.* New York and London, 1976.

Bürgel, J. C. "Die beste Dichtung ist die lügenreichste." *Oriens* 23–24 (1974): 7–102.

———. "Literatur und Wirklichkeit." *Asiatische Studien* 50 (1996): 245–57.

———. "Love, Lust, and Longing: Eroticism in Early Islam as Reflected in Literary Sources." In A. L. al-Sayyid-Marsot, ed., *Society and the Sexes in Medieval Islam.* Malibu, 1979.

Burke, P. "Strengths and Weaknesses of the History of Mentalities." In P. Burke, *Varieties of Cultural History.* Cambridge and Oxford, 1997.

Burton, R. *The Sotadic Zone.* New York [Panurge Press, n.d.].

Cadden, J. "Western Medicine and Natural Philosophy." In V. L. Bullough and J. A. Brundage, eds., *Handbook of Medieval Sexuality.* New York and London, 1996.

Cady, J. "Masculine Love, Renaissance Writing, and the New Invention of Homosexuality." In J. C. Summers, ed., *Homosexuality in Renaissance and Enlightenment England: Literary Representations in Historical Context.* New York, 1992.

Catalogus codicum manuscriptorum orientalium qui in Museo Britannico asservantur. London, 1846–71.

Chamberlain, M. *Knowledge and Social Practice in Medieval Damascus, 1190–1350.* Cambridge, 1993.

Chittick, W. C. *The Sufi Path of Knowledge: Ibn ʿArabi's Metaphysics of Imagination.* New York, 1989.

Cohen, D. *Law, Sexuality, and Society: The Enforcement of Morals in Classical Athens.* Cambridge, 1991.

Cook, M. *Commanding Right and Forbidding Wrong in Islamic Thought.* Cambridge, 2000.

Dover, K. *Greek Homosexuality.* London, 1978.

Dunne, B. "Homosexuality in the Middle East: An Agenda for Historical Research." *Arab Studies Quarterly* 12 (1990): 55–82.

———. "Power and Sexuality in the Middle East." *Middle East Report* 28 (1998): 8–11, 37.

Duran, K. "Homosexuality and Islam." In A. Swidler, ed., *Homosexuality and World Religions.* Valley Forge, 1993.

Ellis, A. G. *Catalogue of Arabic Books in the British Museum.* London, 1894–1901.

Enderwitz, S. *Liebe als Beruf: al-ʿAbbās ibn al-Aḥnaf und das Ġazal.* Stuttgart and Beirut, 1995.

Fackenheim, E. "A Treatise on Love by Ibn Sina." *Mediaeval Studies* 7 (1945): 208–28.

Farrūkh, ʿU. *Abū Nuwās: shāʿir Hārūn al-Rashīd wa Muḥammad al-Amīn.* 3rd edition. Beirut, 1946.

Foucault, M. *A History of Sexuality.* Harmondsworth, 1978–86.

Frazer, E., and D. Cameron. "Knowing What to Say: The Construction of Gender in Linguistic Practice." In R. Grillo, ed., *Social Anthropology and the Politics of Language.* London and New York, 1989.

Freud, S. *Three Essays on the Theory of Sexuality.* Vol. 7 of the Standard Edition of the Complete Psychological Works of Sigmund Freud. London, 1953.

Gardet, L. "Djanna." In *Encyclopaedia of Islam.* 2nd edition. Leiden, 1960–2002.

Gellner, E. "Doctor and Saint." In N. Keddie, ed., *Scholars, Saints, and Sufis: Muslim Religious Institutions in the Middle East since 1500.* Berkeley, 1972.

Gibb, H. A. R., and H. Bowen. *Islamic Society and the West.* London, 1950–57.

Giffen, L. A. *Theory of Profane Love among the Arabs: The Development of the Genre.* New York and London, 1971.

Gilmore, D. *Manhood in the Making: Cultural Concepts of Masculinity.* New Haven, 1990.

———. "Introduction: The Shame of Dishonour." In D. Gilmore, ed., *Honour and Shame and the Unity of the Mediterranean.* Special Publication of the American Anthropological Association, 22 (1987): 2–21.

Goitein, S. D. "The Sexual Mores of the Common People." In A. L. al-Sayyid-Marsot, ed., *Society and the Sexes in Medieval Islam.* Malibu, 1979.

Goldhill, S. *Foucault's Virginity: Ancient Erotic Fiction and the History of Sexuality.* Cambridge, 1995.

Greenberg, D. *The Construction of Homosexuality.* Chicago, 1988.

Halperin, D. "Forgetting Foucault: Acts, Identities, and the History of Sexuality." *Representations* 63 (1998): 93–120.

———. "Historicizing the Subject of Desire: Sexual Preferences and Erotic Identities in the Pseudo-Lucian *Erotes.*" In J. Goldstein, ed., *Foucault and the Writing of History.* Oxford, 1994.

———. *How to Do the History of Homosexuality.* Chicago, 2002.

———. *One Hundred Years of Homosexuality and Other Essays on Greek Love.* New York and London, 1990.

Hamori, A. "Love Poetry (*ghazal*)." In J. Ashtiany et al., eds., *Cambridge History of Arabic Literature: ʿAbbasid Belles-Lettres.* Cambridge, 1990.

Hattox, R. S. *Coffee and Coffeehouses: The Origins of a Social Beverage in the Medieval Near East.* Seattle and London, 1985.

Heyd, U. *Studies in Old Ottoman Criminal Law.* Oxford, 1973.

Hinds, M., and E. Badawi. *A Dictionary of Egyptian Arabic.* Beirut, 1986.

Hitti, P. K., et al. *Descriptive Catalog of the Garrett Collection of Arabic Manuscripts in the Princeton University Library.* Princeton, 1938.

Hodgson, M. S. G. *The Venture of Islam: Conscience and History in a World Civilization.* Chicago and London, 1974.

Homerin, Th. Emil, trans. *ʿUmar ibn al-Fāriḍ: Sufi Verse, Saintly Life.* New York, 2001.

Hopwood, D. *Sexual Encounters in the Middle East: The British, the French, and the Arabs.* Reading, 1999.

Huussen, A. H. "Sodomy in the Dutch Republic during the Eighteenth Century." In R. P. Maccubbin, ed., *'Tis Nature's Fault: Unauthorized Sexuality during the Enlightenment.* Cambridge, 1987.

Imber, C. "*Zina* in Ottoman Law." In J. Bacque-Grammont and P. Dumont, eds., *Contributions à l'histoire économique et sociale de l'Empire ottoman.* Louvain, 1983.

Irwin, R. *The Arabian Nights: A Companion.* Harmondsworth, 1994.

Izutsu, T. *Sufism and Taoism: A Comparative Study of Key Philosophical Concepts.* Berkeley and Los Angeles, 1983.

Jaeger, C. S. *Ennobling Love: In Search of a Lost Sensibility.* Philadelphia, 1999.

Jamal, A. "The Story of Lot and the Qur'an's Perception of the Morality of Same-Sex Sexuality." *Journal of Homosexuality* 41 (2001): 1–88.

Johansson, W., and W. A. Percy. "Homosexuality." In V. L. Bullough and J. A. Brundage, eds., *Handbook of Medieval Sexuality.* New York and London, 1996.

Keen, M. "Chivalry and Courtly Love." In M. Keen, *Nobles, Knights, and Men-at-Arms in the Middle Ages.* London, 1996.

Knysh, A. D. *Ibn ʿArabi in the Later Islamic Tradition: The Making of a Polemical Image in Medieval Islam.* Albany, 1999.

Kohlberg, E. "Shahīd." In *Encyclopaedia of Islam.* 2nd edition. Leiden, 1960–2002.

Lewis, B. *Music from a Distant Drum: Classical Arabic, Persian, Turkish, and Hebrew Poems.* Princeton, 2001.

Loizos, P., and E. Papataxiarchis. "Gender and Kinship in Marriage and Alternative Contexts." In P. Loizos and E. Papataxiarchis, eds., *Contested Identities: Gender and Kinship in Modern Greece.* Princeton, 1991.

Mach, R. *Catalogue of Arabic Manuscripts (Yahuda Section) in the Garret Collection, Princeton University Library.* Princeton, 1977.

Mach, R., and E. L. Ormsby. *Handlist of Arabic Manuscripts (New Series) in the Princeton University Library.* Princeton, 1987.

Manṣūr, Aḥmad Muḥammad. *Dalīl al-maṭbūʿāt al-Miṣriyyah.* Cairo, 1975.

Maqdisi, G. *Ibn ʿAqil: Religion and Culture in Classical Islam.* Edinburgh, 1997.

Marcus, A. *The Middle East on the Eve of Modernity: Aleppo in the Eighteenth Century.* New York, 1989.

Massad, J. "Re-Orienting Desire: The Gay International and the Arab World." *Public Culture* 14 (2002): 361–85.

Matar, N. *Turks, Moors, and Englishmen in the Age of Discovery.* New York, 1999.

McIntosh, M. "The Homosexual Role." In K. Plummer, ed., *The Making of the Modern Homosexual.* London, 1981.

Meisami, J. S. "Arabic *Mujūn* Poetry: The Literary Dimension." In F. de Jong, ed., *Verse and the Fair Sex.* Utrecht, 1993.

Miller, S. G., trans. and ed. *Disorienting Encounters: Travels of a Moroccan Scholar in France in 1845–1846: The Voyage of Muḥammad aṣ-Ṣaffār.* Berkeley and Oxford, 1992.

Monroe, J. T. "The Striptease That Was Blamed on Abū Bakr's Naughty Son." In J. W. Wright Jr. and E. Rowson, eds., *Homoeroticism in Classical Arabic Literature.* New York, 1997.

Montgomery, J. "Abū Nuwās the Alcoholic." In U. Vermeulen and D. De Smet, eds., *Philosophy and Arts in the Islamic World.* Leuven, 1998.

———. "For the Love of a Christian Boy: A Song by Abū Nuwās." *Journal of Arabic Literature* 27 (1996): 115–24.

Murray, S. O. "Homosexual Acts and Selves in Early Modern Europe." In K. Gerard and G. Hekma, eds., *The Pursuit of Sodomy: Male Homosexuality in Renaissance and Enlightenment Europe.* New York and London, 1989.

———. *Homosexualities.* Chicago, 2000.

———. "Some Nineteenth-Century Reports of Islamic Homosexualities." In Murray and Roscoe, *Islamic Homosexualities.*

Murray, S. O., and W. Roscoe, eds. *Islamic Homosexualities: Culture, History, and Literature.* New York and London, 1997.

Musallam, B. *Sex and Society in Islam: Birth Control before the Nineteenth Century.* Cambridge, 1983.

Naṣīr, ʿĀʾidah Ibrāhīm. *al-Kutub al-ʿarabiyyah al-latī nushirat fī Miṣr fī al-qarn al-tāsiʿ ʿashar.* Cairo, 1990.

———. *al-Kutub al-ʿarabiyyah al-latī nushirat fī Miṣr bayna ʿāmay 1900–1925.* Cairo, 1983.

———. *al-Kutub al-ʿarabiyyah al-latī nushirat fī Miṣr bayna ʿāmay 1926–1940.* Cairo, 1969.

Nathan, B. "Medieval Arabic Medical Views on Male Homosexuality." *Journal of Homosexuality* 26/4 (1994): 37–39.

Nicholson, R. A. *Studies in Islamic Mysticism.* Cambridge, 1921.

———. *The Tarjuman al-Ashwaq: A Collection of Mystical Odes by Muhyiʾddin ibn al-ʿArabi.* London, 1911.

al-Nuwayhī, Muḥammad. *Nafsiyyat Abī Nuwās.* 2nd edition. Cairo, 1970.

Oberhelman, S. M. "Hierarchies of Gender, Ideology, and Power in Medieval Greek and Arabic Dream Literature." In J. W. Wright Jr. and E. Rowson, eds., *Homoeroticism in Classical Arabic Literature.* New York, 1997.

Palmer, E. H. *The Koran.* London, 1951.

Pellat, C., et al. "Liwāṭ." In *Encyclopaedia of Islam.* 2nd edition. Leiden, 1960–2002.

Pflugfelder, G. M. *Cartographies of Desire: Male-Male Sexuality in Japanese Discourse, 1600–1850.* Berkeley, 1999.

Philipp, T., and M. Perlmann, eds. and trans. *ʿAbd al-Raḥmān al-Jabartī's History of Egypt.* Stuttgart, 1994.

Pitt-Rivers, J. *The Fate of Shechem; or The Politics of Sex: Essays in the Anthropology of the Mediterranean.* Cambridge, 1977.

Rafeq, ʿA. K. "Public Morality in 18th Century Damascus." *Revue du Monde Musulman et de la Méditerranée* 55–56 (1990): 180–96.

Rey, M. "Parisian Homosexuals Create a Lifestyle, 1700–1750: The Police Archives." In R. P. Maccubbin, ed., *'Tis Nature's Fault: Unauthorized Sexuality during the Enlightenment.* Cambridge, 1987.

Rieu, C. *Supplement to the Catalogue of the Arabic Manuscripts in the British Museum.* London, 1894.

Ritter, H. *Das Meer der Seele: Mensch, Welt, und Gott in den Geschichten des Fariduddin ʿAttar.* Leiden, 1955.

Robson, J. "Ḥadīth." In *Encyclopaedia of Islam.* 2nd edition. Leiden, 1960–2002.

Rocke, M. *Forbidden Friendships: Homosexuality and Male Culture in Renaissance Florence.* New York and Oxford, 1996.

Rosenthal, F. "Ar-Razi on the Hidden Illness." *Bulletin of the History of Medicine* 52 (1978): 45–60.

———. "Fiction and Reality: Sources for the Role of Sex in Medieval Muslim Society." In A. L. al-Sayyid-Marsot, ed., *Society and the Sexes in Medieval Islam.* Malibu, 1979.

———. "Male and Female: Described and Compared." In J. W. Wright and E. Rowson, eds., *Homoeroticism in Classical Arabic Literature.* New York, 1997.

Roth, N. "A Research Note on Sexuality and Muslim Civilization." In V. L. Bullough and J. A. Brundage, eds., *A Handbook of Medieval Sexuality.* New York and London, 1996.

———. "Fawn of My Delights: Boy-Love in Arabic and Hebrew Verse." In J. Salisbury, ed., *Sex in the Middle Ages.* New York, 1991.

Rowson, E. "The Categorization of Gender and Sexual Irregularity in Medieval Arabic Vice Lists." In J. Epstein and K. Straub, eds., *Body Guards: The Cultural Politics of Gender Ambiguity.* New York, 1991.

———. "The Effeminates of Early Medina." *Journal of the American Oriental Society* 111 (1991): 671–93.

———. "Homosexuality." In J. D. McAuliffe, ed., *Encyclopaedia of the Qur'an.* Leiden, 2001– .

———. "Two Homoerotic Narratives from Mamluk Literature: al-Ṣafadī's *Law'at al-shākī* and Ibn Dāniyāl's *al-Mutayyam.*" In J. W. Wright and E. Rowson, eds., *Homoeroticism in Classical Arabic Literature.* New York, 1997.

Saslow, J. M. "Homosexuality in the Renaissance: Behaviour, Identity, and Artistic Expression." In M. Duberman et al., eds., *Hidden from History: Reclaiming the Gay and Lesbian Past.* Harmondsworth, 1991.

Schacht, J. *An Introduction to Islamic Law.* Oxford, 1964.

Schimmel, A. "Eros—Heavenly and Not So Heavenly—in Sufi Literature and Life." In A. L. al-Sayyid-Marsot, ed., *Society and the Sexes in Medieval Islam.* Malibu, 1979.

———. *Mystical Dimensions of Islam.* Chapel Hill, 1975.

———. *As Through a Veil: Mystical Poetry in Islam.* Oxford, 1982.

Schirmann, J. "The Ephebe in Medieval Hebrew Poetry." *Sefarad* 15 (1955): 55–68.

Schmidt, J. "Sünbülzāde Vehbī's *Ševki-Engiz,* an Ottoman Pornographic Poem." *Turcica* 25 (1993): 9–37.

Schmidtke, S. "Homoeroticism and Homosexuality in Islam: A Review Article." *Bulletin of the School of Oriental and African Studies* 62 (1999): 260–66.

Schmitt, A. "Different Approaches to Male/Male Sexuality/Eroticism from Morocco to Usbekistan." In A. Schmitt and J. Sofer, eds., *Sexuality and Eroticism among Males in Moslem Societies.* New York, 1992.

———. "*Liwāṭ* im *Fiqh:* Männliche Homosexualität?" *Journal of Arabic and Islamic Studies* 4 (2001/2): 49–110.

Schmitt, A., and J. Sofer, eds. *Sexuality and Eroticism among Males in Moslem Societies.* New York, 1992.

Ṣidqī, ʿAbd al-Raḥmān. *Alḥān al-ḥān.* Cairo, 1947.

Singer, I. *The Nature of Love.* Chicago, 1984.

Spencer, C. *Homosexuality: A History.* London, 1995.

Ṭawīl, Ṭ. *al-Taṣawwuf fī miṣr ibbān al-ʿaṣr al-ʿuthmānī.* Cairo, 1946.

Thornton, B. S. *Eros: The Myth of Ancient Greek Sexuality.* Boulder and Oxford, 1997.

Tietze, A., ed. and trans. *Mustafa 'Ali's Description of Cairo of 1599.* Vienna, 1975.

Trimingham, J. S. *The Sufi Orders in Islam.* New York and Oxford, 1971.

Tucker, J. E. *In the House of the Law: Gender and Islamic Law in Ottoman Syria and Palestine.* Berkeley, 1998.

al-Tūnjī, Muḥammad. *Bahā' al-Dīn al-'Āmilī: adīban, shā'iran, 'āliman.* Damascus, 1985.

Vanggaard, T. *Phallos.* London, 1969.

Wafer, J. "Vision and Passion: The Symbolism of Male Love in Islamic Mysticism." In S. O. Murray and W. Roscoe, eds., *Islamic Homosexualities.* New York, 1997.

Wehr, H. *A Dictionary of Modern Written Arabic.* Edited by J. M. Cowan. Beirut and London, 1971.

Wensinck, A. J. [L. Gardet]. "Khaṭī'a." In *Encyclopaedia of Islam.* 2nd edition. Leiden, 1960–2002.

Westermarck, E. *Ritual and Belief in Morocco.* London, 1926.

Williams, C. A. *Roman Homosexuality: Ideologies of Masculinity in Classical Antiquity.* Oxford, 1999.

Wilson, L. *Scandal: Essays in Islamic Heresy.* New York, 1988.

Winkler, J. J. *The Constraints of Desire: The Anthropology of Sex and Gender in Ancient Greece.* New York and London, 1990.

Winter, M. *Society and Religion in Early Ottoman Egypt: Studies in the Writings of 'Abd al-Wahhāb al-Sha'rānī.* New Brunswick and London, 1982.

———. *Egyptian Society under Ottoman Rule, 1517–1798.* London and New York, 1992.

Wright, J. W., Jr., and E. Rowson, eds. *Homoeroticism in Classical Arabic Literature.* New York, 1997.

Young, M. B. *James VI and I and the History of Homosexuality.* London, 2000.

al-Zayyat, Aḥmad Ḥasan. *Tārīkh al-adab al-'arabī.* 6th edition. Cairo, 1935.

Index

belles-lettres (*continued*)
in, 60–75; as a source for real-life attitudes, 75–85, 111
Biqāʿī, Burhān al-Dīn Ibrāhīm (d. 1480), 107
bitāʿ al-ṣighār, 16. See also *lūṭī*
Blount, Henry, 40
Boswell, John, 3
boys of paradise (*wildān*), 134–36
Bray, Alan, 44, 75
Buckingham, James Silk, 92–93
Bughyat al-musāmir wa ghinyat al-musāfir (Ibn al-Wakīl al-Mallawī), 70
Buhūtī, Manṣūr al- (d. 1641), 20, 116, 121, 136
Bujayrimī, Sulaymān (d. 1806), 138
Bullough, Vern L., 3, 122
Bürgel, J. C., 76, 78–79
Būrīnī, Ḥasan al- (d. 1615), 23, 29, 50, 55, 84, 90, 91, 135, 141, 154
Būrsawī, Ismāʿīl Ḥaqqī al- (d. 1724), 134
Burton, Sir Richard, 7, 98
Bustānī, Buṭrus al- (d. 1883), 156

Christianity, Social Tolerance, and Homosexuality (Boswell), 3
coffeehouses, 41–42
constructionism and essentialism, 5–6, 43–51
courtship, patterns of, 27–28

Dajjānī, Muḥammad Abū al-Fatḥ al- (d. 1660/1), 36
Dardīr, Aḥmad al- (d. 1786), 22
Dasūqī, Muḥammad ibn ʿArafah al- (d. 1815), 138
Diḥyah al-Kalbī, 104
Dikdikjī, Muḥammad al- (d. 1719), 104
disputation (*mufākharah*), 67–69, 70, 71–75
Dīwān (Abū Nuwās), 158, 160
Dīwān (Ḥafnī), 145
Dīwān (Ibn al-Fāriḍ), 96, 101, 108
Dīwān (ʿInāyātī), 42
Dīwān (Māmāyah), 29
Dīwān (Shabrāwī), 4, 54
Dīwān al-Ḥaqāʾiq (Nābulusī), 100
dream interpretation. *See* oneiromancy

effeminacy. See *mukhannath*
Enderwitz, Suzanne, 76

Fakhr al-Dīn al-Maʿnī (d. 1635), 33
Fāriskūrī, Taqī al-Dīn (d. 1647), 68
Fikrī, ʿAbdallah (d. 1889), 157
Foucault, Michel, 5, 44–47
Freud, Sigmund, 66
Fuṣūṣ al-ḥikam (Ibn ʿArabī), 100

gazing (*naẓar*), 111–17
Ghāyat al-maṭlūb fī maḥabbat al-maḥbūb (Nābulusī), 102–4, 110, 143
Ghazālī, Abū Ḥāmid al- (d. 1111), 54, 94
Ghazālī, Aḥmad al- (d. 1126), 99
Ghazālī, Ibrāhīm al- (d. 1678), 14, 23
Ghazzī, Badr al-Dīn al- (d. 1577), 23
Ghazzī, Najm al-Dīn Muḥammad al- (d. 1651), 41, 51, 58, 83
Ghulāmī, Muḥammad al- (d. 1772/3), 35, 64, 81, 84
Giffen, Lois A., 87

ḥadīth (sayings of the Prophet), 12, 59, 87–88, 98, 113, 114, 120, 125–26, 139, 147, 155
Ḥafnī, Muḥammad al- (d. 1767), 105, 133, 140, 145
Ḥafnī, Yūsuf al- (d. 1764), 89, 145–46
Ḥajjāwī, Mūsā al- (d. 1560), 121
Ḥamawī, Aḥmad al- (d. 1687), 130, 133
Hamori, Andras, 90
Ḥanafī school of law, 22, 115, 118–19, 123, 124, 128, 130–31, 136, 137, 142, 143, 145
Ḥanbalī, Abū al-Mawāhib al- (d. 1714), 99
Ḥanbalī school of law, 120–21, 123, 137, 142, 143
Ḥaṣkafī, ʿAlāʾ al-Dīn Muḥammad al- (d. 1677), 22, 124, 133
Ḥaṣkafī, ʿAlī ibn Muḥammad al- (d. 1519), 67
Hazz al-quḥūf fī sharḥ qaṣīdat Abī Shādūf (Shirbīnī), 37, 60, 160. *See also* Shirbīnī, Yūsuf al-
hermaphrodism, 65
Hijāzī, Aḥmad al- (d. 1471), 64
Histoire de la sexualité (Foucault), 44
Hodgson, Marshall, 3
homosexuality: as absent among animals, 115; as anachronistic concept, 3, 6–8, 15–18, 42–45, 104, 136, 151, 153; transgenerational, 25–33. *See also* constructionism

Muṣṭafā ʿAlī (d. 1600), 21, 33
Muttaqī al-Hindī, ʿAlī al- (d. 1567/8), 139

Nābulusī, ʿAbd al-Ghanī al- (d. 1731), 13, 24, 26, 31, 40, 58, 59, 64, 70, 80–81, 86, 96–97, 100–104, 107, 108, 114–15, 133, 141, 159; *Dīwān al-ḥaqā'iq*, 100–102; *Ghāyat al-maṭlūb fī maḥabbat al-maḥbūb*, 102–4, 110, 143
Nābulusī, Ismāʿīl al- (d. 1585), 23, 24, 54
Nafḥah al-miskiyyah fī al-riḥlah al-makkiyyah, al- (Suwaydī), 81
Nafḥat al-rayḥānah wa rashḥat ṭilā' al-ḥānah (Muḥibbī), 80
Natural History of Aleppo (Russell), 39
Nawājī, Muḥammad al- (d. 1455), 64
Nawawī, Yaḥyā al- (d. 1277), 113–14, 118
naẓar, 111–17
Nuzhat al-albāb fīmā lā yūjad fī kitāb (Tīfāshī), 17–18, 45

oneiromancy, 13–14, 24, 26–27

passive sodomist. See *ma'būn*
pederast. See *lūṭī*
pederasty: and gender segregation, 28–30, 69–70; social context of, 33–43
physiognomy, 47–48
Pitt-Rivers, J., 25
Pitts, Joseph, 1
Plato, 92
poetry. *See* belles-lettres
prostitution, 18, 30

Qalyūbī, Aḥmad al- (d. 1658), 19, 141, 149
Qāri' al-Harawī, ʿAlī al- (d. 1614), 123, 139
Qur'an, 9, 12, 66, 92, 95, 103, 114, 122, 124–25, 126–30, 133–35, 139, 147

Rāfiʿī, ʿAbd al-Karīm al- (d. 1226), 114, 118, 142
Rāghib Pāshā (d. 1763), 93, 141
Rāmī, Qāsim al- (d. 1772/3), 31
Ramlī, Khayr al-Dīn al- (d. 1671), 38, 49, 117
Ramlī, Shams al-Dīn Muḥammad al- (d. 1596), 95, 117, 140
Ramlī, Shihāb al-Dīn Aḥmad al- (d. 1550), 139
Rāzī, Abū Bakr al- (d. ca. 925), 19
Rāzī, Fakhr al-Dīn al- (d. 1209), 47
refinement: as cultural ideal, 11, 57; linked to urban life, 60; and love of beauty, 57–59, 86
Ritter, Helmut, 37, 98–99
Rocke, Michael, 155
Rosenthal, Franz, 76
Rowson, Everett, 7
Rūmī, Jalāl al-Dīn (d. 1273), 104
Rūmī, Shaʿbān al- (d. 1736), 28, 77, 84
Russell, Alexander, 39

Ṣādiqī, ʿAṭāllah al- (d. 1680/1), 72
Ṣafadī, Aḥmad al- (d. 1688), 80, 145
Ṣafadī, Khalīl ibn Aybak al- (d. 1363), 64
Ṣaffār, Muḥammad al-, 2
Saffārīnī, Muḥammad al- (d. 1774), 17, 88, 94, 128, 139–40, 142
Sakhāwī, Shams al-Dīn Muḥammad (d. 1497), 139
Salafī movement, 120, 121, 161
Ṣāliḥī al-Hilālī, Amīn al-Dīn al- (d. 1596), 27
Salīm I (Ottoman Sultan, 1512–20), 107
Ṣaltī, Muḥyī al-Dīn al- (d. 1702), 85, 91, 93, 140
samāʿ. *See* music, listening to
Sandys, George, 41
Schmitt, Arno, 7
serial relationships, 32
sexual intercourse: nonpenetrative, 121, 137–39; as polarization, 13–15; between women, 137–38
Sexual Variance in Society and History (Bullough), 3
Shabrāmallisī, ʿAlī al- (d. 1676), 128
Shabrāwī, ʿAbdallah al- (d. 1758), 3–4, 8, 35, 54, 64, 84, 89, 105
Shāfiʿī, al- (d. 820), 47
Shāfiʿī school of law, 113, 119–20, 123, 137, 140, 142, 143
Shammāmat al-ʿanbar wa al-zahr al-muʿanbar (Ghulāmī), 81
Shaʿrānī, ʿAbd al-Wahhāb al- (d. 1565), 19, 38–39, 40, 60, 108, 109, 123, 127
Sharqāwī, ʿAbdallah al- (d. 1811), 141
Shawkānī, Muḥammad al- (d. 1834), 50, 120, 140